JEAN-MARIE TJIBAOU,
Kanak Witness to the World

Jean-Marie Tjibaou, 1978, in the Hienghène valley leading up to Tiendanite. *(ADCK-Centre Culturel Tjibaou/ James Clifford)*

Pacific Islands Monograph Series 23

Jean-Marie Tjibaou, Kanak Witness to the World

An Intellectual Biography

Eric Waddell

CENTER FOR PACIFIC ISLANDS STUDIES
School of Pacific and Asian Studies
University of Hawai'i, Mānoa
University of Hawai'i Press • Honolulu

Pacific Islands Development Program
East-West Center • Honolulu

Library of Congress Cataloging-in-Publication Data

Waddell, Eric.
Jean-Marie Tjibaou, Kanak witness to the world : an intellectual biography /
Eric Waddell.
p. cm.—(Pacific Islands monograph series ; 23)
Includes bibliographical references and index.
ISBN 978-0-8248-3256-8 (hardcover : alk. paper)—ISBN 978-0-8248-3314-5
(pbk. : alk. paper)
1. Tjibaou, Jean-Marie, 1936–1989.   2. Kanaka (New Caledonian people)—
Biography.   3. Kanaka (New Caledonian people)—Ethnic identity.   4. Kanaka
(New Caledonian people)—History.   5. New Caledonia—History—Autonomy
and independence movements.   6. New Caledonia—History—20th century.
7. New Caledonia—Politics and government—20th century.   I. University
of Hawaii at Manoa. Center for Pacific Islands Studies.   II. Pacific Islands
Development Program (East-West Center).   III. Title.
DU720.T55W33 2008
995.97—dc22
[B]
2008015024

Maps by Manoa Mapworks, Inc, and
Laboratoire de cartographie, Département de géographie,
Université Laval.

University of Hawai'i Press books are printed on acid-free
paper and meet the guidelines for permanence and
durability of the Council on Library Resources.

Designed by University of Hawai'i Press production staff
Printed by The Maple-Vail Book Manufacturing Group

Si la parole manque
il n'y a plus rien
Si tu manques à la parole
si tu ne transmets pas la parole
il n'y a plus rien
    JEAN-MARIE TJIBAOU

If the word is missing
there is nothing left
If you do not respect the word
if you do not pass the word on
there is nothing left

*   *   *

Quand les hommes vivront d'amour
Ce sera la paix sur la terre
Les soldats seront troubadours
Mais nous, nous serons morts mon frère

When men will live to love
There will be peace on earth
The soldiers will be troubadours
But we, we will be dead my brother

. . .

. . .

Quand les hommes vivront d'amour
Il n'y aura plus de misère
Et commenceront les beaux jours
Mais nous, nous serons morts mon frère
    RAYMOND LÉVESQUE

When men will live to love
There will be no more misery
And the good times will begin
But we, we will be dead my brother

Editor's Note

BIOGRAPHY REMAINS the most popular and oftentimes most effective medium of historical expression for a reason. Biography offers a human approach to the life and times of an individual, in a way that intimately links the subject, the author, and the reader. Eric Waddell has produced an eloquent, poetic, moving, and deeply personal account of the life of Jean-Marie Tjibaou, the Kanak political leader and philosopher whose advocacy of his Melanesian people spoke to others within and beyond the Pacific region. The Center for Pacific Islands Studies, through its Pacific Islands Monograph Series, is pleased to join with the East-West Center's Pacific Islands Development Program in the publication of this important work. We wish to acknowledge as well the generous support of the Agence de développement de la culture kanak and its Centre Culturel Tjibaou in Nouméa, New Caledonia.

Roots and routes lay at the core of Tjibaou's life journey. *Jean-Marie Tjibaou, Kanak Witness to the World: An Intellectual Biography* follows the life of this extraordinary man from his village roots in Hienghène to Nouméa, and then to Lyon, Paris, and the Larzac in France. We learn of the modest circumstances of his early years, his training for the priesthood, his student days in France, his disillusionment with the conservatism of the Catholic Church, his courage in the face of danger, his personal losses, and his emergence as a leader whose vision of ultimate independence for the Kanak people was grounded solidly in his Melanesian heritage. Tjibaou treasured Melanesian culture, and saw great strength in its spiritual and communal values. His prescription for the future was at once traditional and forward looking. Tjibaou understood culture as a matter of lived experience, not abstract or untested belief. A restored sense of place, identity, and history allowed the Kanak people to overcome the oppression of French colonialism, and to engage constructively with the forces of modernity. For Tjibaou, living in the larger world was about dignity, self-respect, and recognition. His vision of independence for the Kanak also included a shared land and a shared future.

There is no simple history here. Waddell does not reduce Tjibaou's life to a neat, linear chronology. The book's first chapter focuses on Tjibaou's visit to Hwaadrila on Ouvéa in early May of 1989 to honor the memory of the nineteen Kanak men slain by French forces at Goosana the year before. During the early evening ceremony designed to formalize the ties between visitors and hosts, Tjibaou and his heir-apparent, Yeiwéné Yeiwéné, were shot dead by Djubelly Wéa, an ardent Kanak nationalist who felt betrayed by Tjibaou's endorsement of the Matignon Accords. Djubelly also lost his life that day. Waddell describes this catastrophe as an event that sealed the fate of the Kanak people for the foreseeable future. At the same time, he cautions against viewing Tjibaou's murder as the act of a deranged person. In the chapters that follow, Waddell constructs a very particular and personal life story set against the history of New Caledonia and the French Pacific. In the end, we come away from this detailed, richly nuanced study with a better understanding of the disheartening irony that surrounded the death of a former Catholic priest and Kanak nationalist at the hands of a desperate, former Protestant pastor, equally committed to the future well-being of the Kanak people.

Of particular note is Waddell's attention to the practice of biography. He is acutely aware of the inadequacy of Western scholarly writing to render Pacific realities in a manner recognizable to Pacific peoples. As a result, he seeks to present Tjibaou as faithfully and as completely as possible, while avoiding overtly critical or discursive analysis of the man's life and ideas. In the name of accessibility, he keeps his archival and literature citations to a minimum, while drawing on an extensive body of interviews with those who knew Tjibaou. Waddell freely admits to the editorial selectivity of those with whom he spoke. Many were discreet in what they chose to speak about, out of respect for their friend, colleague, family member, or former adversary. Dealing with the intensity of emotions and lingering wounds from Tjibaou's death necessitated patience, fortitude, and a keen sense of timing. Equally confounding, though in a very different way, were Waddell's hesitations in writing about Tjibaou amidst the prejudice against all things French in the contemporary, Anglophone-dominated Pacific.

Language presented another issue for Waddell in the construction of this biography. The choice between English and French, and a consideration of the more than twenty-eight different languages spoken in New Caledonia were but a part of the biographer's dilemma. There was also a need to recapture to the extent possible the way Tjibaou spoke and its effects on his different audiences. A soft-spoken, self-effacing man, Tjibaou infused his French with Melanesian metaphors and symbols. He spoke with a decidedly Melanesian cadence; he used pauses for effect and often left his sentences unfinished. The challenge facing Waddell was to respect the integrity of the spoken word, and to insure that his translations did not detract from its power and eloquence.

A biography of this sort also requires recognition of the intellectual genealogy of which Tjibaou was a part. He was inspired by Chief Ataï, leader of the 1878 insurrection against the French in New Caledonia, and by more contemporary thinkers, including Roch Pidjot, the first Kanak to occupy a seat in the French Assembly, and Eloï Machoro, the outspoken secretary general of the Union Calédonienne who was assassinated in early 1985. Tjibaou's commitment to the liberation of Kanaky linked him to the plight of indigenous peoples elsewhere. He sought dialogue with them, and with all others committed to freedom and justice in the world. We hope that the publication of Eric Waddell's biography of Jean-Marie Tjibaou will help facilitate this still much needed dialogue.

David Hanlon
CENTER FOR PACIFIC ISLANDS STUDIES

Sitiveni Halapua
PACIFIC ISLANDS DEVELOPMENT PROGRAM

Contents

Illustrations

Maps

Figures

Acknowledgments

IN A VERY REAL SENSE acknowledging the many people who assisted me in the preparation of *Jean-Marie Tjibaou, Kanak Witness to the World* is like relating a *chemin coutumier,* a customary pathway, since in the course of the journey knowledge was shared, counsel provided, encouragement offered and, in a number of cases, new ties were established and others strengthened. It was a remarkable *chemin,* which transcended tribes, countries, and continents, beginning with the capturing of a seemingly timeless *parole* at the University of the South Pacific, in Suva, and provisionally ending with a customary gesture at the Tjibaou Cultural Center in Nouméa, where I presented a copy of the manuscript to Jean-Marie's wife, Marie-Claude Tjibaou. Some key stages in my journey are outlined in the introduction that follows. My purpose here is to identify as many as possible of the people I encountered in my search to learn and to understand.

In New Caledonia: Father Rock Apikaoua, Lêdji Bellow, Joseph Bouarate, Christian Burck, François Burck, Augustin Cidopua, Gérald Cortot, Julien Couhia, Corinne Cumenal, Gilles Dagneau, Alphonse and Thérèse Dinet, Jean-François Dupon, Bernard Gasser, Isabelle Gasser, Patrice Godin, Noël Gohoup, François Jarrige, Christian Jost, Wallès Kotra, Ben and Murielle Lahoussine, Liliane Laubreaux, Caroline Machoro, Victor Mampasse, Louis Mapou, Hamid Mokaddem, Roland Ouckewen, Armand Pala, Jean Pipite, Gilbert Tein, Emmanuel Tjibaou, Mireille Tjibaou, Octave Togna, Billy Wapotro, Aizik Wéa.

In Fiji: Bess Flores, Vanessa Griffin, Epeli Hau'ofa, Tarcisius Tara Kabutaulaka, Yoko Kanemasu, Asenati Liki, Vijay Naidu, George Saumane, Claire Slatter, Konai Helu Thaman, the Reverend Pothin Wete.

In Hawai'i: Linley Chapman, Murray Chapman, David Hanlon, Alan Howard, Bob Kiste, Jan Rensel.

In Australia: John Connell, Helen Fraser, Karis Muller.

In New Zealand: David Gegeo, Raeburn Lange, Moana Matthes, Karen Nero, David Small, Heather Young Leslie.

In France: Jean-Claude Amice, Tamatoa Bambridge, Alban Bensa, Joël

Bonnemaison, Jean Chesneaux, Moniale Chrysostome (Marie-Joëlle Dardelin), Jean Garnier, Mehdi Lallaoui, Philippe Missotte, Michel Rocard, Marizette Tarlier.

In Switzerland: Annabel Chanteraud, Pierre Dasen, Liliane Palandella.

In Belgium: Françoise Raynaud.

In Québec: Jean Morisset, together with my family who suffered my many absences and periods of introspection.

In addition a number of institutions provided me with the material support essential to the undertaking of a research and writing project of this scale: Agence de développement de la culture kanak (Tjibaou Cultural Center), IRD-Nouméa, Université de la Nouvelle-Calédonie, Université Laval (Laboratoire de cartographie, Département de géographie), University of Canterbury (Macmillan Brown Centre for Pacific Studies), and the University of the South Pacific (Oceania Centre for Arts and Culture). Two of them merit my special thanks. The Agence de développement de la culture kanak did everything possible to help and inform me in my search for documentary and audiovisual material over a period of thirteen years. For its part the Macmillan Brown Centre for Pacific Studies awarded me, at very short notice, a six-month position as a research scholar in 2005, thereby creating the opportunity to write my book. Bringing me to the University of Canterbury also allowed me to discover one of the Pacific's best-kept secrets, the absolutely remarkable collection of materials in the Macmillan Brown Library. Gravitating between my office, the library, and my temporary home in the suburb of Sumner, with its extraordinary view onto the Pacific Ocean, I experienced a sense of freedom and exhilaration that made the words flow readily.

There are most certainly other individuals and institutions that I have failed to mention. Hopefully they will accept my sincere apologies in the knowledge that they have, in their silent way, contributed to the elaboration of a portrait of a great Oceanian, arguably the most remarkable personality and voice the region has produced in the course of its entry onto the global stage. My most profound debt is to Jean-Marie Tjibaou himself. I had the privilege of hearing his thoughts and words on neighboring islands, and this experience motivated me to share them with other Oceanian peoples and with fellow global citizens. His hopes and fears with respect to the future of the Earth and of its many peoples and cultures are also ours. The words in the pages that follow are, as often as possible, those of Jean-Marie Tjibaou, while the fabric is mine. I alone am of course responsible for the nature and the quality of the latter.

Sources

IN ORDER TO MAKE the book more accessible to the general reader and at the same time to respect the Melanesian view that the word, hence knowledge, is shared rather than individually possessed, footnotes and references in the body of the text are reduced to a minimum. At the same time, given that the book is the product of a long period of scholarly research, drawing extensively on written and audiovisual materials as well as on interviews with a large number of informants, it is vital that sources be identified. They can best be conceived of as a nested set of materials.

At the core are four essential documents focusing on Jean-Marie Tjibaou himself: the long "conversation" Jacques Violette had with Jean-Marie in June 1987, which was transcribed and published shortly after his assassination (Tjibaou 1989c); the biography of *Le Monde* journalist Alain Rollat, which was published a few months later (Rollat 1989b); the extensive collection of the writings of and interviews with Jean-Marie, prepared by Alban Bensa and Éric Wittersheim (Tjibaou 1996); and, most recently, Hamid Mokaddem's philosophical study of Jean-Marie's political legacy (Mokaddem 2005). An English translation of Bensa and Wittersheim's collection, by Helen Fraser and John Trotter, appeared in Australia in 2005 (Tjibaou 2005).

A first circle around this core comprises major analyses by investigative journalists of two key crises, the 1984 massacre at Hienghène (Duroy 1988) and the 1988 hostage taking and military assault on Ouvéa (Plenel and Rollat 1988).

A second circle consists of contextual overviews of New Caledonia and, more generally, the French Pacific. These include the first and second editions of Alban Bensa's historical study articulated around the notion of a clash of civilizations (1990, 1998); Jean-Luc Mathieu's clinical and Anne Pitoiset's more poetic description of the territory (Mathieu 1995; Pitoiset 1999); and Jacqueline Sénès's chronological overview of events that have marked its history (1985). Jean Chesneaux and Nic Maclellan drew a broad portrait of France in the Pacific (1992). For English-language materials, the best coverage of the French Pacific is provided by Robert Aldrich (1990;

1993), while John Connell's political history of New Caledonia (1987) and Michael Spencer, Alan Ward, and John Connell's collection on nationalism and dependency in the territory (1988) are indispensable reading.

A third and final circle covers principal sources drawn on for the writing of specific sections of the book. These are identified at the beginning of the notes to each chapter.

Unless otherwise noted, all translations from the original French are my own.

Abbreviations

ADCK	Agence de développement de la culture kanak (Agency for the Development of Kanak Culture)
ADRAF	Agence de développement rural et d'aménagement foncier (Agency for Rural Development and Land Management)
AICLF	Association des Indigènes Calédoniens et Loyaltiens Français (Association of French Indigenous Caledonians and Loyalty Islanders)
AISDPK	Association Information et Soutien aux Droits du Peuple Kanak (Association for Information and Support of the Rights of the Kanak People)
CeFA	Centre de Formation d'Animateurs (Center for the Training of Group Leaders)
CRS	Compagnies Républicaines de Sécurité (security and riot police)
DOM-TOM	Départements d'outre-mer et territoires d'outre-mer (French Overseas Departments and Territories)
ÉHÉSS	École des Hautes Études en Sciences Sociales (School of Advanced Studies in the Social Sciences)
ÉPHÉ	École Pratique des Hautes Études (Research Training School in Advanced Studies)
ÉPK	École populaire kanak (Kanak people's school)
FADIL	Fonds d'aide au développement des îles et de l'intérieur (Development Assistance Fund for the Interior and the [Outer] Islands)
FI	Front Indépendantiste (Independentist Front)
FLNKS	Front de Libération Nationale Kanak Socialiste (National Kanak and Socialist Liberation Front)
FN	Front National (National Front)
FNSC	Fédération pour la Nouvelle Société Calédonienne (Federation for a New Caledonian Society)

FULK   Front Uni de Libération Kanak (United Kanak Liberation
            Front)
GFA   Groupement foncier agricole (agricultural land group)
GIGN   Groupe d'Intervention de la Gendarmerie Nationale
            (national police commando group)
IFO   Institut Français d'Océanie (French Institute of Oceania)
INALCO   Institut National des Langues et Civilisations Orientales
            (National Institute for Oriental Languages and
            Civilizations)
IRD   Institut de Recherche pour le Développement (Institute
            of Development Research [formerly ORSTOM])
LKS   Libération Kanak Socialiste (Kanak Socialist Liberation)
ORSTOM   Office de la Recherche Scientifique et Technique
            d'Outre-Mer (Office of Overseas Scientific and Technical
            Research)
PALIKA   Parti de Libération Kanak (Party for Kanak Liberation)
RPC   Rassemblement pour la Calédonie (Assembly for [New]
            Caledonia)
RPCR   Rassemblement pour la Calédonie dans la République
            (Assembly for [New] Caledonia within the Republic)
RPR   Rassemblement pour la République (Assembly for the
            Republic]
SLN   Société le Nickel (nickel mining company)
SMSP   Société Minière du Sud Pacifique (South Pacific mining
            company)
SOFINOR   Société de Financement et d'Investissement de la
            Province Nord (Society for Finance and Investment in the
            Northern Province)
UC   Union Calédonienne (Caledonian Union)
UICALO   Union des Indigènes Calédoniens Amis de la Liberté
            dans l'Ordre (Union of Indigenous Caledonian Friends of
            Liberty with Order)
USTKE   Union Syndicale des Travailleurs Kanaks et des Exploités
            (Labor Union of Kanak Workers and Exploited Persons)

JEAN-MARIE TJIBAOU,
Kanak Witness to the World

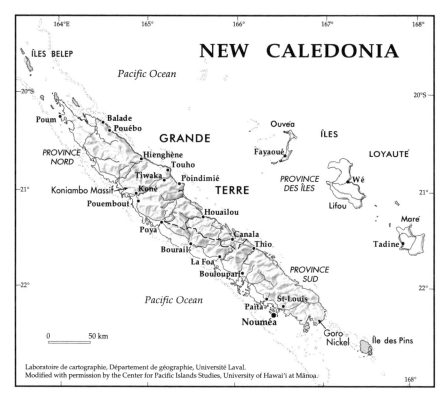

Laboratoire de cartographie, Département de géographie, Université Laval.
Modified with permission by the Center for Pacific Islands Studies, University of Hawaiʻi at Mānoa.

Map 1

Introduction
The Challenge of Writing about Jean-Marie Tjibaou

> You walked into my home as if it were your home. How, then, could I make you welcome?

WRITING ANY BOOK is invariably an intense personal experience, no matter how detached one is from the subject matter. It absorbs, even possesses the author, from the moment the first sentences are formulated until the final polishing of the manuscript. Writing biography is even more emotionally charged because it involves entering the life of another human being and establishing an intimate relationship with that person, be it real or simply through the mediation of the spoken or written word. My thoughts on this account are drawn spontaneously to David Marr's biography of Patrick White (Marr 1991). Although no more than a simple admirer of White's writing, I wept when I arrived at the last few pages, both at the thought of a dying man, the finished manuscript in his hands, tearfully reading the painful story of his own life, and at his biographer's fear that the portrait he had drawn may have accelerated his subject's departure, in 1990, from this world.

The second time I wept over biography was in 1993. The evening before, in the context of the institution's Twenty-Fifth Anniversary Lecture Series, I had given a public lecture at the University of the South Pacific entitled "Jean-Marie Tjibaou: Kanak Witness to the World." Tjibaou was the deceased leader of the Melanesian independence movement in neighboring New Caledonia. I had been very nervous in the preceding weeks, and I don't think I have ever spent so much time fine-tuning a presentation, essentially because I had chosen to reveal a Melanesian person and mind to a Pacific Island audience. In addition, that person's words and thoughts were already of inestimable importance to me, a *palagi,* who, on and off over several decades, had traveled, lived, and worked in Oceania, in other words who had been materially and, above all, spiritually nourished by the region.

There was no question of my filtering the man through academic discourse, constructing and deconstructing him, or clothing him in alien theory. I was aware that my audience knew little about him, but that his name was, for reasons unclear to me at the time, of great significance to them. I felt I was adventuring into a potential minefield. So, in preparing the lecture, reading about Jean-Marie, delving into his writings and speeches, listening to interviews, and meeting people who had known him, I had come to the most natural of decisions: I would let the man speak for himself, in his own words, simply assuming the responsibility of translating them, giving them a semblance of order, with a view to sharing them with my Suva audience. I received numerous messages from island friends, scholars, and students following my talk, one in particular coming from a Solomon Islands colleague:

> I sat up late last night, thinking about the man within me. A man who has lived for thousands of years. He adopted me when I was given birth by a mother he adopted before me. He inherited me as I inherited him and he lived in me as I in him. . . . Since the end of the sixteenth century he has become subjugated, marginalised and may even have been obliterated by strangers he accepted as visitors to his home. For years he remained dormant, dying in silence and in indifference on my part. I whom he nourished and fed for years with the word of his wisdom and the experience of living in this land for centuries.
>
> I do not know how to say thankyou to you, white man, who has resurrected the man within me. It is because the man within me does not have a word for "thankyou." Not because he is unappreciative but rather because appreciation is so deep that no word could express it. Also it is because the man within me understands that what is given will come back one day. Giving is reciprocal. Maybe it won't come back tomorrow, but it will one day. Not in your lifetime maybe, but in your grandchildren's. This is because, for the man in me, human relationships and human values have no time limits.
>
> From the man within me there are words that come in bits and pieces. My grandpa used to tell me: "When I die, throw the soil into my grave, but do not throw away my words." I guess he is right. The man within me is the word that lives on. He is what anthropologists and other scholars call "The Melanesian Society." But he is part of me and I am part of him.
>
> I am proud he exists and I respect him as he respects me. Through him and the experiences I gather elsewhere, we can build a better society for all. We have always existed, two persons in one, but sometimes forgetting. (Tarcisius Tara Kabutaulaka, 7 October 1993)

Such spontaneous responses confirmed in my own mind what I had already grasped in the context of my experience teaching at several Pacific

Island universities: that island students do not recognize themselves in the vast majority of social science writing on Oceania that they are required to read, assimilate, and reproduce in the course of their studies. It is not simply a question of Western scholarly obsession with footnoting, or with academic language, but more fundamentally, of the actual subject matter that characterizes much of the writing of metropolitan scholars, for they are largely driven by theoretical and ideological debates in vogue in their home countries and institutions. Their writings are frequently colored by arbitrary distinctions between tradition and modernity, and between the village (tribe or bush) and the town. They tend to celebrate distance and isolation. In other words they are too often concerned with the differences between the authors as Westerners (real, or assimilated by education) and Islanders—the normal and the norm versus the strange and the exotic. Precious little attention is given to what is shared, by virtue of belonging to a single "family of man" and to the fast emerging global community. Their writings reveal what Margaret Jolly described in a 2003 workshop, "Learning Oceania," held at the Center for Pacific Islands Studies, University of Hawai'i, as "the desperate inadequacy of anthropology."

As another Pacific Island colleague and friend said to me a few years ago:

> Nothing has changed. With a few notable exceptions, the Pacific Islands world is a world of property—intellectual property, "my people"—which is traded on the global academic stock exchange, often for high stakes. Local knowledge, intellectual debate, great theory: it is all so disembodied, and yet eminently marketable.
>
> I eavesdrop on their conversations on electronic bulletin boards. It is a world of ethereal, mesmerising and oft-times incomprehensible chit-chat which finds its ultimate expression in academic conferences, articles and disciplines; conferences Pacific Islanders don't attend, articles they don't read and disciplines they don't study.
>
> Most of these dealers in Pacific Islands knowledge are certainly good people, kind and generous. They all have friends down there in their little communities, but they don't participate in the larger fabric of Oceanian society. One can't expect them to. Theirs is another culture, another place, where they are born, marry, raise children and die.
>
> The drama lies in the fact that it is they who accumulate the knowledge on the Pacific, translate it into their languages, their forms, their media, their preoccupations. And it is the educational institutions of the region who work hard at erasing, or at least belittling, what remains behind.
>
> In the new forms of cultural transmission it is largely this scholarly Western version which trickles back, the language filtered by the Church and the substance interpreted by the University. No wonder there is shame and confusion. And also anger. No wonder, too, figures like Jean-Marie Tjibaou emerge from

this cultural and intellectual war zone to deliver their message to their world, if not indeed to the world as a whole. (3 August 2002)

Of course, anthropology is not alone in its disembodied regard and its culturally determined introspection.

Despite the parachuted theories, and despite being inundated by data generated within the region to nourish those theories, Oceania has, as Pacific Islands scholars constantly stress, always produced its people of ideas and its philosophers. It is just that they have passed largely unnoticed and unrecognized, their thoughts having rarely been committed to paper.

On that memorable evening the words and dreams of Jean-Marie Tjibaou had clearly bridged the gap between the observer and the observed, as another Solomon Island colleague was to tell a couple of years later. For George Saumane, Jean-Marie's evocation of a distinctive "Melanesian Way," in terms of engagement in the modern world, was much more meaningful than that of Bernard Narakobi, the New Guinean who was the first to formulate the expression (1983). Particularly with respect to the spoken word, or *parole,* and to his references to land and to the ancestors, Tjibaou's vision offered sense and meaning because it was, in his case, clearly lived and experienced. It evoked and legitimized a specifically Melanesian way of navigating the living world. For George, the strength of the message resided in its assertion that the spoken word belongs to everybody and nobody, that it flows through people and is shared, that it creates and cements relationships, thereby giving sense to an individual as a member of a group; it encapsulates a place, a point in time in a long trajectory, a rank, a sense of meaning and of purpose. What a contrast it was with the daily drama of Melanesian students at the University of the South Pacific, confronted by a Western academic discourse where the word is considered to be individual property, to be claimed and recognized, its parentage to be inscribed in "sources." For island students, to ignore this essential, scholarly fact is to risk reproach, even sanctions, and perhaps failure for not having summarized and transmitted knowledge in a responsible, transparent, and even honest manner!

In the days following my lecture I also learned, to my absolute astonishment, that the thoughts and loyalties of several of my Oceanian colleagues lay with Djubelly Wéa, the man immediately responsible for Jean-Marie's death on Ouvéa, in the Loyalty Islands, some four years earlier. Two or three of them had spontaneously written poems in memory of him. While they had known Djubelly well, Jean-Marie was an obscure and unfathomable personality, a few recalling a solitary experience in Sydney where he had refused their invitation to publicly take a position against Sitiveni Rabuka as perpetrator of the 1987 coups in Fiji.

Such sentiments and revelations were largely at the origin of my decision to delve further into the life, thoughts, and actions of Jean-Marie

Tjibaou, and also of my decision to present the results in as direct as possible a manner, where I would purposely avoid theoretical constructs and searching critical analysis. For me, it was an avenue fraught with risk, since I had never met Jean-Marie and was absent from and, to all intents and purposes, out of touch with the Pacific during the 1980s, the period when he had been projected by history onto the public scene. I also knew little or nothing of New Caledonia, apart from having briefly set foot in the capital, Nouméa, in 1967, in the course of a journey from Port Vila to Sydney on a Messageries Maritimes *paquebot mixte* (mixed passenger-cargo steamship), the *Tahitien*.

It was not the Pacific as an object of study that had initially drawn me to the man, but the sum of my own adult life experiences, and of my personal values. The Pacific was a part of both, but my spontaneous response to the words and actions of Jean-Marie Tjibaou was above all inscribed in the preoccupations of the postwar generation to which I belonged. In 1991 I had been asked by *The Contemporary Pacific* to review a special issue of the journal *Ethnies* entitled *Renaissance in the Pacific* (Chapman and Dupon 1989a). One of the two editors, Murray Chapman, was a long-standing friend and colleague, and he was no doubt at the origin of the invitation. Some twenty papers, written for the most part by Islanders, addressed the question of cultural identity among the peoples of the region. The publication had been trapped in the turbulent events of New Caledonia in the 1980s, a colony and a country hovering on the verge of civil war. The *événements* (events), as the dramatic situation is still euphemistically referred to in the territory, had led to the canceling of the Fourth Pacific Festival of Arts, which was to have taken place in Nouméa in 1984, and to the planned appearance of the collection. It took five years to find another publisher. One contribution in particular struck me—an interview the second editor had conducted with Jean-Marie Tjibaou, about which I wrote:

> [He] speaks of the parallel "search for identity and the acquisition of elements from other cultures" (78), the need to fully grasp the configuration of self in order to handle the confrontation with other. He reflects on the revalorization of "Custom" as a strategy for self-recognition and dignity: "It is in its totality that tradition must give a sense to the life of a Melanesian" (76). But at the same time he sees this reappropriation of the past not as an end in itself but as providing "models for the integration of the traditional and the modern" (76). . . . Tjibaou makes a plea for reconciliation, not only between Kanaks and non-Kanaks, but also between the town and the country, the state and the tribe. . . . he invokes themes which . . . he alone has the capacity to translate into one broad and fundamentally generous vision of the world. Now that he has gone we can only hope that we will have more time to linger on his words. (Waddell 1992, 216–218)

Jean-Marie's death had occurred at the very moment of *Renaissance in the Pacific* going to press, allowing just enough time for the editors to insert a brief statement on the opening page. In dedicating the issue to him they quoted a reflection made by a man whose personality, dignity, and stature had clearly inspired them: "In our view of life, the important thing is always to share, to give what one has, all that one is. It may be a smile, a word of wisdom, or a custom, with the words that give it meaning. If a person has been able to live thus, on the day of his death, customary rites will be held over his tomb. He will be remembered as someone who knew how to give; and when he dies it will be like a music vibrating gently into silence. This is what, in our eyes, defines the greatness of a man" (Tjibaou, quoted in Chapman and Dupon 1989a, 3).

My immediate reaction was that such words were addressed to me too, and to my world, to all possible worlds, and I decided forthwith that I must go to New Caledonia in search of Jean-Marie Tjibaou. It was 1993. Jean-François Dupon, a geographer working at the French government's Institut de Recherche pour le Développement (IRD, formerly ORSTOM) in Nouméa, took me straight to the Agence de développement de la culture kanak (ADCK) and introduced me to the director, Octave Togna, and to Lêdji Bellow, their public relations (information and communication) officer at the time. Mme Bellow, a journalist originally from West Africa, immediately opened up doors, archives, and her heart to me. Although she had only met Jean-Marie toward the end of his life, she was an *inconditionnelle* (ardent supporter), describing him as "one of the most lively and warmest beings she had ever met" (Bellow 1989b, 28). This spontaneous expression of enthusiasm at having had the privilege of knowing Jean-Marie Tjibaou was to be repeated, with one solitary exception,[1] by everyone I met in the course of my research over the following years, invariably by recourse to such epithets as "simple," "down to earth," "totally honest," "warm," "a true humanist," "profoundly moral." All were eager to meet with me, to share their knowledge and their emotions with respect to someone they were convinced was a remarkable man. They were also invariably keen to know what had drawn me to him and to learn of my intentions. In other words, there was a concern to share what was for everyone a transforming encounter.

Given the forceful and moving nature of so many of these observations and of the repeated expressions of generosity on the part of all the people I met over the years, I quickly came to the conclusion that my unique responsibility in writing about Jean-Marie Tjibaou must be to present, as faithfully as possible, the man, his ideas, and his itinerary, and to avoid engaging in what may be described as a critical analysis or study. In so doing I prefer essentially to leave to the reader the task of judging and interpreting his view of Kanak civilization, both in the immediate New Caledonian context and in the larger contexts of Oceania and the modern world. While I run the risk of being taxed as naive and idealistic in proceeding in this manner, I am convinced that it is the most appropriate way of opening Jean-Marie Tjibaou's vision of his people, and of the world into which they were projected, to a Pacific Island audience. It is also the best way of demonstrating to a Western scholarly audience the manner in which a Pacific Island life embraces the present and prepares to engage the future. In other words, in opting for this approach, Jean-Marie Tjibaou's life, knowledge, values, and vision reveal themselves to be simultaneously traditional and modern—or to be neither, because they are constantly evolving from firmly grounded Melanesian roots into the rapidly changing global community, thereby transcending all boundaries, real or imagined.

The focus of the book being the word, and in particular the spoken word, rather than the man, little or no attention is given to the very considerable literature on "writing biography" or to delving into Jean-Marie Tjibaou's personal life. There is no plot, but simply periods in a man's life, that life being a brief moment in the trajectory of a civilization, which civilization is but a speck in the modern world. It is the voice of a man who spoke on behalf of "a people so few in number that it runs the risk at any moment of disappearing," as Jean-Marie repeatedly took pains to explain, whether in Nouméa, Paris, Geneva, or New York.

If what follows is biography at all, it is what I prefer to call intellectual biography, that is, an attempt to highlight the complex web of one man's experiences, and of the ideas and knowledge gained from them, with a view to establishing the foundations of his political philosophy, of his conception of culture and identity, and of his commitments and worldview. This approach will demonstrate, I believe, that his vision—"the whole"—is the fruit of a lifetime's journey that was embarked on and articulated around a firm and, above all, confident and extremely articulate Melanesian base. Jean-Marie's itinerary, from his tribal home, crossed many intellectual and geographical territories, territories that, in his view, were largely complementary and not conflictual, and that he succeeded in blending into a seemingly creative and coherent whole. In the story of his life the terms *roots* and *routes* take on all their meaning, for Jean-Marie was a traveler who never lost sight of home, a *passeur*, a crosser of frontiers, who sought both to nourish his own world with the wealth of experience gained elsewhere and to nourish the larger world with the accumulated experience of his own people.

In principle, an essentially descriptive exercise should be conducted relatively rapidly, and yet this study of Jean-Marie has taken the best part of fifteen years to complete. I can offer many reasons for this, the most banal being my administrative responsibilities within academia, changing jobs and continents, and the difficulties of writing on the Pacific in a Québec that is too distant from the region to be even mildly interested in its destiny. In addition, there was the very considerable task of retracing Jean-Marie's journey, from his village in the hills behind Hienghène to Nouméa and then on to Lyon, Paris, and the Larzac; or of meeting the many people who crossed his path—in Fiji, France, Switzerland, and Australia. There were so many routes to follow in the search for information and understanding. At the

same time, far more important considerations account for the slow matu-
ration of the book, considerations grounded in the realities of Melanesian
history and of life in New Caledonia.

First among them was the sentiment, attributed to Marie-Claude
Tjibaou, Jean-Marie's wife, that it was important to produce biographies of
his spiritual and intellectual predecessors, or ancestors—Chief Ataï, Roch
Pidjot, Eloï Machoro—before writing one on Jean-Marie. It may have been
a simple question of humility and of respect on her part, but it was perhaps
also a way of expressing how the spoken word moves through people and
generations, with Jean-Marie being the temporary depository of the knowledge and wisdom of an ancestral civilization. The essential fluidity of this
parole ensures that it can adapt and respond to changing realities, while its inherent mobility means that it can never be identified with any one person.

Second, very early in my research I met Father Rock Apikaoua, the
Kanak priest who had officiated at Jean-Marie's burial ceremony. He told
me that he had read nothing on Jean-Marie since his death five years earlier
because he felt that there was something indecent about it all. To illustrate
his point, he recounted a visit to a bookshop that he had made with one of
Jean-Marie's sons, then an adolescent. The boy's eyes were drawn to a book
on his father, with his face on the front cover. He was both attracted to and
troubled by what he saw, and it prompted Father Apikaoua to assure him
there would come a time and a place for him to read it, but it was not yet.

The third and, perhaps for me, the most important cautionary note
was expressed by Gérald Cortot, who had been *chef de cabinet* (principal secretary) for Jean-Marie at the time of his death. M. Cortot, a métis from
Nouméa, had spent fifteen years working closely with him, preparing his
speeches and becoming a close family friend. When I met him in the late
nineties he was director of a company investing in the tourist industry and
was also associated with the Société Minière du Sud Pacifique (SMSP), which
was committed to the development of a majority Kanak-owned nickel mining and processing initiative in the Province Nord. M. Cortot was quite obviously eager to meet me. A man who was both open and discreet at the same
time, concerned to protect a close friend for whom he had an immense respect—"I don't want to reveal the man in all his intimacy. There are things I
will probably never say"—he was nevertheless keen to talk about Jean-Marie.
He also wanted to listen to me, so that I might both reveal my intentions
and disclose my perspective on the man. When I had made them known, he
proceeded to share his thoughts as to the shortcomings of many outsider
observers of Melanesian society:

> This tendency [on the part of foreign researchers] to make mistakes, to conduct
> an analysis on the basis of Western thought, and hence to impose a perspective
> which is more their own—their analytical and theoretical framework, their intel-
> lectual preoccupations—and hence never arrive at the essential, never really

listen. They ignore the Melanesian roots of Jean-Marie Tjibaou's reasoning and actions. They impose another framework on his words, thereby deforming them and ignoring their essence. In addition they skim over the events in which the words are inscribed, ignoring the fundamental link that exists between the word and the act. (Gérald Cortot, 7 May 1997)

For me, it was a powerful observation and it concluded with Gérald Cortot's advice to me to proceed *slowly*, thereby allowing me to assimilate the reasoning of Jean-Marie and the broad cultural context in which it was articulated.

Needless to say, I was moved by the counsel I received. I thought about it for a long time as I crisscrossed New Caledonia, visited the *terre* and *case kanak* (Kanak land and house) on the Larzac in southern France, discussed with close friends of Jean-Marie, and sat with his assassin's brother at Goosana. And I took note. Indeed it was only in late 2002 that I gained sufficient confidence to set foot on Ouvéa, an island that was, at the time, still an open wound in the body of Kanaky. My patience was rewarded. Some at least of the intense pain and suffering of the 1980s has now receded, as has the sense of loss and tragedy. A new generation has largely displaced the one that occupied the center stage during the *événements*. The light breeze in the valleys of the Central Chain and the breaking surf along the East Coast have replaced the sounds of gunshot and the cries of pain. Important and deeply moving acts of reconciliation have been completed. While the time of mourning has passed, and some of the suffering fades into distant memory, the spoken word remains. The time is now opportune for the thoughts of an exceptional man, who dedicated his life to his people, to be freely shared with a generation and with peoples and nations of the Island Pacific that did not have the privilege of knowing him.

My own long journey has been motivated by another, more personal conviction regarding the essential wisdom of what the West calls indigenous peoples. I share, with the likes of Jean Malaurie, the conviction that those "first" communities and civilizations that still survive on their ancestral lands are, in a very real sense, "the sentinels of our planet":

We must pay attention to rooted peoples, these first-comers, in order to learn that the truth comes not only from above, from the Heavens, but also, humbly, from below, from that which is at the origin of the universe, from that which constitutes the texture of the earth, from its water, and from the air which gives us life. *Nolens volens,* we are moving towards a merging of thought, that of the sacred books and that of pantheistic peoples. . . .

Michelet wrote, "To see what no one sees, that is second sight." To see what one senses is to come, what will be born, that is prophecy. They are two things which astonish the masses, attract the mockery of the wise, and which are typically a spontaneous gift of simplicity. This gift, rare among "civilized" people

is, as we know, widespread among first nations, regardless of whether they are
called "savages" or "barbarians." (Malaurie 1999, 28)

Let me be clear: I'm not suggesting that indigenous peoples are intrin-
sically nobler or purer than later comers, that there is something ethnic or,
indeed, genetic, about their superiority. They too have feet of clay, know
cruelty and violence, pain and oppression. They are responsible for major
biological extinctions, and they are in the process of being shattered by alcohol, violence, the rape of the environment, urbanization, self-interest, and
the cynical manipulation of customary practice. However, in today's world
there are still survivors of such peoples, who remind us of the vital significance of having an uninterrupted experience of a particular place, of being
able to conceive a local world in terms of long (or deep) time, of possessing
a warm and intimate knowledge of the land, and of transmitting that knowledge through the entire fabric of society, such that it is universally shared
and possessed. Memory and dignity are of inestimable importance to these
communities, the former being constantly nourished by the natural world
and the latter fused with a great sense of humility in relation to it.

Such a grounded and fast-disappearing indigenous world stands in
stark contrast to, and defiance of, a largely atomized and narcissistic urban-
industrial world, where its individual members are locked into the present
and the immediate future, are isolated from and largely ignorant of the
natural world, and are totally committed, with their political leadership, to a
logic of unlimited accumulation of material wealth and unconstrained economic growth. One has only to juxtapose, in this respect, the words of Ralph
Klein, until recently premier of Alberta, Canada, with those of Jean-Marie
Tjibaou, to appreciate the gulf between two fundamentally different ways of
inhabiting the earth. Klein, expressing his opposition to the Canadian government's intention to sign the Kyoto Protocol, announced, "I'm not going
to be here in thirty years' time and neither are most of the people around
me. I don't care a fuck." A few weeks before his assassination, Jean-Marie
affirmed, with regard to the natural world in general and to his responsibility
to others:

> Me? I'm only momentarily here. But I must do everything in my power to en-
> sure that the country I will leave to my sons is the most beautiful possible. For
> it to be rich in thought, in wisdom, in flowers and in food. (Quoted in Bellow
> 1989a, 39)
>   One is accountable, in time and in space, from the day when one first appears
> before the sun to the day on which one disappears. Regardless of the place one
> finds oneself in, one has the same responsibility with regard to present and
> future generations. (Quoted in Bellow 1989b, 29)[2]

This tragic confrontation of small communities that are bearers of an
intimate, generous, aesthetically pleasing, and ritualized knowledge of their

local geographies by an all-conquering industrial civilization of planetary dimensions is what makes the message of Jean-Marie so important in my mind. It is not nostalgia that motivates me but a sense of tragedy and crisis, of an inability to engage in any real form of intercultural communication, one that once again he so eloquently expressed when speaking of the particular challenge facing New Caledonia in the 1980s:

> If today I can share with a non-Kanak of this country that which I possess of French culture, it is impossible for him to share with me the universal element of my culture. (1989a, 78)

Jean-Marie's knowledge, intrinsic simplicity, and intelligence set him resolutely apart. He was much more than a big man (or tribal chief), from Hienghène, an articulate interpreter and promoter of Melanesian culture and identity, or the president of the Provisional Government of Kanaky. He was a great man. His disarming eloquence and his total honesty constituted the outward expressions of this unique status.

The spoken and written word—language: therein lay another of my hesitations with respect to writing about Jean-Marie. Which language should I express it in, French or English? The dilemma was not simply a function of being fluent in and writing easily in both. Language is the linchpin of culture, essentially the medium through which that culture is diffused within a group and transmitted from generation to generation. At least twenty-eight Melanesian languages are spoken in New Caledonia, none of them dominant. For the Kanak, French is the common language, just as Bislama is the acknowledged lingua franca of Vanuatu and English of Fiji. Many speak French extremely well, and in this sense Jean-Marie was simply a primus inter pares. His command of French was remarkable, and in public he infused it with Melanesian metaphors and symbols and graced it with a Melanesian rhythm. He often paused before he spoke and left his sentences suspended, as if relaying a *parole* that reached far back into the past and would pursue its course unbroken into the future. In these circumstances, my natural response was to seek to respect the integrity of his essentially spoken word rather than to deprive it, through translation, of much of its intrinsic force and beauty.

Yet another consideration accounted for my lengthy hesitations. Strange as it may seem, in the broad regional context of a now dominantly anglophone Pacific, all things "French"—a term broadly and indiscriminately used to cover language, culture, politics, a metropolitan state, and anything associated with the French, Frenchness, and the French presence in the region—are even today often considered to be a source of some irritation, if not inherently retrograde. Everything perceived as French is seen as a reality that makes little sense and runs counter to the great forces of history. The roots of this ambivalence plunge far down into the Pacific Ocean, embracing competing imperial designs in the late eighteenth and nineteenth centuries, deep-seated rivalry between the Protestant and Catholic Churches, the Pritchard affair in Tahiti, and, in recent decades, metropolitan France's resistance to powerful independence movements in its Pacific territories, the absurdity of nuclear testing on Moruroa and, linked with it, the sinking in 1985 of the admiral ship of the Greenpeace fleet, *Rainbow Warrior,* in Auckland harbor.[3] Australia and New Zealand, first as British colonies and then dominions, not to mention the merchants of Sydney, have played a crucial role in this continuing drama. Responsibilities as regional gendarmes, and interests as trading and themselves colonizing nations, have served to nourish this animosity for more than a hundred and fifty years.

In such a context, the boundaries between rationality and irrationality, empirical knowledge and particular interests, reason and emotion, are all too easily blurred. Even in a scholarly world it can easily become a situation where, to quote Wittgenstein, "The limits of my discourse are those of my universe" and the writings of a tiny minority of reactionary French academics are characterized as being the voice of French scholarship as a whole. The outcomes can be quite absurd, as I discovered on joining the University of the South Pacific in 1990 and being cautioned by several colleagues about the dangers of speaking French in the corridors of the institution! As if English were not also an imperial language, and as if French speakers from Canada were condemned to the same regional dialectic! If the tide has turned somewhat in recent years and a new understanding has been reached between France, Australia, and New Zealand, as well as with the historically ambivalent independent Melanesian states, it is essentially by virtue of a convergence of strategic preoccupations, notably the concern to buttress "failed" island states and the need to protect the region from what are perceived as destabilizing forces originating in Asia.

More seriously, such partiality becomes problematic in any attempt to understand and appreciate Jean-Marie Tjibaou, not to mention other intellectuals and thinkers from the French-speaking Pacific. Their references, networks, and friends extend to and pass through France, on to Africa, the Caribbean, and other parts of the francophone world. They are marked by events, struggles, and debates taking place within that universe, and many of their references and values are drawn from it. Jean-Marie Tjibaou was not allergic to France, and he was not alone in that respect. There was much he liked about French civilization, as there was much that angered and frustrated him. In the final analysis, France and the French language were part of his identity, his window on the world, and he had no wish or reason to reject them. Because this was the larger world that nourished him and within which he navigated, he remained relatively unfamiliar with the anglophone Pacific and the Anglo-American realm at large. At the same time his anchor was unequivocally Kanak, and this ensured an intuitive understanding of and complicity with other Oceanians.

In a context where, in regional terms, any specific group is disadvantaged with respect to power relations and to something that can broadly be described as "understanding," it is a natural tendency for its members to withdraw into their familiar cultural and intellectual space, where they are more likely to be intuitively understood. Fortunately the growing number of publications in French on Jean-Marie Tjibaou, beginning with the moving portrait drawn by the journalist Alain Rollat in the months immediately after his death (Rollat 1989b), followed by the important collection of interviews with and writings by him prepared by Alban Bensa and Éric Wittersheim (Tjibaou 1996, 2005), and most recently Hamid Mokaddem's scholarly study of his political philosophy (Mokaddem 2005) all deterred me from gravitating toward such shelter. An invitation to join the Macmillan Brown Centre for Pacific Studies as a visiting scholar in 2005 settled the matter. I could finally write the book and thereby fulfill a debt to my friends and former colleagues of the University of the South Pacific who responded with such enthusiasm back in 1993 to my first lecture on Jean-Marie. They encouraged me to delve further, even though their hearts lay with the man who was immediately responsible for his descent into what he described as "the big black hole." Therein lies my decision to offer his words, his thoughts, and his life "in translation," in the belief that they will thereby transcend those barriers that are mere artifacts of imperial design.

1 "The Big Black Hole"... and the Open Wounds of Ouvéa

> I would say that perhaps the hardest is not to die; the hardest is to remain alive and to feel that one is a stranger in one's own country, to feel that one's country is dying, to feel that one is incapable of rising to the challenge and of reasserting our claim to reconquer the sovereignty of Kanaky.

THE TOURIST literature is frightening in its naivety and ignorance. The brochures prepared principally for the Japanese who frequent the luxury hotel at Mouly assert that Ouvéa is the "closest island to Paradise... the dazzling purity of the combined colors of the sky, the lagoon and the vegetation, the exceptionally clement climate, the natural hospitality of its inhabitants, the gentle way of life in an island protected from any impurity." Certainly that is how it appears to those privileged few for whom this partly raised atoll is a brief holiday destination, blinded as they are by the sun, the sand, and the glistening water of the lagoon (figure 1). However, such international tourists are simply another manifestation of what the inhabitants of neighboring Tanna call "drifting men." Their perceptions and experience of the island bear absolutely no resemblance to those of the *man-ples*,[1] whose roots plunge deep into its earth, and for whom Ouvéa is an open wound of seemingly immeasurable form and depth. In a very real sense it is a brooding place, steeped in a succession of dramas, broken dreams, and a distinctive historical experience—dark and even defensively hostile to the inquisitive outsider... until the silence is broken and the island begins to tell its own story—a story that is crucial to understanding what Jean-Marie Tjibaou lived and died for. It helps explain why it was a fellow Kanak independentist[2] who shot him and, the ultimate irony, why it was a former pastor who, in one last gesture of desperation, resorted to killing a former priest.

The latest, most tragic of Ouvéa's many wounds is the product of two gestures of seemingly incomprehensible violence, one inflicted at Goosana in 1988 and the other at Hwaadrila in 1989. Both have served to accentuate

15 km

N

FIGURE 1. Ouvéa atoll as seen from space in November 1990. The southeast portion is slightly raised, resulting in a continuous landmass embracing the districts of Fayaoué (at bottom) and Saint-Joseph (at right). The island of Mouly (left) is linked to Fayaoué by a bridge. The largely submerged atoll of Beautemps-Beaupré is visible at the top. *(Image Science & Analysis Laboratory, NASA Johnson Space Center)*

a deep cultural and geographical rift within the Kanak community, a rift much more profound than the one that separates loyalists and independentists into distinct political camps. Ouvéa is steeped in blood, with a total of twenty-eight violent deaths inscribed in the minds and thoughts of all its inhabitants, but most particularly in those of the Goosana tribe and their chiefdom of Imwene, located at the northern end of the island (map 2).

The first catastrophe was provoked by the killing of four French gendarmes on 22 April 1988, in the assault, by a group of independence militants, on the police station at Fayaoué, situated in the center of the island.

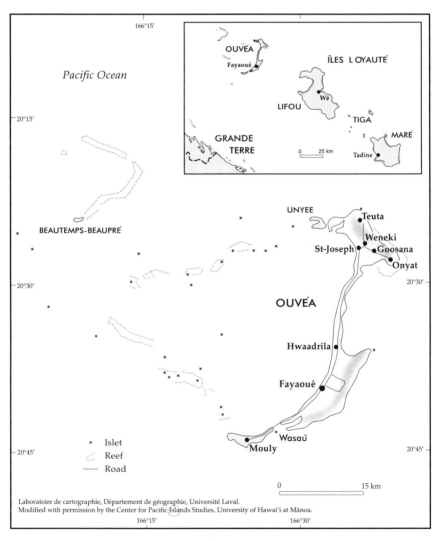

Map 2. Ouvéa and the Loyalty Islands (Îles Loyauté)

Twenty-six more gendarmes were taken hostage by the militants, and sixteen of these were transferred to a sacred cave on Goosana land in the north of the island, where they were held hostage for almost two weeks. On 5 May highly trained French military launched an all-out assault on the cave, which resulted in the deaths of nineteen Kanak militants from throughout Ouvéa and of two French soldiers.

The second catastrophe has, in a sense, sealed the destiny of the Kanak people for the foreseeable future. It occurred in the early evening of 4 May 1989, just after sunset, in front of the communal grave containing the bodies of the local victims of the assault on the cave. Jean-Marie Tjibaou, accompanied by his close collaborator and heir apparent, Yeiwéné Yeiwéné, had just been received at the *chefferie* (chiefdom) at Hwaadrila ("the mythical heart of the island" according to many outside observers) and made his customary speech and presentation of gifts designed to seal the ties between the visitors and the hosts: a *manou* (laplap), sacred money, yams, and rice. These offerings were made as marks of respect, confidence, and generosity that in their very nature evoke time past and time present, the cycle of the seasons and the web of exchanges, linking tribes, creating alliances, sharing obligations, celebrating in times of joy, and communing in times of suffering. In his speech Jean-Marie spoke of life and of death, of shared dreams and of collective loss:

> [A]s the elder said a few minutes ago, the living blood flows and it continues to live. And we rush forward because this blood of the dead and of the living calls out to us. It is our blood; it is the blood which demands liberty for our people. . . .
>
> This sacrifice, the anniversary of which we are celebrating today, is inscribed in the long line of martyrs that our people have lost or have given in order that our existence be recognized, in order for us to be respected. (Tjibaou 1989a, 40)

The customary presentation concluded, a fellow Kanak militant from Goosana, Djubelly Wéa, unexpectedly stepped forward, ostensibly to present the next day's program that was designed to mark the end of the twelve-month period of mourning. He invited the visiting delegation to line up in front of the bleached white communal grave so that the local people could shake their hands (figure 2). Then, when Djubelly arrived in front of Jean-Marie, he drew a pistol from his woven bag and shot him at point-blank range. In the chaos that followed Yeiwéné too was shot and, finally, the assassin himself. As he lay writhing on the ground Djubelly cried, "Vive Kanaky! Vive l'indépendance!" All three, mortally wounded, were rushed to the island's medical center, dying either on the way there or before they could be transported to Nouméa.

Le grand trou noir (the big black hole): death, violent death, had always haunted Jean-Marie Tjibaou. He spoke of it often in the context of the re-

FIGURE 2. Hwaadrila: The communal grave of the nineteen Kanak militants killed in the French military assault on the cave at Goosana, 5 May 1988. *(Eric Waddell)*

peated risks he took, but also because it was inscribed in the history of his immediate family and of his tribe at Tiendanite, in the hills behind Hieng-hène, on the Grande Terre almost due west of Ouvéa. Once he entered the political arena it was an ever-present concern, although deep down he believed it would only occur after the independence of his country. In a sense he was not afraid of death; it was his destiny as a chief, while as a devout Catholic and former priest he saw himself as being "in the hands of God": "With God there is no such thing as chance. I was born for that, for service . . . and to die" (quoted by Gilbert Tein, 3 April 1997). The convergence of the two loyalties, both nourished by a Kanak sense of destiny, if not of fatalism, meant that he was motivated by a profound and unswerving sense of responsibility. He prepared his family and, in particular, his own children for the eventuality of an abrupt and violent end to his life. Immediately after he made the decision to enter the political arena, his wife, Marie-Claude, chose to devote all her time to their children, assuring a continual presence in the face of what were to be his constant absences, but also to prepare them in the event of his departure from this world. The family rarely traveled together, for fear of an attack on his life, while whenever he left home on a trip he was never sure he would return. After the terrible ambush of December 1984, in the valley leading from Hienghène to Tiendanite, where ten men from his tribe, including two of his own brothers, were killed by local settlers, and where it was intended that Jean-Marie himself would be one of the victims, he was always accompanied by bodyguards.

Although such logic of service involved personal sacrifice and led to the ultimate sacrifice, it did not mean that Jean-Marie aspired to become a martyr. He was too warm and down-to-earth a person, too deeply attached to his family, his friends, and his tribe, to his vegetable garden, good food, and fine company, to have such thoughts. In his case it was simply awareness that death, violent death, was the heavy price he expected to pay for the role he assumed in leading his people into the twenty-first century. However, he never imagined that he would die at the hands of a Kanak—until Ouvéa, where he was confronted, for the first time in his life, by fellow Melanesians whom he openly feared and who did not share his vision of the way to achieve an independent Kanaky.

Jean-Marie did not want to go to Ouvéa on that fateful day in May 1989. He had turned to his friend Armand Pala in search of an excuse to cancel the visit. Failing that, he had asked his wife to accompany him, because of his fear of not being able to hold back his tears in front of the widows of those who had been slaughtered at the cave at Goosana. Since signing the Matignon Accords the previous year, he had been overcome by doubt and plagued by dark thoughts, he was not sleeping well, and he felt increasingly alone. In a speech he intended to deliver the next day to formally mark the end of mourning, and that, exceptionally, he had written down,[3] these words figured:

> It is already one year ago . . . the thunder was rumbling, lightning was zigzagging all around, the sky was sharing the anger of the Kanak people and the mourning of the tearful Iaaï families. Nineteen FLNKS militants had just fallen on the path of our people's struggle for liberty. That day I cursed the sinister individual who had authorized the slaughter on Ouvéa. May the deaths of those who fell at the cave at Goosana gnaw at his conscience and may their spirits accompany him forever in his sleep. (1989b, 3)

Jean-Marie was angry, even bitter. He had, in his constant questioning, even begun to doubt the loyalty of his lieutenant and heir apparent Yeiwéné, by virtue of his being a Loyalty Islander (from Maré) and having worked at one time in the post office on Ouvéa. So when he finally caught the plane, he wore a dark suit rather than his usual short-sleeved shirt, and he spent the day of 4 May alone. Then, just before the ceremony began, he took Yeiwéné aside and walked with him toward the sea, talking to him quietly. Finally, once the ceremonies were underway, he asked the members of his delegation to "come closer, these people frighten me." It was as if he sensed the imminence of "the big black hole."

It would be a grave error to interpret the killing of Jean-Marie and, perhaps incidentally, of Yeiwéné as a solitary act, committed by a maverick and deranged person, a man with an insatiable thirst for personal power. Without doubt, Djubelly Wéa made the decision alone, despite there being, according to the records, a second assassin.[4] At the same time his desperate act should be considered the logical outcome of his failure to impose his personal vision of the future of the Kanak people as a whole or to contribute in any way to the negotiations of the preceding year. However, it was also an act grounded in the specific historical experience of the Loyalty Islands in general, of the particular form that experience had taken on the island of Ouvéa, and of the trajectory of his own tribe at Goosana, a tribe of which he was the spiritual leader.

In an immediate sense Ouvéa was, and still is, an embittered, solitary island, steeped in anger and guilt, as well as in a deep sense of not being understood, either by fellow Kanak or by outside observers. In its frustration and anger it turned in on itself during the 1980s, nourished by a past that was less and less known or understood by the larger world. Djubelly, like other Pacific Island thinkers who had become prisoners of their own marginalization and powerlessness, affirmed, "In silence the old men and women reflect and await our guide that is for us the spoken word. In silence they protect the secret of our people, which no researcher can discover" (quoted in Gauthier 1996, 27).

The death of the militants was the direct consequence of an attack on the local police post that had gone terribly wrong, and of the failure of the Political Bureau of the Front de Libération Nationale Kanak Socialiste (FLNKS) to intervene in negotiations that might have led to the release of the hostages taken and held in the cave at Goosana.

The years 1986 to 1988 were the most dramatic in the recent history of New Caledonia. Bernard Pons, the French minister in charge of overseas departments and territories (DOM-TOM), had adopted a strategy of outright confrontation with the Kanak independence movement. He imposed a direct military presence in tribal communities, abandoned any attempt at a more even distribution of economic investment in the country, and excluded representatives of the movement from the territory's principal institutions. This strategy of *nomadisation* was approved through a referendum on 13 September 1987, its avowed objective being to crush Kanak political aspirations once and for all. In this context the FLNKS had no choice but to urge its supporters to boycott the referendum, and its call resulted in abstention rates of more than 70 percent being recorded in all the communes in which Kanak constituted a majority of the electorate. In contrast, Europeans and the allied ethnic minority groups turned out en masse. They voted in favor of the Pons proposals, thereby accentuating the division between Nouméa and the bush and undermining most of the political achievements obtained by the FLNKS in the preceding decade. Jacques Chirac, then French prime minister and candidate in the upcoming presidential elections, came to Nouméa a few days later, to be welcomed by a vast rally of loyalists at the Place des Cocotiers. The event created the firm impression in right-wing political circles in Paris that the independence movement was coming to an end, and it prompted Pons to make yet another provocative gesture with respect to the Kanak people, namely to hold the New Caledonian territorial elections on the same day as the first round of the presidential elections in France, 22 April 1988.

The FLNKS, its back to the wall, had no choice but "to organize resistance by all possible means." Since neither active participation in the established democratic institutions nor recourse to nonviolence through electoral boycott had worked, more aggressive forms of confrontation were the one remaining option. Even the Union Calédonienne, the most moderate of the political parties forming the FLNKS, recommended an "active" rather than "passive" boycott of the upcoming elections, a decision approved by its Political Bureau. As party leader, Jean-Marie, more and more frustrated by the Pons initiatives, also favored the radicalization of the independence movement. Increasingly, he despaired of the possibility of achieving independence through dialogue and negotiation, or through impassioned appeals to the intelligence and principles of elementary justice on the part of his French counterparts. With regard to election day on 22 April, decisions were taken to set up roadblocks on the Grande Terre and to occupy, at five-minute intervals, the police stations on Ouvéa, Lifou, and Maré, having recourse to arms if necessary to achieve these objectives. According to the Ouvéans, the specific decision to take over the police stations was made at a meeting of Loyalty Islands FLNKS representatives held on Lifou on 21 April.

Although roadblocks were set up on the Grande Terre on the morning of 22 April, and the Ouvéa police station was attacked at 8:00 AM, nothing happened on Lifou or Maré. Furthermore, the attack at Fayaoué was bungled, with a gendarme shooting and wounding one of the Kanak militants. In the scuffle that followed, two gendarmes were killed and a third would later die of his wounds. The remaining twenty-eight gendarmes were taken hostage. The perpetrators of an attack designed to be at once a simple, nonviolent, and carefully coordinated physical occupation were henceforth trapped in a spiral of events over which they exercised little control. They obtained no support from militants elsewhere in the Loyalty Islands or on the Grande Terre, and they became pawns in a confrontation that extended far beyond Ouvéa and New Caledonia. It was as if they were destined to become the ultimate victims. The fact that Djubelly Wéa and the Goosana tribe were, almost from the outset, projected onto center stage only served to fuel the quasi-inevitable tragedy.

While some of the hostages were released in the south of Ouvéa in the aftermath of the attack, others were shifted around the island for four days, before being regrouped in the cave on Goosana tribal land. The decision to take them to Goosana was made by Alphonse Dianou, one of the architects of the assault on the police station and leader of the youth wing in the Union Calédonienne. Alphonse was a militant well known to the French administration, as was Djubelly Wéa. However, Djubelly had played no role in the hostage taking, having been at home sick at the time. Alphonse was a Catholic from the same tribe as Djubelly, although from the nearby village of Teuta, while Djubelly was a Protestant from Goosana. Both had received religious training in Fiji, Alphonse at the Pacific Regional Seminary and Djubelly at the Pacific Theological College.

While Djubelly completed his studies and became a pastor on Ouvéa (before being excluded from the Evangelical Church in 1981 for his radical views), Alphonse left the seminary before the end of his training for the priesthood and returned to New Caledonia to engage in political action.[5] He assumed responsibility for the Commission des Jeunes, and he was also a member of the executive of the Union Calédonienne, both positions within the party bringing him into close contact with Jean-Marie, whom he much impressed. One of his most memorable initiatives as a youth leader was to travel from one Kanak tribe to another to present the film *Gandhi*. Yet in spite of his widely recognized preference for passive resistance, Alphonse was shot and wounded by a French soldier after the assault on the cave and the release of the hostages, and, following further aggressions, was "allowed to die."

As for Djubelly, the moral leader of the Goosana tribe, the French military were convinced that he was one of the organizers of the attack on the police post at Fayaoué. As a result he was abused and tortured along with others from his tribe. He nevertheless continued to provoke the military with cries of "Vive l'indépendance! À bas l'armée française!" Djubelly's father, an eighty-year-old man, died shortly after the military occupation of Goosana, no doubt in part because of the abusive treatment he received at their hands. Consequently he came to be regarded by many on the island as the twentieth victim of the massacre. Finally, following the assault, thirty-two suspects from Ouvéa, Djubelly among them, were flown to France for imprisonment.

From the French point of view, the hostage taking could not have occurred at a more critical time. Prime Minister Jacques Chirac was a candidate in the presidential elections, while Bernard Pons was still his minister for overseas departments and territories. The first-round results showed Chirac trailing François Mitterrand, with less than 20 percent of the vote, while the extreme right-wing candidate, Jean-Marie Le Pen, came close behind him with 14 percent. Counseled by Pons, Chirac chose the obvious strategy with a view to impressing the right-wing electorate: he immediately adopted a hard line with respect to Ouvéa, using such terms as *order, security, force, honor.* If the FLNKS was "a kind of political party," it was nevertheless, according to Chirac's logic, drifting toward "terrorism" and in the process of becoming a "terrorist group." Given such reasoning, it was necessary to declare "war" on the "rebels" rather than negotiate with them. With negotiations underway at the same time for the release of two French hostages in Lebanon, it was all the more important for him to demonstrate "authority and leadership." Such was the tone Chirac gave to a nationally televised debate between himself and Mitterrand on 28 April.

A favorable denouement to the Ouvéa crisis had to occur before 8 May, the date of the second and deciding round in the presidential elections. Already, on 22 April, General Vidal, commander of the military forces in New Caledonia, had announced to Djubelly Wéa and the chiefly council at Goosana that "France, as of now, declares war on you. France declares war on the Kanak" (Plenel and Rollat 1988, 96). The means eventually used to release the hostages on the morning of 5 May—parachutists, commandos, marines, the special operations branch of the national police—bore precious little relationship to the real nature of the military task at the cave. It was an action designed to fuel a political debate occurring half a world away, and it ultimately failed, as Mitterrand was reelected president on 8 May. By then the act had been consecrated on Ouvéa, blood had been spilled, and lives lost.

As far as Djubelly and the people of Goosana in general were concerned, more and more of their bitterness was directed not at the French, but at fellow Kanak, in particular the FLNKS. They felt, quite reasonably, that once again they had been abandoned. Not only had the coordinated action to occupy the police stations on the Loyalties fallen through, but the Political Bureau had refused to act on repeated requests from the Ouvéans to intervene in negotiations with the French military and government, their response to the frantic appeals being simply to advise them to "sort it out themselves." The sentiment of being increasingly marginalized, if not openly ignored, within the context of the national independence movement was now strengthened by the trauma of military occupation and the loss of human lives in violent circumstances. It was as if a point of no return had been passed. With the island progressively turning in on itself during the 1980s, old internal divisions were resurfacing, to be cruelly expressed by the rapid release of hostages by Kanak militants in the south of the island following the attack on the police post, by public declarations about where the other hostages were being held, and by the role of high chief Bazit, from the neighboring tribe at Weneki, in directing the French military to Goosana. History was repeating itself, with Bazit using his privileged relations with France to assert his authority over the smaller, recalcitrant chiefdom of Imwene.

Goosana had always been a major actor in the Kanak independence movement. In a sense, it was a model community, addressing at the local level much broader educational, cultural, and economic as well as political concerns. It possessed a variety of communal structures, including a bakery and a dynamic École populaire kanak (ÉPK, Kanak people's school). It was a tribe in a hurry, demanding unconditional independence "now." It was also a community that reached far out into the Pacific Islands, motivated by the saying that recurs in many forms throughout the region: "You cannot be alone. You must look for someone" (A Wéa, pers comm, 21 Nov 2002). During the mid-nineteenth century that "someone" took the form of the English-speaking trader and missionary. With respect to European discovery, contact, and appropriation, this reality points to the distinctive place occupied by Ouvéa in New Caledonia and, in some respects, in Melanesia as a whole.

Neither Cook nor D'Entrecasteaux saw the Loyalties when they visited New Caledonia in the late eighteenth century, probably because the islands were too low-lying. They were no doubt seen and probably visited by other explorers in the early decades of the nineteenth century, yet they remained virtually unknown for some time. Those who did visit judged them to be of no obvious interest, Ouvéa, Lifou, and Maré being essentially coral and limestone formations with limited soil development and groundwater. Then, at the beginning of the 1840s, everything changed, and all three islands, together with the Isle of Pines, entered what was for them something of a golden age of intense commercial activity that only petered out in the 1870s.

Sandalwood traders operating out of Sydney came to the Loyalties from the 1840s to the early 1860s and for many of them Ouvéa became an important island of call. Sandalwood traders were followed by pearl divers, island produce and bêche-de-mer traders, labor recruiters, and, in the 1860s and 1870s, whalers. The traders were predominantly English speakers, variously English, Australian, and American. Even the island produce traders operating out of Nouméa at the time were mostly Anglophones. This intense commercial activity opened up a brief but extremely important window of opportunity for the Loyalty Islanders. Concerned to "open roads," and living on islands with very limited resources, they leaped at the opportunities provided by the European visitors, rapidly developing an excellent reputation as sailors and laborers. They worked on ships that took them to Hobart and Sydney, China and California, not to mention the many intermediate ports of call, and they no doubt had Hawaiians, Marquesans, and other Oceanians as fellow crew members. They were employed on the docks of Sydney and in the cane fields of Queensland, and they dived for pearls in the Torres Strait and among the Admiralty Islands. Ships' captains married local women. This diverse and remarkably intense network of relations between English-speaking traders and Loyalty Islanders was much appreciated by both parties. Moreover, for a long time the interactions took place in a political vacuum. Although France took possession of "New Caledonia and its dependencies" in 1853, it was only in the 1860s that the colonial authorities asserted their presence beyond the Grande Terre. The last of the three Loyalty Islands to be occupied was Ouvéa, in 1865.

The dynamic commercial environment meant that many Ouvéans acquired a working knowledge of English as early as the 1850s, some becoming quite fluent. Such was the pervasiveness and prestige of English that it was widely spoken until the early twentieth century. For instance, Djubelly's grandfather spoke it, and most of Djubelly's generation can recall the time when it was still known. This knowledge and experience meant that Ouvéans and other Loyalty Islanders became confirmed Anglophiles. Until at least the 1880s, if not later, they were often overtly hostile to any French presence and to the idea of working for French traders and, by extension, French Catholic missionaries. This reaction simply reflected that the English provided much greater opportunities for them, opening pathways across the ocean to a variety of Pacific Rim countries and bringing tangible benefits to the islands. Nevertheless, this privileged relationship came to a relatively abrupt end in the 1870s, essentially because resources were exhausted and no more local labor was available to crew ships or to work on plantations in Queensland. The French were in no way responsible for the commercial decline, but they were demonstrably in no position to redress the situation.

This golden age directly attributable to "the English" is still alive in the minds of many Ouvéans and other Loyalty Islanders, and perhaps above all in those of the inhabitants of Goosana. It was a flame that continually nourished the thoughts and actions of Djubelly Wéa.

The onset of missionary activity largely coincided with that of the traders. Christianity, like commerce, had an English face, and it exposed the Loyalty Islanders to a larger world and to new opportunities. In the 1840s and early 1850s the London Missionary Society, expanding out of Polynesia into Melanesia, placed Cook Island, Samoan, and Tongan "teachers" (catechists) on all the Loyalty Islands. Permanent English Protestant missionaries followed. Anglican "teachers" also assumed a brief presence on Maré and Lifou in the 1850s but then withdrew in favor of the London Missionary Society, which started training local "teachers" on Maré and Lifou as of the 1860s and also sent Loyalty Island students to Samoa and the Cook Islands for training. During its brief presence, the Anglican Church sent upwards of forty Islanders to St John's College in Auckland. In turn, trained Loyalty Island teachers were sent farther into Melanesia as pioneer evangelists: to the Grande Terre, and also to Vanuatu and Papua.[6]

French Marist missionaries arrived from the Grande Terre in the late 1850s and 1860s, too late to become a dominant force on Lifou and Maré. Only on Ouvéa did they eventually succeed in converting a majority of the population to Catholicism. Since the two other Loyalty Islands remained predominantly Protestant, this proved to be another factor in setting Ouvéa apart and, ultimately, fueling the crises of 1988–1989.

Missionaries, like traders, were actively solicited by the Islanders, and to a certain extent they were also instruments of imperial design. Although concerned principally to introduce "civilization," "enlighten" the Islanders, and protect them from the ravages caused by the traders, they were as well directly or indirectly committed to promoting their respective national interests. Rivalry between Protestant and Catholic missionaries was bitter and steeped in prejudice. It was a powerful, sometimes voluntary sometimes involuntary, expression of the larger rivalry between the English and French colonial empires.

In the minds of the local populations and particularly their leaders, attracting missionaries and traders was a part of the same ancestral logic of accepting and integrating Polynesian migrants into their communities and naming strangers as chiefs. It was motivated by the concern to establish social and economic ties over great distances—in order to ensure ecological and economic survival, to strengthen the fabric of society, and to increase political power and influence. Needless to say, in the case of Ouvéa, as elsewhere in the Pacific, it took a long time for the European latecomers to appreciate the complexity of the island society they were engaging with.

Ouvéa, like Lifou and Maré, lies at the interface of the Melanesian and Polynesian worlds. Its inhabitants are drawn from both, a reality finding tangible expression in the two languages spoken there—Melanesian Iaaï and Polynesian Faga Uvea. When the missionaries and traders arrived, two powerful chiefdoms were each vying with the other for exclusive control of the island. One, led by Bazit, was centered on the village of Weneki in the north; the other, led by Wenegueï, head of a group of recent immigrants from the Grande Terre, was centered at Fayaoué. Both took advantage of traders and missionaries to increase their power and thwart their rival. Missionaries in particular, and by extension the French colonial authorities, were instrumentalized in such a way that the consequences are still felt today. The long series of tribulations of the Goosana tribe is one expression of this situation, as were the deaths in the cave and the killings of Jean-Marie-Tjibaou, Yeiwéné Yeiwéné, and Djubelly Wéa at Hwaadrila.

Wenegueï moved very quickly to establish profitable ties with Europeans. In 1856 he succeeded in attracting two London Missionary Society "teachers" to Fayaoué from Maré, and in the same year two Sydney-based merchants established sandalwood stations on the island. Andrew Cheyne bought the islet of Wasaü, at the southern end of Ouvéa, while Andrew Burns operated out of Fayaoué. Burns lived there for extended periods over the following five years, using the station to assemble sandalwood from throughout the southwest Pacific, cleaning and processing it prior to shipping it to China. Strong links between the central chiefdom and the English-speaking world were thus established. Not to be outdone, Bazit invited French-speaking Marist missionaries to Heo, and they arrived a year later, renaming it Saint-Joseph. The Marists quickly obtained the support of the French commandant in Nouméa and established a second Catholic mission at Fayaoué in 1858. Hence, as a result of an alliance of mutual convenience between an Ouvéan high chief, French Catholic missionaries, and the colonial authorities in Nouméa, Bazit rapidly extended his authority over much of the island, and Ouvéa became predominantly Catholic. In the late twentieth century, this historic alliance was affirmed in the form of a strong loyalist political tradition.

When Europeans first established their presence on Ouvéa, a number of smaller chiefdoms were refusing to recognize Bazit. One of the ways in which they chose to express their resistance to his authority was through attachment to the Protestant faith and to the English-speaking world. One of these smaller, rebellious chiefdoms was located at Hwaadrila-Fayaoué and the other at Goosana-Onyat. In this extremely volatile situation on Ouvéa, where chiefly authority was constantly challenged, religious wars were also tribal wars and vice versa. In 1864, the year preceding effective French annexation, the resident Catholic priest allied with Bazit to chase the Protestant tribes from the northern end of the island. In consequence, the people of Goosana spent the next thirty-four years in exile among the Protestants of Hwaadrila-Fayaoué. Although they were able to return home at the end of the nineteenth century, they learned that the French regime would not recognize their chiefdom, Imwene, but only that of their historic rival, Bazit. Condemned to social and political oblivion, the Protestants decided to withdraw farther into the northern interior, finally settling at Goosana:

> This name, Goosana, was given at the time of our ancestors' return from exile. It is a name that can be found in the Bible, linked to the history of the people of Israel. It is like the Promised Land, it is the place where the children of Israel rested before continuing on to Canaan.[7] It is a bit of that journey, the one of our ancestors, which we have adopted as an important reference in our modern history. Our ancestors were, then, already in that situation, always moving, attacked by the system in place at the same time as was their faith. (M Wéa 1999, 39)

Such are the roots of the Goosana people's vision of themselves, of their relations with other tribes on Ouvéa, of the place of their island in the Pacific world, of their radical political discourse in the 1980s, and ultimately of their sentiment of isolation, persecution, and betrayal. It was largely on the basis of this specific historical experience and psychosocial configuration that their charismatic leader, Djubelly Wéa, sought, with ever-growing desperation, to build a future for Kanaky. He had studied at the Pacific Theological College in Suva in the 1970s. These were the early years of the University of the South Pacific, an institution essentially created and nourished by a first generation of political leaders of newly independent states, with the material support of Australia and New Zealand, and an institution that was in the process of training the next generation of island political leaders and professionals. Its teachers spoke of and practiced a new and exciting regional consciousness. Distinctive pathways to a free and independent Pacific future were being explored, Pacific ways that had international repercussions—of political nonalignment and of freedom from nuclear testing and weapons, for example. Close academic and personal ties were maintained between the university and the theological college. Djubelly learned to speak good English and he mixed with people from throughout the region who, in the context of their studies and daily lives in Fiji, all shared that language. He became a part of an Oceanian *wantok* network, and he wrote a thesis entitled "An Education for Kanak Liberation" (D Wéa 1977).

Following his return to Ouvéa the Protestant Church, finding him too radical, soon relieved him of his pastoral duties. Thereafter he moved progressively from institutionalized religion to politics, and on to the politics of independence. But above all he invested his energies in his own community and island. In this capacity he played a crucial role in the establishment of one of New Caledonia's most successful Écoles populaires kanak, an educational innovation that involved teaching in the local language and transmitting local knowledge (both spiritual and practical), as well as promoting the teaching of French and, above all, English as second languages. For Djubelly, English was the unifying language of the new Pacific, the logical way forward, and at the same time a resurrection of the past. He not only wanted the children to learn it, but also, thanks to funds provided largely by Vanuatu, over a decade or so he sent a number of young Loyalty Islanders to study at the University of the South Pacific. He even dreamed of establishing a campus of that university at Goosana.[8] According to Simon Aporonou, as a part of this initiative an institutional framework (Embryon universitaire des Écoles populaires kanak) was established on Ouvéa in 1986, with teaching and research conducted in five departments: Sciences of Kanak Culture (languages, sociology, psychology, history . . .); Humanities (cultures, French, English, Iaaï, and Faga Uvea); Political and Economic Sciences (national liberation struggle, Kanak socialist independence struggle, socialism in Kanaky . . .); Ecological Sciences (protection of nature and of humanity); and Politico-Religious Sciences (theology of liberation) (Aporonou 1986, 14). Whether any of these initiatives were actually implemented is highly doubtful, and no Université de Kanaky ever materialized. Likewise, few tangible benefits were recorded from the students attending the University of the South Pacific, their prior academic training and English language skills being insufficient to ensure success in their studies.

Djubelly was a radical, a purist, a pacifist, and a Christian. In the last year of his life he announced, "I am still a Christian and I will die a Christian."[9] His logic was implacable, and he was in a hurry: "There must be an immediate solution." He was also uncompromising: "Our sovereignty, our independence are nonnegotiable" (quoted in Rollat 1989a, 7). By March 1989 he had isolated himself and his community at Goosana, had "seceded from France," intending that Ouvéa would make a unilateral declaration of independence in 1990, in expectation that the other Loyalty Islands would follow.

His was a vision clearly nourished by the specific colonial experience of the Loyalties, and there was an obvious rationale to it. Not having any evident economic value, the islands had been left very much to themselves by the late nineteenth-century French colonial authorities. Their principal concern, apart from bringing an end to religious and tribal fighting, was to integrate them into a French-speaking New Caledonia.[10] No European settlers were sent, and in contrast to the Grande Terre, the Islanders suffered little from the ravages of European contact in terms of syphilis, alcohol, warfare, and the disruption of entire communities. No significant population decline occurred, no land was alienated, and there were no violent revolts against the European presence. No major imported administrative structures were imposed, and in 1900 the islands as a whole were declared "native reserves." In a sense they never endured systematic colonial repression, except for Goosana, and in their case it was at the hands of fellow Kanak—those of the Bazit chiefdom and their French Catholic allies.

Condemned in the late twentieth century to living on the distant economic margins of New Caledonia, the Loyalty Islanders had only the memory of a "golden age" to nourish their dreams. Because their colonial reality was much less complex than that of the Grande Terre, it facilitated the formulation of straightforward solutions to the independence struggle and simple models for the future of the Kanak people. "Independence now" made good sense in such a context as, perhaps, did imported models and ideologies.

Against this perspective, the 1989 Matignon Accords signed by the principal independentist and loyalist political movements, the FLNKS and the Rassemblement pour la Calédonie dans la République (RPCR), could only be viewed as a terrible betrayal. It was not simply that Djubelly had been abandoned in Ouvéa in April 1988 and had been excluded from the negotiations following his release from prison, despite his being in Paris at the time. It was that his people had not even been consulted with regard to the outcome of the negotiations, even though the "martyrs" had died on their land and several of them had come from their own ranks. For the people of Goosana, it was the terrible realization that the accords meant, "We've gone back thirty years, just when we were on the finishing line. Is that what you call solidarity?" (M Wéa 1999, 51).

The larger context of Goosana and Ouvéa helps to explain why Djubelly committed the most desperate of acts at Hwaadrila—a place of considerable symbolic importance, where his people had been exiled before. The Matignon Accords had condemned them to a new, political exile almost a century after their return from an earlier, physical exile. Djubelly probably also realized, at least subconsciously, that in assassinating Jean-Marie and

Yeiwéné, he would himself be killed, thereby in one tragically symbolic act eliminating all possible ways to the future. History and geography, time past and time present, all converged with the setting sun at Hwaadrila on 4 May 1989.

If Djubelly always insisted on *l'acte d'abord et la parole ensuite* (first the act then the word), for Jean-Marie it was precisely the opposite. In his view it was the *parole*—the spoken word—which comes from afar that determined actions, nourished reflection, and was the bearer of memory. The memory of the Grande Terre is very different from that of the Loyalties. History had made the Grande Terre a shared and, simultaneously, a cruelly divided land, a land in which the Kanak people were numerically, politically, and economically disadvantaged. In 1986–1988, under Pons and Chirac, their backs were driven up against the wall. The country was on the verge of civil war. Jean-Marie had come to the conclusion that a strategy of nonviolence was taking his people nowhere. More aggressive action was necessary.

On 24 December 1987 he had written:

> To envisage at this time large-scale initiatives is to gamble on one's own death in order to attract national and international attention. It means we offer ourselves as victims, resolved to win without recourse to violence. It means running the risk of being killed, while continuing to advance, irrespective of the number of victims. Insofar as I'm concerned, I'm ready. But how many deaths will oblige us to change tactics? (1996, 235)

Ouvéa had provided the definitive answer to that question, even though the acquittal of the perpetrators of the massacre of ten members of his own tribe near Hienghène in December 1984 was still firmly on Jean-Marie's mind. Or perhaps it was precisely because they were firmly on his mind? No one will ever know. What is certain is that Jean-Marie's own, much larger, island was bathed in blood and steeped in the memory of a violent past, a situation that had prevailed for well over a century. From the perspective of the Grande Terre the Kanak people had no choice but to come to terms with the fact that they shared their land with European settlers and other immigrant communities. In outright confrontation they would only lose, individually and collectively, time and time again. It was inconceivable, from Jean-Marie's perspective and from those of his associates, that a model for Kanak independence could come from Ouvéa and the Loyalties.

That conclusion would cost him his life.

2   The Roots of Identity
Hienghène and Its *lourd héritage*

> We want . . . to turn back towards the past . . . in order to draw the
> strength and the references necessary for supporting our word now
> and for the future. Our ancestors are not Gauls, nor the immediate
> heirs of Mozart, and in order to participate in history, it is necessary
> first for us to be a people rooted in our fundamental specificity.

HIENGHÈNE, LIKE OUVÉA, is a place of immense beauty, its distinctive
characteristic being that it evokes Melanesia rather than Polynesia. A dramatic pinnacle structure, La Poule Couveuse (The Brooding Hen), rises out
of the sea to mark the entrance to a sheltered bay into which two navigable
rivers flow (figure 3). A high mountain range, deep valleys, and dense vegetation form the backdrop to the bay, while a narrow surfaced road hugs the
coast, with occasional dirt tracks branching off to serve the tribes that are
tucked in the hills (map 3).

Here, as on the smaller islands, the casual visitor experiences the same
sense of being at the "world's end." In neither Hienghène nor Ouvéa are
there any significant outward manifestations of material affluence. Further,
the sophisticated infrastructures that characterize so much of the French
Pacific territories are absent. Roads seem to peter out quickly, the few administrative centers have a vaguely run-down air about them, stores contain
essentially "trade goods," life is slower, and, in the eyes of the passing *palagi,*
"not much seems to be happening." Both are quiet places, through which
strangers quickly pass, oblivious to the presence of the past and to the pattern and density of local life—unnoticing, but not unnoticed.

To the undiscerning eye it is geography that defines the difference between the two. The omnipresent lagoon and ocean at Ouvéa give the impression of a certain openness, of being able to "look to infinity," and of
boundless opportunities. Hienghène, by contrast, evokes a more secluded
and private world, shielded from the harsh realities of contact, trade, and
empire. However, that first impression is an illusion, for the local popu-

FIGURE 3. Looking east across Hienghène Bay to La Poule Couveuse. *(Eric Waddell)*

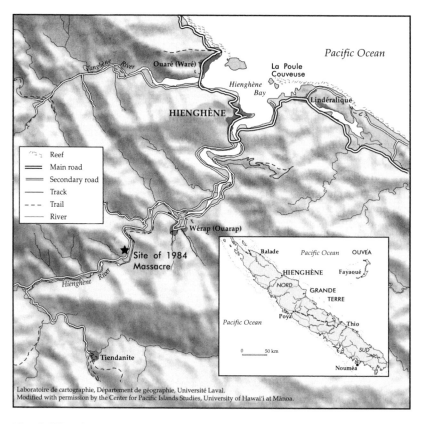

MAP 3. Hienghène and the Grande Terre

lation has always expressed a concern to establish contact and exchange with the world beyond the horizon. Yet here the experience of contact with Europeans took on a very different configuration. Apart from a brief period of opportunity and high expectations in the 1840s, the century and a half that followed at Hienghène and in its immediate vicinity was deeply scarred by a seemingly endless succession of confrontations with all-powerful newcomers, pain, exile, and violent death.

This was the *lourd héritage* (heavy burden) that Jean-Marie Tjibaou was born into and carried throughout his life. It was at the origin of the terrible misunderstanding that was the immediate cause of his death on Ouvéa.

If the landscape of Hienghène has a distinctive Melanesian air, its inhabitants embrace forms of social organization that, much as on Ouvéa, are strongly influenced by Polynesia. There are chiefly lineages where rules of primogeniture are applied, and authority is transmitted through them from generation to generation. The existence of clans within tribes, of minor chiefs, and of high chiefs points to nested, hierarchical structures. There is also the practice of welcoming the stranger and bestowing on him the title of chief. That stranger was often a Polynesian, arriving from the east, a drift voyager or an exiled person, member of a group that arrived unannounced on the coast.

Both inherited leadership and adoption were necessary cultural practices, serving to exercise control over territory and to construct networks of relations with other, sometimes distant, groups, both on the Grande Terre and across the sea on the Loyalty Islands. The high chief Bwaarhat, whose name is intimately associated with the early European contact experience of the area, spoke Faga Uvea, because that was the language of his first wife and of some of his subjects living on the eastern side of the bay of Hienghène, if not, indeed, of his own ancestors. It was but one expression of the many ties that linked Hienghène and Ouvéa, ties that were brutally fractured with the killings of Jean-Marie, Yeiwéné, and Djubelly at Hwaadrila in 1989, only to be reestablished some fifteen years later, in July-August 2004, through a deeply emotional process of pardoning and reconciliation.[1]

Although Captain Cook had set foot at Balade, some seventy kilometers north of Hienghène, in 1774, the Grande Terre, like the Loyalties, remained little known and little visited by European explorers and particularly traders until well into the nineteenth century. The reputed hostility of its Melanesian inhabitants and the difficulties of establishing contact with relatively small, linguistically and culturally diverse communities were, no doubt, the principal reasons for this neglect. As far as Hienghène was concerned, all this changed with the arrival in 1843 of Captain Richards, an English sandalwood and bêche-de-mer trader, and of his meeting with the high chief, Bwaarhat. As with his counterparts on Ouvéa, Bwaarhat was concerned to seize the opportunity provided by the presence of Richards and the traders who followed him. His objective was to increase his personal power and prestige by developing reciprocal ties with these rich and well-connected visitors. In turn, these new alliances would result in considerable benefits flowing to his people. Bwaarhat rapidly acquired a reputation among the European traders as being an exceptionally powerful and charismatic chief and also a particularly intelligent person. Mutual appreciation and an evident convergence of interests resulted in an important but brief opening of Hienghène to the larger Pacific world. During the decade following Richards's first visit, Bwaarhat received firearms and other gifts. On two occasions he traveled to Sydney, where he was received by the governor of New South Wales and described in the local press as the "King of New Caledonia."

In the process, the high chief became an avowed Anglophile and he encouraged other English-speaking traders to place agents at Hienghène. Local men were taken on as crew on trading vessels, but as a group they did not develop the same reputation in trading circles as the Loyalty Islanders did. The benefits of trade and the European presence probably accrued principally to Bwaarhat himself as a power broker, and to his immediate entourage, serving thereby to strengthen his ascendancy over the inhabitants of much of the northeastern part of the Grande Terre. The population as a whole acquired opportunities to trade, otherwise simply benefiting indirectly from his increased power and prestige, and hence from his protection. In turn the visiting traders were protected and well served by the high chief.

His high status and visibility among the English meant that Bwaarhat rapidly attracted the attention and the wrath of the French Marist missionaries who had established themselves at Balade in the same year that Captain Richards had moored at Hienghène. Given the overlapping interests of church and state, and given that France took possession of New Caledonia at Balade in 1853, it was hardly surprising that one of the colonizing power's first actions following the declaration was to send two hundred soldiers to Hienghène to ensure that Bwaarhat would publicly declare his loyalty to the new regime.

A decade of instability followed, where, as on Ouvéa, the missionary and colonial presences served as catalysts and unwitting agents in local intertribal rivalries and conflicts. Believing those to be rebellions against their own presence, the French dispatched armed forces to Hienghène in 1857, and Bwaarhat was arrested and sent into exile in Tahiti for six years. Troops returned again in 1859, and this time they spent fifteen days burning villages and destroying food gardens. "The people of Hienghène, demoralized, were obliged to ask for peace. The English who were fighting with them were captured, brought before a Council of War and they were shot immediately" (Saussol 1979, 84).

This was just the beginning of a long period of destabilization and violence, both within the Melanesian community itself and between the Melanesians and the French. While, on the one hand, the ascendancy of Bwaarhat was such that he successfully absorbed the Poowe, one of Hienghène's two other tribes, on the other, the Melanesians quickly learned that it was impossible for them to establish effective channels of communication with the colonial authorities.

Celebrated by the early English traders, Bwaarhat himself was variously used and silenced by the French administrators and military. For his part, he was unable to play one group against the other, the traders progressively losing interest in the Hienghène area as they moved on to more profitable commercial activities elsewhere in Melanesia. In 1864, after two decades of intense interactions with those whom he considered business partners, Bwaarhat summarized his sentiments to Jules Garnier, the French engineer who discovered garnierite, the mineral from which nickel is extracted:

> I liked these English a lot . . . they paid me well and treated me as a chief; I even agreed on one occasion to follow them across the sea as far as their big village of Sydney; it is there that I best understood our weakness; however, and in spite of the good reputation in which I was everywhere held, I soon became homesick for my island, and it was with happiness that I saw my mountains again and that I heard the cries of joy of my tribe.
>
> It was then that your warring nation arrived; at first I didn't take much interest; but because my young men had killed an enemy Kanak from Houagap, who was protected by the missionaries, I witnessed the arrival in my harbour of an enormous ship (the *Styx*); instead of fleeing, I went aboard, at the Captain's demand: it would be a long time before I saw my tribe again, I was made prisoner, carried far away to Tahiti, and I only returned six years later . . . , to be among my own people, who were already weeping for me.
>
> But what had happened during this time? My warriors were planning ven-

geance; the French got word of it; they came back, fired cannon-shot at my people who had come down to the shore and were looking with curiosity at these strangers; overcome with fright, my Kanak hid themselves in the woods; the soldiers, who had disembarked, came to look for them once again; for three days your countrymen burned our homes, destroyed our gardens and cut down the coconut trees; several of my warriors were killed; it is true that it was a matter of revenge, for my young men were overjoyed to see some of these invaders fall under our fire; one of them was the chief (Captain Tricot). And at this time, sighed bitterly old Bwaarhat, I was in Tahiti, weaving baskets in order to make a little money, and the worries of banishment were prematurely whitening my hair. (Bwaarhat in Garnier 1871, 312–314)

Interestingly, according to Garnier, Bwaarhat spoke "Tahitian, French and English well, but prefers to express himself in this last language" (1871, 225–226).

By 1864 the window of opportunity had closed on the people of Hienghène, and the world with which they were henceforth constrained to negotiate was a very different one from that of Ouvéa. Certainly the Ouvéans were confined to silence, to loss, and to memories—memories that in the 1970s and 1980s would nourish new, seemingly unfettered dreams. At Hienghène, however, this constraint meant entry into an increasingly violent world, one marked by conflict between two radically different civilizations as the French progressively asserted their presence throughout the Grande Terre. Although conflict was often only latent or simmering, it occasionally exploded into brief periods of rebellion, marked by destruction and death, where Melanesians were always the losers, both in armed confrontation and before the courts. As the nineteenth century drew slowly to a close the people of Hienghène had in all probability already come to the realization that they were condemned to living in a shared land. They were physically and legally powerless to set the terms of, or even propose, a partnership that might recognize their presence and take into consideration their particular needs and interests, if not their ancestral rights as the people of the land. At the very best they might be tolerated as a source of cheap labor, while at the worst they were considered an impediment to a model of development that was conceived solely in terms of European settlement and the development of a commercial economy.

Although New Caledonia was destined initially to be simply a penal colony and a place to which political prisoners were exiled, by the end of the nineteenth century a new governor, Feillet, had decided to transform the territory into a free settler colony. The aim was to create a *France australe*, a French counterpart of Great Britain's Australian colonies. This colonizing mission necessitated a progressive pushing back of the Melanesian population onto marginal land at the heads of valleys, confining them to reservations, and co-opting them for public works and to provide labor for the settlers. It was the logic of a superior, conquering civilization:

> It is evident that the Kanak, like all primitive peoples, live miserably on land that would support with abundance fifty times more European inhabitants (we have noted that this colony could support two million inhabitants, while the indigenous population numbers scarcely 30,000); isn't it just that they give way to those who, by patient and active study, have over the course of many centuries, assembled a sum of knowledge and of materials that enables them to arrive at this remarkable outcome of being able to draw from the soil fifty times more than the native can, and isn't it also a law constantly sanctioned in the natural world by thousands of events, that the skilled displaces the unskilled, and the strong displaces the weak! (Garnier 1871, 214–215)

Even the merging of the two peoples on the most unfavorable of terms was not an option: "a progressive mixing of the conquering and the conquered race is impracticable here, for the native and the white, by natural instinct, repel each other and can agree about nothing" (Garnier 1871, 214).

The first European settler arrived at Hienghène in 1879, and a few others followed over the next ten years or so, establishing properties in the Hienghène and Tanghène valleys. However, it was not until the mid-1890s that serious land alienation commenced, at a time when the local population had already developed a reputation as successful coffee producers. Naturally, the Melanesians resisted the expropriations, but without success. Entire communities were destabilized, provoking disputes between the various tribes. As punishment, Bwaarhat's grandson was sent into exile on the Isle of Pines in 1894, but to no avail. A further outbreak of violence in 1897 resulted in the French authorities carrying out a major punitive raid, hanging "rebels" and torching villages. Again Bwaarhat's grandson was considered to be the rebel leader, and this time he, together with several others, was exiled to Tahiti for four years. While the 1859 punitive raid had focused on the villages of Lindéralique, on the coast, and Kalégone, in the lower Hienghène valley, in 1897 the attack was directed at Tiendanite, Jean-Marie Tjibaou's birthplace.

Land alienation in the fertile valley bottoms and the progressive displacing and confining of the Melanesian population to the surrounding hills was accelerating. If in 1895 only 470 hectares had been expropriated in the Hienghène valley, by 1905 this figure had risen sharply to 1,200 hectares, and by 1930 had almost doubled again to 2,200 hectares. It finally peaked in 1970 at 2,600 hectares, with all the alienated land in the hands of a few dozen European and mixed-race landowners, aided by Asian laborers. The last allocations of land to new settlers occurred in the late 1950s.

In addition to the arbitrary and often violent expropriations, the Melanesians' carefully managed food gardens were subject to increasing damage from the settlers' freely roaming livestock.

Already in 1878 a massive insurrection against systematic land expropriation and the creation of native reservations had occurred on the western side of the central range, under the leadership of Chief Ataï. In the course of it, some one thousand Melanesians and two hundred European settlers were killed in the area between Bouloupari and Poya (see map 1). While the people of Hienghène had no reason to be involved in this revolt, having still to experience the advancing front of pioneer European settlement, they would certainly have learned of it. Their turn was to come almost forty years later, in 1917, following the surge in land expropriations at the turn of the century and the hostility of the new settlers toward their Melanesian neighbors. However, the immediate catalyst for the crisis was a renewed drive on the part of the French colonial administration to recruit Melanesian "volunteers" for the war in Europe.

> [T]he initiative came from the Bwaarhat chiefdom, infuriated by the abuses of the settlers . . . and, in general, by the constraints the colonial regime imposed on the Kanak communities. . . . Messages were sent to all the regions in the North—probably as early as 1912; meetings were held in 1913 at Pamale and in 1915 at Tiendanite. Hostilities finally broke out in 1917. On the Kanak side the death total was very heavy: more than one hundred killed. [There were three victims among the Europeans.] The high chief Bwaarhat who, on the surface, was not involved in the matter . . . was, on the occasion of the trial that was held in Nouméa, openly denounced as the instigator of the rebellion, and he committed suicide. Numerous reshapings of reservations and displacements of populations followed. (Godin 2003, 40)

The Bwaarhat chiefdom included the village of Tiendanite, which, for the second time, was the focus of the violent riposte of the colonial military forces. Much less costly in terms of loss of life and displacement of people than the 1878 uprising under Chief Ataï, it proved to be the last Melanesian revolt on the Grande Terre. It was also what Alain Saussol described as a "traditionalist and cultural outburst" against the French authorities in New Caledonia:

> Everything in this enterprise, if you ignore the recourse to new techniques like the rifle, the horse, or barbed wire, had the air of a revival of customary and ancestral rights. The secret diplomacy in preparation for the alliances had been undertaken using traditional symbols, war bouquets, black money, and knots of *balassor*.[2] The recourse to magic, ritual murders, cannibalism, proprietary fumigations of weapons and of belts, the unrolling of banners of bark, all endowed this "revolt" with a sudden burst of cultural identification or, as M. Leenhardt sensed, a return to triumphant animism.

> The defeat of the rebels was also the defeat of this revival of the cult of the ancestors. (Saussol 1979, 322)

This final armed confrontation with the colonial authorities was followed by half a century of silence and despair on the Grande Terre.

At the same time, because it had taken place in and around Tiendanite, it was an important part of Jean-Marie Tjibaou's specific tribal heritage and memory—and it was inscribed in the history of his immediate family.

> In 1917, at the time of the repression, the soldiers had pursued the people of Tibatchi and Tiendanite. They had chased after them, continuing to shoot, and when they reached Tiendanite they burned everything. Several women and girls who had been with the mother of my father, a woman from Coulna, decided they wanted to return to Tiendanite with some wounded men. The people of Tendo were afraid to take them in . . . and so the women were at Gavatch. They climbed by the river, fleeing Tiendanite toward the north. The valley is deeply entrenched. They traveled up early in the morning. The soldiers in fact were following them. They must have been informed. At sunrise, while they were climbing up the right bank, the soldiers fired at them from the left bank. It was at that moment that my grandmother was killed. My father was being carried by his mother; he was only a baby. He rolled down in the ferns and his big sister picked him up. They continued walking. My father was four years old. (Tjibaou 1996, 257–258)

The crucial shot had been fired by a man from Houaïlou, the French military having once again recruited local auxiliaries in order to set Melanesians against Melanesians, purposely exploiting old enmities to help crush the rebellion.

With these images of desperate resistance and survival against all odds, the pathway of Hienghène into the twentieth century diverged radically from that of Ouvéa. Although Ouvéa and the other Loyalty Islands were condemned to the margins of the young and aggressively ambitious colony, the fabric of their society remained largely intact, population numbers were maintained, and, in the case of the Protestants, a high degree of institutional autonomy was ensured. They even provided the Grande Terre with a first generation of "teachers." Opportunities for educational advancement were also greater than on the Grande Terre, perhaps contributing to a certain Polynesian sense of superiority with regard to Melanesians. The Loyalties as a whole presented an apparently contradictory face, as they increasingly portrayed themselves to be both very "traditional" and very "modern," as well as uncompromising in their reading of the world, in marked contrast to the Melanesians of the Grande Terre. The mix was an explosive one in the sense that it eventually led to serious misunderstandings as to the nature and objectives of the Kanak independence movement as a whole. These misunderstandings had crystallized in the late 1960s and rendered effective dialogue and communication between the Grande Terre and the Loyalties extremely difficult if not at times impossible, as the 1988–1989 crisis on Ouvéa so cruelly demonstrated.

The colonial experience on the Grande Terre, including Hienghène, was characterized by repression, loss of food gardens and commercial plantations, destruction and displacement of entire communities, deadly new diseases, individual and collective despair, population decline, . . . and the ever-expanding presence of European settlers, accompanied initially by Javanese and then Japanese immigrant labor. In the first half of the twentieth century, Hienghène was a thriving, albeit relatively small, colonial community, while neighboring Tiendanite was both witness to and victim of the development of the town and its surrounding European settlements in the Hienghène, Tanghène, and Tipinjé valleys. Its inhabitants remained in the hills behind, once rebelling, but nevertheless silently observing the newcomers, and also no doubt seeking to understand, hopefully to accommodate, and above all concerned to have their rights restored and their dignity respected.

With the Grande Terre the object of an ambitious imperial project, its Melanesian inhabitants were in a very real sense condemned from the outset to resist—and to fail. Their repeated appeals to reason and for justice fell on deaf ears. Even efforts to communicate the Melanesian distress, through recourse to European analogies, were met with silence for, in the absence of mutual respect and comprehension, no dialogue was possible.

"One day when it was question of assigning land to Whites, he [Bwaarhat] said to me, knowing that there was no question of me having come to take some from him: 'What would you say if the Kanak were to take some in your country?'"[3] Jean-Marie Tjibaou was to pose the same rhetorical question a century later, little having changed in people's day-to-day lives during the intervening period. However, the moral and legal contexts were very different. The Melanesians had by then acquired French citizenship, democratic institutions had been created, the rule of law prevailed—in principle at least—and the international community was beginning to express interest in the fate of a distant colony and its indigenous inhabitants. Jean-Marie's questioning could no longer be met with silence by the imperial authorities.

In 1897, the arrival of Marist missionaries to build a mission station at Ouaré, on the northern side of the bay, sealed the destiny of the people of Hienghène. It meant that the Catholic rather than the Protestant Church came to dominate that part of the coast as well as most of the adjacent valleys. Most of the time this church received the favors of the colonial administration, because it espoused the same national and civilizational objectives. As well, it was organized in such a manner that authority was unequivocally vested in Rome, and its missionaries in the northeast of the

Grande Terre were for long exclusively European. Indeed, the first Melanesian to break this hegemony was Jean-Marie, who was ordained at Ouaré
in 1965 and celebrated his first mass among his own people at Tiendanite
immediately afterward.

For all these reasons, the history of Hienghène merged progressively, in
the postwar years, into the modern history of New Caledonia and into the
political project of its Melanesian people—demanding the creation of an independent country to be called Kanaky. Gradually it became prominent in a
debate that was personified in and led by a man who was deeply marked by
the memory and experience of a dynamic Melanesian people who struggled
to survive in the shadow of a small settler town and its surrounding valley
properties.

Jean-Marie Tjibaou was born in 1936 into a highly politicized Melanesian tribe, one that had been marked by exceptional leadership and that
had also resisted and paid the price for its rebellious reputation. The people
of Tiendanite were recently assimilated members of the large and powerful
Bwaarhat tribe, centered on the Hienghène valley but extending to and
along the coast. Created out of the voluntary fusion of two major tribes in
the wake of contact with the English traders, the Bwaarhat and the Poowe,
it had become the largest and most powerful tribe in the northeast of the
Grande Terre. Jean-Marie's father, Wenceslas (Ty), was chief of the Tiendanite clan, while his mother, Herminie, was a Bwaarhat, given in marriage
by her father, the high chief, to mark the renewal of ties with the Tiendanite
clan.[4] The language they spoke at home and in the village was Pijé. The second of eight children, Jean-Marie was destined, following the early death of
his elder brother, to become a minor chief.

By virtue of the merging of the two tribal lineages in his person and of
his inherited chiefly status, as a young child Jean-Marie was already endowed
with a broad and important set of expectations and obligations. This biological and genealogical heritage was reinforced following the decision of
the high chief of the third major Hienghène tribe, Goa, to confer on Jean-
Marie the status of a high chief.[5] This initiative, taken with the agreement
of Bwaarhat, made it possible for all the Melanesian people of the Hienghène area to again speak with one voice, as they had in the mid-nineteenth
century. The broad-based responsibilities of his status were nourished by
a context in which Jean-Marie spent the first eight years of his life at Tiendanite. Within his immediate family, he experienced day-to-day subsistence
living, marketing of the few commercial crops, and initiation into customary
practices and myths by a maternal uncle.

> Jean-Marie grew, once he was old enough to imagine the hidden side of
> things, above all in the shadow of his maternal uncle, Fidéli, a grave and gentle
> man, charged, according to custom, with the responsibility of initiating him into
> the fundamental rules of life.

He had first learned that, since the beginning of time, the human species was subject to the rhythm of the cultivation of yams, a noble tuber if, indeed, there is one. . . .

Following that, Uncle Fidéli had revealed to him the secret of the origins of the world. In the beginning was the Earth. Everything came from the Earth. Without the Earth there would be nothing. The Earth created the trees, then human beings. The first man came out of a big male tree that grows in the mountainous chain of the Grande Terre, the *houp*. The first woman was born of another, smaller tree that often grows among the boulders, the *poué*, a female species which is also called the taboo. . . .

The young Jean-Marie Tjibaou was fond of taking long walks in the company of this uncle who had an answer for everything and who knew the history of each stone, each leaf, every inch of the ground and every person in the valley. Guided by his expert hand, he learned the genealogical map of his ancestral land. Because everything came from the Earth, the Earth was also the living memory of each and every person, and all that was needed was to speak in silence to this spring, that mound of earth, that rock, to have news of the ancestors. Nature is simply an open book, the Kanaks' catechism. (Rollat 1989b, 49–50)

A senior journalist with *Le Monde,* Alain Rollat covered events in New Caledonia in the 1980s and came to know and above all to admire and respect Jean-Marie. Despite an element of poetic license in his depiction of Jean-Marie's childhood, he highlighted a defining feature that is confirmed by many Melanesians who knew him well—that by the age of nine, when Jean-Marie left Tiendanite for school at Canala, he already had a firm grounding in his culture, with respect to both substantive knowledge and symbolic and mythological references (figure 4).[6] They proved to be his essential bearings in the larger world to follow.

It is impossible to construct in detail the contours of these first formative years, the principal adult actors being long departed, yet their legacy was manifest in many of Jean-Marie's preoccupations and gestures in later life. He regularly escaped from Nouméa to the peace and quiet of Tiendanite, in order to be among close kin, to tend his food garden, to feed his pigs, and to think about village tasks to be undertaken and relatives to be cared for. The tribe and the food garden were never far from his mind, even when he was on official missions in New York, Paris, or Geneva. After a grueling day's work he would often call New Caledonia, to enquire about someone's health or to determine whether a task on behalf of another had been carried out. Moreover, whenever he received an important *palagi* visitor in Tiendanite, that person would invariably be subject to a test well described by Alain Rollat:

[E]ach time he received a stranger judged to be worthy of interest, he took plea-sure in submitting him to a test. After having welcomed him with open arms,

Figure 4. Student days at the *petit séminaire,* Saint-Tarcissius, in Canala. Jean-Marie is on the right. *(ADCK-Centre Culturel Tjibaou)*

a smile on his lips, after having shown him the hillside where his grandmother had been killed in 1917, the tombs of his two brothers, killed in the ambush at Hienghène in 1984, after having shown him his trees, his plot of yams, he invited him to sit on the grass, like him, in a suit, on this gently sloping piece of land. Then, his eyelids lowered, his mouth closed, he meditated at length, pretending to ignore his visitor. A heavy silence followed, made even more oppressive by the majestic mystery of the place. Jean-Marie Tjibaou was seeking to establish whether his guest was capable of respecting the meditation of others,

the silence of this place that was sacred to his people, to take the measure of
Kanak time, which is different from the time of people coming from Europe.
He wanted particularly to determine the depth of the person in front of him.
(Rollat 1989b, 47)

If his Uncle Fidéli played a crucial role in revealing his Tiendanite inheritance—a world defined by the rhythm of nature and the presence and
counsel of the ancestors—Jean-Marie's father, Wenceslas, was concerned to
facilitate his entry into the pressing reality of contemporary New Caledonia.
The circumstances surrounding the death of his own mother, Jean-Marie's
grandmother, no doubt nourished him in this endeavor. Wenceslas was the
protégé of a Marist priest, Father Alphonse Rouel, who was in charge of the
mission at Ouaré. The priest felt Wenceslas could play a crucial role in promoting Catholicism among the Kanak living in the hills behind the coast. In
turn, Wenceslas was attracted to the priest for the knowledge he possessed
of the European world and for his practice of defending Melanesians in the
many conflicts that occurred with the local settlers and the authorities. He
became a *moniteur* (assistant) in the mission school Father Rouel established
for them, teaching the rudiments of French and the catechism. Then, following his marriage, he ran the small school that the priest established in Tiendanite. By the age of eight, Jean-Marie had acquired some knowledge of the
French language. Most probably his father had also sown in him the seeds
of a certain political consciousness, for, soon after the war, Wenceslas became a member of the Union des Indigènes Calédoniens Amis de la Liberté
dans l'Ordre (UICALO). This group was closely associated with the Catholic Church and, together with its Protestant counterpart, the Association
des Indigènes Calédoniens et Loyaltiens Français (AICLF), they constituted
the first expressions of a modern indigenous political consciousness in New
Caledonia, following the granting of French citizenship to Melanesians in
1946. The Union Calédonienne, an avowedly multiracial political party, was
subsequently born of the fusion of the two movements. It sought recognition of and justice for the indigenous population, and an equal partnership
between the "Black" and the "White" people of New Caledonia, as expressed
in the motto *Deux couleurs, un seul peuple* (Two colors, a single people). That
vision proved dear to Jean-Marie in later life.
    Wenceslas even went so far as to stand on a multiracial list in the 1954
municipal elections at Hienghène, and to win. In the same year, Jean-Marie
returned to Tiendanite after a prolonged absence.
    If history, geography, and lineage were crucial formative influences, it
was Father Alphonse Rouel who charted the specific path that took Jean-
Marie Tjibaou from the tribe to the school to the seminary and on to priesthood, for the priest had developed a close relationship with three generations of the Tjibaou family. Jean-Marie was his spiritual son, his hope for the
future of New Caledonia. For his part, Jean-Marie was to affirm much later

in life that "the person who will always remain my source of inspiration is a Marist priest who taught us to reflect a lot" (1996, 185).

Father Rouel was a remarkable man. An Auvergnat of peasant origins, fluent in the patois of that region of the Massif Central, he arrived in New Caledonia in 1913 at the age of twenty-six. Despite his being a priest, he was soon conscripted into the army and served as an involuntary agent in the crushing of the revolt of 1917. "Alphonse Rouel discovered the cruelties of war and the absurdities of colonial injustice. He observed the horror of this inequitable, iniquitous and crazy repression. . . . Very quickly, this priest, somewhat of a nonconformist, took a position against the excesses of colonialism" (Mokaddem 2004, 20). In 1918 he was appointed vicar of the parish of Hienghène and took up residence at the mission at Ouaré, remaining there until his death in 1969. It was an exceptionally long reign, even for a missionary. Over that entire period of fifty-one years he made only three return visits to France. In addition he was deported to Nouméa and then Sydney during the Second World War for having avowed loyalty to Marshal Pétain. During the half-century he spent at Hienghène he devoted as much of his energies to the defense of the interests of the Melanesian community, faced as they were with the injustices of the colonial regime and the multitude of problems posed by the presence of a hostile settler community, as to the propagation of the Catholic faith. To be more accurate, he acted according to his Christian convictions, seeing no distinction between the two. Father Rouel rapidly became fluent in Fwâi, the language of the dominant Bwaarhat tribe, and probably got to know on a personal basis the entire Melanesian population of the immediate region. Intimacy, commitment, and longevity meant that he played, directly and indirectly, a crucial role in the life and politics of Hienghène. "In the configuration of the relations of authority (the settler, the gendarme, the priest), Father Rouel took the place of the official in charge of indigenous matters, attributed to the police, and was considered by the Kanak to be their preferred representative. In contemporary terms, one could say that Rouel acted as the cultural intermediary between the Kanak and the administration" (Mokaddem 2004, 27).

That administration was concerned first and foremost to defend the interests of the settlers, whose interests were in turn its own. Inevitably, the peasant priest was perceived as a troublemaker by the local European community and as something of a charismatic leader by many of the Melanesians, with the result that "[t]he fifty-one years spent at Hienghène made this man a major agent of social change" (Mokaddem 2004, 38). Regardless of his renowned authoritarian character, Jean-Marie went so far as to characterize him as an "anti-colonialist" (1996, 183).

As a committed promoter of social change in the interest of the Melanesians, Father Rouel was quick to seize on Jean-Marie's potential, ensuring he obtained a formal education that would continue on to the seminary and, it was hoped, the priesthood. For this reason Jean-Marie never attended the mission school at Ouaré. Instead, Father Rouel sent him directly to the *petit séminaire* (minor seminary) at Canala, Saint-Tarcissius. Jean-Marie spent four years there, from 1946 to 1949, and then went on to study with the teaching brothers on the Isle of Pines for a further four years, completing what was the equivalent of a primary education. By this time the religious authorities had decided that he would become a *frère auxiliaire,* an indigenous teaching brother responsible for basic religious and secular education in the Catholic school system. So, rather than proceed to the seminary, he returned to the Isle of Pines in 1954 and 1955 for his *noviciat.* On completion of these studies he was sent to teach in a Catholic primary school on Lifou and, subsequently, to Thio, back on the Grande Terre. However, before embarking on his new career, in 1956 he returned briefly to Tiendanite. He had been away for more than ten years without once returning home. A road was in the process of being bulldozed to the village, and he went up much of the way in a truck.

The experience of being reunited with his family was a moving and traumatic one that would mark him for the rest of his life. If French had been the sole language of instruction for Jean-Marie, and the only one tolerated outside the classroom, it also served as a natural and vital lingua franca for the Melanesian students who came from a country where some twenty-eight indigenous languages were spoken, none of them widely. For an emerging generation of teachers and leaders, the French language was immediately recognized as an essential instrument of communication, the basis for a new pan-Melanesian solidarity, and a source of strength to meet the challenges of postwar New Caledonia. However, Jean-Marie learned the price he had paid for his prolonged absence and for his commitment to this new language only on his return to a home and family that he had left as a child and rediscovered as a young adult. Again the journalist Alain Rollat has offered a powerful evocation of that occasion:

> Jean-Marie Tjibaou will relive a thousand times the same scene, and a thousand times the scene will unfold in an inexplicable obscurity. His mother crying with joy. His father, proud as a Pope, recounting to all and sundry the exploits of the valorous seminarian. His father places him suddenly in front of four boys from the tribe. Jean-Marie recognizes Louis, his younger brother, but not the other three. "They are your brothers," Wenceslas says. David, Tarcisse, Vianney, born during his absence, look at him as if he is a stranger. They timidly say a few words. Jean-Marie opens his mouth. But his tongue remains frozen, silent, struck with stupefaction. He is overcome with dizziness. He stops in his tracks, petrified. No, it is not a spell. He suddenly realizes that he can't understand what his brothers have just said to him; that he hasn't grasped the sense of their words; that he is unable to answer them; that he can't communicate with them. He discovers with terror that in nine years of exile[7] he has forgotten the language of the people of Hienghène, Fwaî,[8] his mother tongue! . . .

The haunting memory of a first scar, experienced as a mutilation, the loss of a root, analyzed later on as the commencement of an interminable journey in search of a lost identity. (Rollat 1989b, 84–85)

Irrespective of whether the details of Rollat's description of Jean-Marie's return to Tiendanite are entirely accurate, it is certain that the discovery of the loss of his mother tongue (or at the least of the capacity to speak it), and of the implications of that loss, was a critical factor in determining many of his core preoccupations and actions in the years to come. He would make little or no distinction between his own personal drama and that of his people. This experience helps to explain why his primary concerns were always cultural: identity lost and rediscovered, identity affirmed and recognized, and identity reformulated. It reveals why, for him, culture served as the foundation for political action, and why he was so concerned to rediscover his own particular culture, understand and build on it, searching for what is universal in specific human experiences in order to make intercultural communication and sharing with others possible. It probably also helps to account for why he never ceased to study and seek to understand. Finally, it no doubt explains why Jean-Marie favored pragmatism over ideology, a middle path and consensual actions, rather than the radical, uncompromising solutions that history had encouraged Ouvéa to adopt.

3   C'était la logique du système
Negotiating the Catholic Church in New Caledonia

You bring the good news but you eat separately.

JEAN-MARIE WAS NOT satisfied with being a teaching brother and insisted that he wanted to pursue his studies, proceed to the *grand séminaire* (theological seminary), and train to be a priest. In making this choice he was no doubt counseled by Father Rouel, but above all he was expressing a personal commitment to his mentor. The Catholic and Protestant Churches were the only institutions that had, since the beginning of the colony, been consistently close to the Melanesian people, defending them in times of crisis, offering counsel, and providing opportunities for significant educational advancement.

In Jean-Marie's case, training to become a priest meant returning to the *petit séminaire* (minor seminary) in Canala for two years before entering the *grand séminaire* in Païta for a further six years of study. When he arrived at Païta in 1958 he was twenty-two, older than many of his fellow seminarians, and he was constantly questioning and searching. Both seminaries were exceptionally fertile intellectual environments at the time, and a new generation of leaders within the francophone Pacific was to emerge from their student bodies: François Burck, Eloï Machoro, and Gabriel Païta in New Caledonia; Gérard Leymang in Vanuatu; and Oscar Temaru in French Polynesia, to name only a few. For the students it was a first step beyond the boundaries of kin and islands into a much larger Oceanian world. They shared a new language, they spoke of national and regional identities, and they engaged in broad-ranging political debate. Several were to become close friends and collaborators for life, activists in New Caledonia and elsewhere in the Pacific with whom the aspirant priest shared ideas, experiences, strategies, and an overarching vision.

Jean-Marie was always at ease in Christianity and in Catholicism, and even at the height of political action in a purely secular world he would never renege on his faith. It was an integral part of his nature and identity. Yet it was something he rarely talked about—except when he had to justify it before a European audience, at the University of Geneva in 1981, for instance. There he explained, simply and with remarkable lucidity, why he saw no contradiction in being both a Catholic and a Melanesian, a Christian and an animist. For Jean-Marie there was a great deal in common between the two visions of Man on Earth. Melanesians had the same spiritual preoccupations as Europeans. However they were grounded in a distinctive human experience:

> How is life and hence the birth of man conceived? I would say that the Melanesian world, as with every human group, has sought answers to the questions that preoccupy all societies: Where do we come from? Who are we? Where are we going? And the answer to the question "Where do we come from?" on the New Caledonian earth has been translated into genealogies by the people. They say "The people of such and such a clan," "it's the clan . . . Aramoto." Well the Aramoto, they come from straw, a particular kind of straw, that grows on such and such a mountain, and from this straw came that clan, and in that clan. . . . You recall, those of you who know the Bible, the genealogy of Jesus, "son of David, son of Abraham, son of Adam." We have the same scheme. However, at the end, we have a tree, or an animal, or a stone, or thunder. It is the relationship with the land, with the environment, with the country, with the local, inhabited earth. *We are not people from elsewhere. We are people who come from this earth.* Ethnologists, psychologists, psychiatrists will be able to discuss at length the psychoanalytical significance of such "origins," but that is not my intention. I'm simply pointing out, that is how it is. (Tjibaou 1981, 84; emphasis in original)

Myth, genealogy, the Word, the word of the firstborn; Jean-Marie believed, no doubt, that through Christianity, it was possible to reach out to the universal, appeal to both emotions and to intelligence, and arrive at the essential humanity of all mankind. Hamid Mokaddem, author of a significant corpus of writings on him, considers that for both Jean-Marie Tjibaou and Father Apollinaire Anova, another Melanesian priest whose writings had a profound influence on Jean-Marie, the Melanesian and the Christian worlds were complementary rather than conflicting belief systems. "I believe that an intermingling or juxtaposition is structured at two levels: the level inherent to Kanak civilization that conceives Nature as being the hierarchical expression of the principle of life, structuring the ancestor, the clan of the chiefdom and the proliferation of lineages; and the transcendental level of the Christian God which is superimposed alongside the Melanesian conception of the sacred" (Mokaddem 2000, 79–80). As complementary belief systems they also assumed complementary roles. Jean-Marie saw priestly responsibilities as being closely linked to his responsibilities as a chief. Service lay at the heart of both: serving his people, receiving and sharing the word—the word of the ancestors and the word of God—and being prepared to give his own life as the ultimate sacrifice. Perhaps, in his case, the decision to become a Catholic priest was a natural consequence of his being a tribal chief, and perhaps he made no distinction between the two. While interpretations may differ in detail, they converge with respect to Jean-Marie's central preoccupation. According to the French journalist Antonio Raluy, "He had chosen this path [of priesthood] . . . not so much as a vocation but 'because of the wish to serve his people'" (1990, 171).

However, Jean-Marie's beliefs and commitments were confronted right from the outset by his experience within the institution of the Catholic Church in New Caledonia, where the gulf between discourse and practice was profound. As a teaching assistant, he had already become aware of some if its contradictions, had experienced petty injustices, and had quickly learned how to subvert them.

> The first thing that angered me when I arrived on Lifou: at the table there was white coffee for the Father, because we ate in the same pavilion, and we were entitled to tea. And one day, the Sister asked: "But wouldn't you prefer to drink white coffee in the morning?" We said: "Of course!" However she didn't tell the Father, and the priest kept the coffee for himself. So we didn't eat or drink anything.
>
> Then when the school bell rang, we hadn't eaten anything, hadn't drunk anything . . . but my colleague there. . . . He had relatives where we were. He told them. As a result, at the break, all the kids went to inform the village that the Father hadn't given us anything to eat. They brought bottles of coffee, baskets of provisions . . . from then on it was every morning, the table there was full of . . . things to eat. (Tjibaou 1989c, 12)

Being denied café au lait at breakfast was a minor irritation compared to the institutional segregation that Jean-Marie experienced on arrival at the *grand séminaire* in Païta.

> [W]hen I entered the seminary, what struck me the most . . . was that [segregation]! In the refectory there was a table for the Europeans . . . two tables for the Europeans, and then a table for the priests, the people in cassocks . . . and then the other tables for the black students there . . . for everyone [else]. . . . that upset me, that traumatised me . . . and then the dormitory too. We had big dormitories for everybody, those that weren't white. The older ones who were at the seminary, in rooms, that was o.k. For the Europeans, [there was] a special dormitory next to the chapel . . . that appalled me. But you got over it . . . it was the logic of the system.[1] (Tjibaou 1989c, 13)

It was the logic of a system where to be Melanesian was to be set apart and be considered inferior, in other words be condemned to silence in a colony located at "the end of the earth." However, the political climate was changing rapidly, the expectations of the Melanesian people were rising, and the system was under stress. The Second World War and its immediate aftermath challenged all the perceptions, the prejudices, and the rules that had been imposed since France had taken possession of the country almost a century before. The Bataillon du Pacifique (Pacific Battalion), made up of European, Melanesian, Tahitian, and ni-Vanuatu volunteers, had been formed to fight alongside the Free French in the European theater. Following the entry of the United States into the war, Nouméa became the military headquarters in the battle for the South Pacific. Tens of thousands of American troops arrived, with the attendant displays of immense material power. Among them were large numbers of black soldiers. Occasionally, white soldiers were seen to receive orders from higher-ranking blacks, suggesting a degree of racial justice that was unheard of in New Caledonia. Generous salaries were paid to Melanesian workers, and friendly relations were established, regardless of the opposition of the French authorities and the local European community.

The year after the war ended the French government abolished the Code de l'Indigénat (Code of Native Regulations), including compulsory labor and limitations on movement and residence outside the reservations for Melanesians. It also granted French citizenship to all the inhabitants of New Caledonia. This new legal reality, combined with rising economic and social expectations, initiated a process of detribalization through urbanization for a growing number of Melanesians. In this context of the fracturing of ethnic and geographical boundaries and of renewed hope, Jean-Marie embarked on his studies as a seminarian. The Church offered the best if not the only possible way to serve his people: "a refuge for the oppressed and a dispenser of knowledge" (Jean Pipite, pers comm, 17 July 2006). In the words of a fellow student who was later to become a close political collaborator, François Burck, "It was the reason why we were all there" (pers comm, 22 Jan 1998).

Both the Catholic and the Protestant Churches, historically committed to the defense and promotion of the Melanesian people, were concerned to canalize their new aspirations out of fear that they might abandon their faith in favor of secular political ideologies. Already a Parti Communiste Calédonien had emerged in the wake of the Second World War. It was the first political organization operating at the level of the whole country to direct its attention to the indigenous population. Speaking openly about racial injustice and about political, social, and economic ideals, the small but vocal "revolutionary" party attracted the attention of many Melanesians and proved particularly appealing to returned soldiers. As an explicit countermeasure, in 1947 the Catholic Church created the Union des Indigènes Calédoniens Amis de la Liberté dans l'Ordre (UICALO), and the Protestants, in the same year, the Association des Indigènes Calédoniens et Loyaltiens Français (AICLF). Both groups were initially designed to focus on social and cultural issues to the exclusion of politics. But that policy was to no avail, for under the leadership of the Catholic Roch Pidjot and the Protestant Doui Matayo Wetta, they rapidly linked up with reformist elements among the European population to create, in 1953, the Union Calédonienne. This national political party, led by Maurice Lenormand, called for the emancipation of the Melanesian people through the provision of equal rights, equal services, and equal salaries. At the same time, voting rights were progressively extended to all the inhabitants of New Caledonia, Melanesians included, the process being completed by 1957.

The Protestant Church was able to assimilate and respond to this rapidly evolving social and political context without too much difficulty, its members being largely Melanesian and its pastors almost exclusively so. However, the majority of the members of the Catholic Church were European, as were virtually all its priests, and it was poorly placed to even adjust to the new reality. As late as the 1980s, it was often referred to as *l'Église des Blancs* (the White People's Church). Yet at the same time, the Melanesian population was divided roughly fifty-fifty between the two faiths. The Catholic Church found itself caught in a Gordian knot, with its Melanesian priests too often treated as *pupilles* (wards) to be overseen and "counseled" by their European counterparts, if not quite simply constrained to silence. For their part, the same priests were acutely aware of the preoccupations and aspirations of their own people.

This broader institutional and national context gave a very particular configuration to Jean-Marie's experience as a priest in the Catholic Church. He was ordained in 1965 and, faithful to his principles of loyalty and service, the ceremony was held at Ouaré, near Hienghène, in the presence of Father Rouel and several other European priests and Melanesian seminarians (figure 5). The bishop of Nouméa, Monsignor Martin, officiated. Jean-Marie then proceeded to celebrate his first mass in his village, Tiendanite, giving communion to his parents and kin. He had no doubt that "It was the day of glory for Father Rouel," the man who had guided him thus far (Tjibaou 1996, 260). Appointed first as priest at Bourail, a markedly Caldoche community on the west coast, he then became a chaplain at Nandaï, the nearby army camp, again serving a very cosmopolitan group (including Eloï Machoro), before being appointed second priest (curate) at the cathedral in Nouméa in 1967. That proved to be another transforming experience in his life. The cathedral served a largely European community, but through urbanization an increasing number of Melanesian Catholics were gravitating to it, and this was the group that Jean-Marie had the specific responsibility of serving, along with the first priest, Father Joseph Kapéa, another Melanesian.

The Church's decision to send the two Melanesian priests to the cathedral was undoubtedly very necessary but also extremely difficult, fraught with institutional and political risks. For the priests it was at once a formative

FIGURE 5. Jean-Marie's ordination at Ouaré in 1965. *(ADCK-Centre Culturel Tjibaou)*

and troubling experience. "During the year I was curate in Nouméa . . . what a lot of drunks I gathered up in the evening, especially Fridays and Saturdays . . . to take home. . . . And I often experienced that discourse, cries in the bottom of the dungeon . . . the tears that recall the lost land . . . and who proclaim . . . who get angry, who fight, who struggle . . . but who find comfort in alcohol. . . . There they become men again, when they can insult the Whites, assume their role as men, and . . . rebel, something they cannot do coolly, in all conscience" (Tjibaou 1989c, 19).

On the one hand Jean-Marie listened to the cries of despair of a people who had lost their bearings in the modern world, who were spiritually and materially dispossessed; on the other he witnessed and was subject to the constant manifestations of European prejudice and discrimination, where Melanesians were described as "boys" and constantly addressed in the diminutive *(tutoyer)*. Adrift in the city, they were neither respected nor had they any respect for themselves. Inevitably the Melanesian diocesan priests debated these issues, drawing no boundaries between religion and the secular world into which they and those they were sent to serve had been projected.

> [W]e held a lot of meetings, among ourselves, among the diocesan priests, on those problems . . . and also on the Church's difficulty in this situation. Then there was Vatican I, with John XXIII, and afterwards Vatican II, which made very important openings. And also the position adopted by the Evangelical Church.
>
> With Kapéa, we always attended Union Calédonienne meetings, more so than those of UICALO, for the people's protests and for their difficulties in getting satisfaction, and for us, the difficulty of defending their causes within the institution of the Church. (Tjibaou 1989c, 14–15)

Jean-Marie and his fellow Melanesian priests became increasingly preoccupied by the larger context within which the Church operated, and their preoccupations inevitably began to find expression in their sermons. The reaction was immediate. The influence and the actions of the Melanesian priests, notably Jean-Marie Tjibaou and Joseph Kapéa, had to be curtailed. "There I began to see something of the political problems, the difficulties one had in standing up for the poor. Speeches were closely controlled. It was Father Jacob Kapeta [Kapéa] who was the first curate. He was the Union Calédonienne's chaplain, hence highly politicized. When it became necessary to appoint the cathedral priest, there was a long story aimed at preventing him from being appointed. He was brilliant, and preparing a doctorate in theology at Rome" (Tjibaou 1996, 260–261).

"It was a time when there could be no freedom of speech" (Apikaoua, pers comm, 20 July 1994). It was also a moment of truth for Jean-Marie, the immediate crisis at the cathedral in Nouméa being influenced by much broader forces that were at work. By the time he had completed his studies at the *grand séminaire* and arrived in Nouméa, the position of France and of the local Catholic Church with respect to New Caledonia had changed radically from that prevailing in the early postwar years. Jean-Marie, like his fellow Oceanian seminarians, had been profoundly marked by the values of the Fourth Republic, values that were basic to the political transformations of the late 1940s and early to mid-1950s. Already, in his speech to open the Brazzaville Conference, in January 1944, Charles de Gaulle had firmly stated his intentions with respect to France's colonies. "[I]n French Africa, as in all the other territories where people live beneath our flag, there would be no progress that is [true] progress, if the people, in the land of their birth, could not profit morally and materially, if they could not raise themselves little by little up to the level where they will be capable of participating in their place in the management of their own affairs. It is the duty of France to ensure that it is so" (de Gaulle, 1944).

In the decade or more following the end of the war, de Gaulle proved faithful to his declaration. Independence was offered to the African colonies in 1958 and, in 1960, accepted by all but one of them. (New Caledonia voted in favor of becoming a *territoire d'outre-mer*.) In December of the same year the United Nations General Assembly adopted resolution 1514, which "Solemnly proclaims the necessity of bringing to a speedy and unconditional end colonialism in all its forms and manifestations."[2] At the same time the Catholic Church was being transformed under the leadership of Pope John XXIII, with Vatican II offering a new approach to the world, a new ecumenism, and new religious practices that were adapted to local realities—including a concern with the material conditions of people's lives. Appointed in 1958, Pope John XXIII died in 1963.

These winds of change had been felt in New Caledonia too, stimulating the young Melanesian seminarians and priests in their reflections and their searching. However, New Caledonia was not Africa, and the practice of Catholicism there was not receptive to the message emanating from the Church in Rome. New Caledonia was a settler colony and it possessed significant mineral resources. Consequently, the door that had started to open in the aftermath of the Second World War had, by the beginning of the 1960s, begun to close again. In 1956 the National Assembly in Paris had approved a *loi-cadre* (governing law) whereby, in the case of New Caledonia, the General Council, a purely advisory body, was replaced by a Territorial Assembly elected by universal suffrage, which in turn elected six ministers and a vice president to a Government Council presided over by the governor. A year later this resulted in the majority of seats in the Territorial Assembly being held by the Union Calédonienne and in a Melanesian, Michel Kauma, being elected as vice president. This situation provoked the wrath of European settlers and residents, and they successfully pressured France into revoking, in 1963, what had come to be known as the *loi Defferre* (Defferre's law). It was replaced by the *statut Jacquinot* (Jacquinot legislation). The Territorial Assembly was dissolved and an advisory body established in its place, with executive power vested once again exclusively in the hands of the governor. The political gains of the 1940s and 1950s for New Caledonia, and in particular for the Melanesian community, were thereby largely dissolved.

However, considerations internal to New Caledonia did not completely explain this political retreat. By 1962 France itself had changed radically, as had de Gaulle's vision of the role his country was called on to play in the global arena. Algerian independence, achieved in that year after a bloody eight-year war, had left deep scars on the country. The French people were demoralized and divided. Successive right-wing governments were elected, beginning in 1959 and continuing without a break until 1974. In New Caledonia the natural allies of these governments were, inevitably, the European settlers. The year 1958 marked de Gaulle's return to power, the end of the Fourth Republic, and the beginning of the Fifth. His avowed intention this time was to build a country that was both strongly nationalistic and internationally aggressive. Rather than remain a middle-range power in a Western alliance dominated by the United States, France would, according to this design, move back to the global center stage, and reestablish itself as a great power. Being a great power required a geographical and geopolitical presence throughout the world and the possession of nuclear weapons. Those were the attributes that guaranteed a permanent seat on the United Nations Security Council.

In the wake of the 1958 revolt in Algeria and of its subsequent independence, France's remaining overseas territories were endowed with a new vocation. De Gaulle and the new political leadership stressed that their overseas possessions had played a vital role during the Second World War, in structuring and launching the movement for liberation of an occupied France. From this novel geostrategic perspective, New Caledonia and the other Pacific territories were now seen as crucial to the acquisition of great-power status and to ensuring the territorial integrity of France. So, in 1966, when Jean-Marie was already a priest, de Gaulle returned to Nouméa and delivered a message that bore no resemblance to his first—one that had been enthusiastically received a decade earlier: "You are *France australe* [antipodean France]. You have a French role to play in this part of the world" (quoted in Rollat 1989b, 116). Immediately afterward, he went on to French Polynesia, specifically to Moruroa atoll, in order to witness one of his country's first aerial nuclear tests. In the same year, France withdrew from the NATO Joint Strategic Command. The message was clear and uncompromising.

In this context, the interests of the European settler community in New Caledonia largely coincided with those of metropolitan France, with the Melanesian people once again marginalized by history and relegated to the status of second-class citizens in their own country. They were reminded that they were inconsequential pawns in a global game, condemned to live out their lives "at the end of the world." This time, however, a new generation of educated Melanesians was emerging; they were not prepared to accept such a fate and were increasingly conscious of the forces of change that were sweeping across Europe—France included—Africa, and Asia. There were also more and more unskilled fellow Melanesians seeking work outside the reservations and responding to the demands of an expanding economy. The paths of both intellectuals and laborers converged in Nouméa.

In this atmosphere, in 1967, Father Apollinaire Anova's thesis began to circulate. Jean-Marie hadn't known the priest personally, for Anova had been ordained in 1957 and had gone to France in 1959, first to act as a parish priest in Chartres, and then to pursue his studies in Paris. He returned to New Caledonia in November 1965 a sick man, and three months later he died of leukemia, at the age of thirty-seven. Conscious of his intellectual strength, the Catholic Church in New Caledonia, in the hope he would teach at the seminary, had decided to send him to the Institut Catholique de Paris to do a *licence* (bachelor's degree) in theology.[3] Following his two years at the institute, however, Father Apollinaire insisted on staying on two more years in order to undertake postgraduate studies (DES) in social science and economics, this time at the Institut des Sciences Sociales et Économiques. There he wrote a thesis entitled "Histoire et psychologie des Mélanésiens." After it was defended and accepted with the *félicitations du jury* (congratulations of the jury), his wish was that it would be published in New Caledonia. With this in mind he revised the manuscript and prepared a brief "cautionary note":[4] "[T]his book wishes to keep its dual character: First of all that of being the work of a student, and then an investigation into the socioeconomic, political and religious realm of New Caledonia. This book also seeks to strengthen the ties of friendship between black and white Caledonians and metropolitan French. May it achieve its goal" (Ataba 1984, 21).

Whether Monsignor Martin had approved its publication prior to its author's death is unclear. He asserted he had informed Father Apollinaire in Paris that "this document wasn't publishable as it stood, not because of its content, but on account of its unfinished state" (Lenormand, Gauthier, Guiart, and Martin 1969, 198). However, it is most likely that the bishop did authorize publication of the revised manuscript only to reverse his decision following Father Apollinaire's death. A special issue of the *Journal de la Société des Océanistes,* entitled *Les missions dans le Pacifique* and published in 1969, contains the chapter "L'insurrection des Néo-calédoniens en 1878" (The Revolt of the New Caledonians in 1878) and part of a second chapter entitled "Pour une économie humaine" (Toward a Humane Economy; Apollinaire 1969, 201–237), the two excerpts being published under the rubric "Deux exemples de réflexions mélanésiennes" (Two Examples of Melanesian Thought). They are preceded by a portrait of the author based on the remarks of four religious, political, and academic authorities who had known him reasonably well (Lenormand and others 1969). The same issue of the journal contains an article by Father Gérard Leymang entitled "Message chrétien et mentalité néo-hébridaise" (The Christian Message and the New Hebridean Mind; Leymang 1969, 239–255). It is unlikely that news of this scholarly publication would have filtered back to New Caledonia before 1970, if then. Rather, what Jean-Marie Tjibaou saw in 1967 was a roneod version of the whole manuscript. It was not until 1984 that the revised thesis was published, under the title *D'Ataï à l'indépendance* (From Ataï to Independence), with a lengthy explanatory introduction written by François Burck. Even then its publication provoked controversy, for obvious reasons. Father Apollinaire was the first to provide, from a Melanesian perspective, an overview of the colonial history of New Caledonia in which he linked economy, politics, and religion. Even more provocatively, his analysis proposed the High Chief Ataï, leader of the 1878 rebellion, as a hero and a model for the Melanesian people. "We must be proud of our past. We must be proud of our struggles and of our collective victories. The indigenous person must be proud of he who was the soul of the Insurrection of 1878: the High Chief Ataï. He has to see in him the symbol, the 'incarnation' of he who must be his model in the building of his country" (Ataba 1984, 46).

Throughout his thesis, Father Apollinaire was concerned to highlight Melanesian values. He believed that his people's failure to confidently assume them and reveal them to the European residents of the country were at the root of their suffering. Melanesians needed to become conscious of their common heritage, irrespective of specific tribal loyalties, and Europeans had to recognize, out of respect, the very considerable differences between the two cultures and civilizations. "For the indigenous person, the world carries in itself its ultimate meaning. For the European, the world is only a means for ensuring his existence; and its ultimate sense is deferred to an extra-cosmic world beyond" (Ataba 1984, 53).

Having addressed a first taboo, Ataï, Father Apollinaire then proceeded to consider a second, land tenure. Here he affirmed that, for Melanesians, land was not a commodity to be valued purely in economic terms. Rather, it lay at the very roots of identity. "[W]hat counts [for the indigenous person], is above all to be in possession of the land of his ancestors" (Ataba 1984, 84). He stressed that the Church has a responsibility to engage in debates on these issues, for as the economy is influenced by politics so it is by religion. "[I]t is a neglect of our priestly duty to fail to undertake the political training of the faithful. . . . policy or politics are of concern to man in his totality, with his secular and religious values. There is not one side which is Christian and the other Civic. Rather there is the Christian Citizen" (Ataba 1984, 168).

Finally, he identified three political options for the future of New Caledonia: one, a Département d'Outre-Mer; two, independence; and three, a federation of all Pacific Islands. The first he rejected, the third he considered a long-term objective; his preference and prediction were unequivocally vested in the second: "It is what New Caledonia is destined to be one day" (Ataba 1984, 170).

The whole approach of the thesis was pervaded by a search to identify shared values, a shared history, and shared concerns for the Melanesian people as a whole. Father Apollinaire attributed the same quest to Ataï, whose last words, after he was struck down by two Melanesians from Canala who had been co-opted as auxiliaries by the French troops, were: "You too, my brother" (Ataba 1984, 67). In other words, in proposing Ataï as a symbol of Kanak liberation, he made a plea for a common Melanesian identity. He also affirmed that once a common identity had been established, intercultural dialogue would be possible, and the union of the Melanesian and European peoples of New Caledonia could be advanced as a desired outcome.

Without a doubt, "Histoire et psychologie des Mélanésiens" was a revolutionary document at the time of its writing and initial circulation. It was powerful and articulate and, at the same time, generous in its approach. It was a Melanesian voice that emerged from a wasteland lacking any Melanesian literature or modern voices for priests like Jean-Marie Tjibaou to reflect on. As François Burck wrote in his introduction to the first published edition of the thesis, "Apollinaire Anova-Ataba is without a doubt the first Kanak intellectual to have spoken out in order to proclaim the distinctive personality of the Kanak people in the context of their liberation. His writings, and in particular his thesis, signal the birth of a modern Kanak thought that is grounded in Myth and in History, and that gives on to economic development and social progress. A Christian and a priest, Apollinaire engages at one and the same time in criticism of the Caledonian Church and in support of the involvement of Christians in the political organization of the Kanak people" (Burck 1984, 13).

Obviously, Father Apollinaire's vision of his responsibility as a Kanak intellectual, and of his role within the Church as a Kanak priest, closely reflected Jean-Marie's preoccupations, as well as those of other Oceanian priests of the same generation. Seeing no conflict between their priestly vocation and their Melanesian identity, they found themselves confronted by an inflexible colonial Church in the form of the Marist mission. This local institutional reality was the source of a tension that Gérard Leymang, the ni-Vanuatu priest and friend of Jean-Marie, clearly identified in his own contribution to the 1969 special issue of the *Journal de la Société des Océanistes*. "How can one give the Hebridean the possibility of becoming not a Western-style Christian, but an Oceanian Christian who does not turn his back on his race or his traditions in order to remain authentically Christian without ceasing for all that to be Hebridean; this in the context of a traditional conception of the Church that expresses itself through a dogmatism and a moralism that does not facilitate the adaptation of Christianity to the Oceanian mentality?" (Leymang 1969, 243). At the same time, for all of them, it was a preoccupation that transcended the narrow boundaries of the Catholic Church. As Leymang stated at the end of his article, "It is not only the non-Western world which poses a problem for the Church. The Western world also creates difficulties for Oceanians" (1969, 255).

Significantly, Father Apollinaire's thesis and Father Leymang's article were written during their studies in France. It was the nature and pertinence of this European experience, far removed from the colonial reality of the South Pacific, that was no doubt a revelation for Jean-Marie. With respect to this experience, Father Apollinaire wrote of his first year spent as a parish priest, "The year that I spent at Rechèvres was, then, profitable for me. It revealed many things to me, for instance another side of France. A France that was conciliatory with regard to other peoples, generous, and that was voluntarily Christian. It also revealed to me another aspect of the Church, alas much less known in our lands: its universality" (Ataba 1984, 180). François Burck elaborated on this point in his introduction to *D'Ataï à l'indépendance*.

In Paris, where he undertook his studies, he had the necessary detachment to get a good perception of the situation in the country, that of the Church and that of the Kanak people. It is perhaps why the Bishop asked him to come back. Apollinaire refused, for he needed also to escape from the straitjacket of the Caledonian Church: in Paris he mixed with Whites who were not colonials and, above all, with Africans. . . . Apollinaire's combat . . . was that of an intellectual who . . . remained outside (yet attentive to) the political struggle, but who was committed as an intellectual to supporting the process of affirmation of the Kanak people and identity, and who had the courage to speak out with respect, at one and the same time, to the Kanak past, present and future. (Burck 1984, 18)

Curiously, Jean-Marie made only passing reference to Father Apollinaire in the long interview where he recounted the story of his life to Jacques Violette (Tjibaou 1989c). Neither Father Apollinaire nor his thesis figures elsewhere in Jean-Marie's public statements, for several possible reasons. One consists of the hazards of interviewing; another is that Father Apollinaire had already left the seminary by the time Jean-Marie arrived and was in France by the time he was ordained. It is also conceivable that, later on in life, Jean-Marie was not comfortable with the way in which radical Melanesian groups, notably the Foulards Rouges, had appropriated Ataï and used him as a symbol in a struggle driven by ideology rather than the reality of daily life in New Caledonia.

Regardless, it was almost certainly Jean-Marie's reading of the thesis that led to his decision that he too must go overseas for further study.

It was 1968, and France and the Western world were in turmoil.

4 The Desire to Understand
University Studies in Lyon and Paris

I didn't leave to study; I left above all in order to look for analytical tools that would help better understand the situation here.

ALREADY IN 1967 Jean-Marie was actively exploring the possibility of going to France. Pierre Métais offered him a scholarship to study ethnology at the University of Bordeaux, and he was given leave by the Church to prepare for the entrance exams in June of the following year. However, because of the events of May 1968 the exams were canceled. In the meantime Jean-Marie obtained a *Croissance des jeunes nations* (Growth of Young Nations) scholarship to study at the Faculté Catholique de Lyon, commencing in September 1968. There he joined his ni-Vanuatu friend Gérard Leymang, who had left a year or two before and who was later to become the last prime minister of the Franco-British Condominium of the New Hebrides.[1]

The bishop of Nouméa had approved Jean-Marie's departure, expecting no doubt that, like the Melanesian priests who had gone before him, Jean-Marie would pursue his religious studies with a view to returning to teach at the seminary. But, as with Apollinaire Ataba, who had gone to France a decade earlier, the wish proved to be of no avail.

Father O'Reilly: "That was a mistake to thrust them into 'Sociology.'"

Father Laurenge: "But the Bishop never sent them to France for that. He should have done clerical studies: theology, Holy Scriptures, etc., however straight away, they branched off and confronted the Bishop with a fait accompli." (Fassael, quoted in Mokaddem 2004, 17)

Rather than remain condemned to silence within the Church and in a colony that was "at the world's end," Jean-Marie was intent on becoming an actor "within the world," in order to bring his people from the distant margins of humankind and of empire onto the global stage. With this objective clearly in mind, there was no question of his being constrained to theological studies. He turned to economics, political science, sociology, and so forth, whenever possible with reference to development studies. Thanks not only to the subject matter of the courses he took in Lyon, but also to the third-world origins and experience of many of his fellow students and teachers, he quickly acquired a conceptual understanding of the colonial situation in his homeland.

> [T]hey were above all adults, people who had already worked. Africans . . . people from South America, people coming from underdeveloped countries.
>
> Our time was divided between courses at the Institut politique de Lyon, the State University, and also the Institut de sociologie and the Institut social.
>
> In "social" there was above all Roger Nordon, in economics . . . on economic analysis, state budgets, financial systems, banks, the economic system in general.
>
> There was a politics professor too, Latournel, who also taught at the State University. . . . Two people who taught courses in law . . . and then there were also cooperatives. (Tjibaou 1989c, 16)

The intellectual and political climate in France at the time also nourished a context in which a wide range of experiences were debated and a variety of analytical tools proposed for interpreting them. "[T]here were group practical exercises. . . . That provided the opportunity for people to discuss with each other. Then, in the sociology of development, there was also an African professor who was himself working on dependencies. . . . The unequal terms of exchange. It is as clear as crystal! The colonial powers have left, they've decolonized, granted independence, but they arranged things in such a way as to maintain a presence, an economic domination with the complicity of the new regimes" (Tjibaou 1989c, 17).

Outside the classroom Jean-Marie observed French reactions to immigration from North Africa and witnessed the formation of ghettos in Lyon, all the while benefiting from the explosion of ideas in the wake of May 1968. He was at once stimulated and preoccupied by much of what he saw and heard. For the recently arrived Oceanian with a thirst to learn and to understand, it rapidly became apparent that political independence without economic independence was proving to be a hollow victory for many former colonies. Likewise, the upheaval in France suggested that political debate not rooted in a particular place and grounded in a specific human experience made little sense. In this respect, Jean-Marie's reaction to the crises of 1968 is revealing. A number of Western countries, in both Europe and North America, had been engulfed in a major student protest movement. In France the movement had quickly spread to the trade unions, feminist groups, left-wing political parties, and even the military and the churches, with a massive national general strike as the outcome. A manifestation of the thinking of the first postwar generation to enter the adult world, the movement had a utopian air in its challenging of a civilization dedicated exclusively to material gain, and it provoked a major political crisis in the country. However, many of the actions had an unequivocally festive air about them too, and a number of observers now consider May 1968 to have been the first major expression of the hedonistic preoccupations that have since come to the fore in the developed world. Unlike Nidoish Naisseline and several other Melanesians who were studying in France at the time and who went on to form the Foulards Rouges and the Groupe 1878,[2] Jean-Marie was not seduced. "Sixty-eight didn't 'liberate' me. And I'm really happy not to be 'liberated'" (1996, 106). Although he had not witnessed the revolts, demonstrations, and strikes, he experienced their aftermath on his arrival in Lyon several months later, and his judgment was severe. For him they were expressions of despair rather than of hope. "These people no longer have an identity. The right questions aren't asked" (Godin, pers comm, 29 April 1997).

The right questions? In his sociology course in Lyon Jean-Marie was introduced to the writings of Maurice Leenhardt. A Protestant missionary who first arrived in New Caledonia in 1902, he had been welcomed by the mayor of Nouméa with the remark, "What have you come here for, pastor sir? In ten years there won't be any Canaques left." Leenhardt went on to spend a total of twenty-five years in the country, delving into and revealing Melanesian society and culture through his writings and his actions. As a missionary and, increasingly, a humanist he was not interested in arbitrarily imposing the beliefs of one civilization on another. Rather he was concerned with real peoples' lives, with the future of the Melanesian people, with interactions between cultures, and with mutual respect and understanding. He approached society in its globality (language, art, myths, cultural practices . . .). He was particularly fascinated by myth, which he considered an integral part of the fabric of civilization, and he was deeply moved by the humanized landscapes of the Grande Terre — the terraced food gardens, the cultivated forests, the *grandes cases* (chiefly conical houses) with their *flèches faîtières* (roof spires) reaching to the sky, and the majestic avenues lined with cordyline and araucaria leading up to them. He recognized these structures and forms as landscapes whose great beauty somehow expressed their role as mediators between the visible and invisible worlds; they were like an open book, to be read, absorbed, and meditated on. He explored the many *sentiers de la coutume* (customary exchange networks), traveling from valley to valley across the Grande Terre. He came to appreciate the role of language and of *la parole* (the spoken word) in assuring the perennity of human existence, and of chiefs and elders as conveyors of collective experience. In absorbing Melanesian culture, Leenhardt arrived at the inevitable conclusion that "The shock of defeat [at the end of the nineteenth century] was aggravated by separation, physical and spiritual, from the moorings of mythic geography" (Clifford 1982, 45).

Maurice Leenhardt's message was not lost on Jean-Marie. Neither was his itinerary in life, for if he had arrived in New Caledonia at the dawn of the twentieth century a missionary, he had rapidly developed a complementary interest in anthropology. Further, his independent nature and his persistent *parti pris* (commitment) in favor of the Melanesian people and of Melanesian spirituality meant that his relations with both the Société des Missions Évangéliques de Paris and the colonial administration in New Caledonia were frequently ambiguous if not openly conflictual. Committed more and more to learning from as distinct from teaching Melanesians, he focused his activities increasingly on anthropology with the result that, in 1933, he was appointed a *chargé de cours* (lecturer) in ethnology at the École Pratique des Hautes Études (ÉPHÉ)[3] in Paris. From this point on, his primary concern was to translate the Melanesian world to non-Melanesians, while never losing sight of his overriding Christian and humanitarian convictions. Once the professional transition from missionary to educator had been completed, he was committed to teaching French university students rather than to training Melanesian pastors and evangelists. Appointed to the chair of ethnology at the ÉPHÉ in 1942, he went on to introduce the teaching of Oceanic languages at the Institut National des Langues et Civilisations Orientales (INALCO), to establish the Institut Français d'Océanie (IFO) in Nouméa, and to play a key role in founding the scholarly Société des Océanistes.

In a very real sense Maurice Leenhardt was a source of inspiration and a model for Jean-Marie, for he had creatively merged Christian convictions and academic scholarship in his life, and in so doing had demonstrated his immense respect for the Melanesian people of New Caledonia. He had also revealed in his writings some of the core convictions Jean-Marie himself was seeking to formulate. Jean-Marie highlighted them almost a decade later, on the occasion of celebrations organized at Houaïlou to mark the one-hundredth anniversary of Leenhardt's birth.

> I am indebted to Pastor Leenhardt for having . . . taken account of Kanak culture. He wrote in effect in 1913: "The greatest sacrifice . . . required of a missionary is that of his culture; not that you should show contempt for it, but one must be able to put it aside, as a given, in order to acquire a new, indigenous culture—at the Sorbonne one would say pre-logic—and that is not easy. Consequently so little has been achieved with the indigenous people, because little application has been given to this effort to penetrate their mentality, to reformulate the substance of our concepts in order to arrive at concepts which are acceptable to them with our own truths, these truths being purged in order *to keep only that which is the heritage of mankind and not the superficial lustre of Westerners.*" (Tjibaou 1978a, 94; emphasis in original)

Serving in the triple capacity of pastor, ethnologist, and friend, Maurice Leenhardt had given the Melanesian people of New Caledonia cultural credibility, legitimacy before the law, and hope. For these reasons Jean-Marie terminated his "Hommage à Maurice Leenhardt" with the words, "In the name of this people whom he loved and for whom he gave the best of himself, I pay tribute to his memory and I wish for him and his family the benediction of the ancestors" (1978a, 97).

In all probability it was his reading of *Do Kamo* (The Person in His or Her Authenticity) (Leenhardt 1947) that most of all marked Jean-Marie, in its concern to describe and explain the plenitude of Melanesian life, with its foundations in both reason and myth. Without a doubt, the book is the most important of Leenhardt's writings, by virtue of both its scholarship and the way its missionary-anthropologist author revealed a profound humanity in his corresponding desire to understand himself and his own civilization.[4]

Stimulated by his discovery of Leenhardt, motivated by his experience at the cathedral in Nouméa, and encouraged by his rapid academic progress, Jean-Marie stayed only six months in Lyon. Rather than complete a broadly based undergraduate program there he moved on to postgraduate studies in ethnology in Paris. "I went to Paris to study ethnology at the École Pratique des Hautes Études. When I was at the cathedral in Nouméa, I looked after drunks, Kanak, and something had struck me: they always talked about their land, their tribes that were occupied by Whites. So I worked, with Professor Roger Bastide, in ethnology and in psychiatry, on mental problems" (Tjibaou 1996, 261).

Roger Bastide had spent many years teaching and engaged in research in Brazil. He was fascinated by religion, spirituality, and myth in the context of societies in transition and of the interpenetration of civilizations. He had witnessed rituals with deep African roots, rituals that evoked, for uprooted peoples, "their cries for the country left behind." He was interested in race relations and in social psychiatry, in the links between cultural change, mental illness, dream, and the sacred, that is, in what Henri Desroche described in his introduction to Bastide's *Le sacré sauvage,* as the "speleology of the soul" (1975, 10). The feelings and experiences of living human beings were important to him, not the explanations and conceptualizations of scholars.

Bastide also expressed a deep respect for Leenhardt's writings.

In Lyon Jean-Marie had already written a research paper addressing the twin tragedies of alienation and resignation that marked his people. He concluded it with the affirmation that

> we had to take initiatives which enable people, the group to . . . regain an image . . . a gratifying image of themselves, because they had got to the point where they had swallowed an alien indeed a contemptuous image of themselves . . . which they drowned in alcohol in an effort of rediscovery. But they are alienated anyway, they no longer accept that the people . . . have the right to exist [or] be proposed as a model.
>
> People, there are some who have even changed their name, who have Europeanized their name to become whites. . . . Because our own society no longer

offers the pride of being a complete man. You have to be ashamed of being
Kanak . . . and proud of being White. . . .

To become White, that's . . . the aim . . . to be accepted by the Whites, to speak
French well, to be shrewd, to swagger, to put down others . . . that's the model
which is proposed.

To eat like Whites, to live on the margins of the tribe, ultimately . . . not to
engage in customary exchanges, what? To save up, to have fancy cars . . . to de-
spise the Kanak a bit too . . . that's part of the status of self-righteous modernity,
accepted as a model for the future. (Tjibaou 1989c, 21–23)

The other anthropologist to have a direct impact on Jean-Marie was
Jean Guiart. A student of Maurice Leenhardt, Guiart had commenced his
career in 1947, at the newly established Institut Français d'Océanie (IFO),
and he went on to acquire an encyclopedic knowledge of Melanesian languages and cultures as well as a deep commitment to the Melanesian people
of New Caledonia. Guiart and Bastide had very different personalities and
scholarly interests, and each had a distinctive impact on Jean-Marie. Guiart
undoubtedly informed him, in a substantive sense, setting him off on the
trail of deepening his understanding of (if not relearning) his own culture
and enriching his knowledge of Melanesian civilization in general. Bastide,
on the other hand, influenced him in a personal and in a broad-based intellectual and moral sense. He was by all accounts a warm, attentive person,
unpretentious and of evident integrity. He also welcomed students into his
home, a practice Jean-Marie much appreciated. Although Bastide had retired from his teaching position at the Sorbonne in 1969, he still supervised
students, and Jean-Marie had the good fortune to attend a course he offered
at the Collège Coopératif, at Montrouge in the suburbs of Paris.[5] It was entitled "Les mutations religieuses dans le Tiers-Monde" (Religious Change
in the Third World). Guided by Bastide, Jean-Marie entered the universe of
myth and of the sacred, or what Ravelet described, in his overview of Bastide's life and work, as "the mysterious journey down from the rational to the
irrational" (Ravelet nd). It was a journey that fitted well with Jean-Marie's experience of his own culture, and of the tensions and misfortunes his people
were suffering. Furthermore, Bastide's approach appealed to Jean-Marie in
its intellectual generosity and its search for synthesis based on lived experience. "Bastide mistrusted all-embracing theories, or ideologies, preferring
obscure and confused thought to the grand explanatory systems, be they Marxist
or structuralist" (Ravelet nd; emphasis in original).

An "a-conformist," Bastide stood apart from the debates of 1968, opening his students' doors to a particular kind of applied anthropology, one
concerned with human beings struggling emotionally and mentally with
cultural change and what can only be described as "the soul." He directed
attention to the spiritual universe that lay beyond and prior to the material
conditions of human existence. The absence of spirituality in the revolt of
1968 had already intuitively struck Jean-Marie, and Bastide explored this

dimension in his teachings, revealing in the process the sense and the vital importance of the Melanesian worldview. Bastide's teachings convinced Jean-Marie that this spirituality was something his people had, at all cost, to carry forward with them in their journey into the modern world.

> Power to the imagination, that was the cry in May 1968, and not: power to reason. Imagination, in other words instituted emotions. And not reason, in other words the opposing of new systems of laws as a remedy for anomie, the rejection of the established order. . . .
>
> We have only [to underline] . . . the factors that influenced individuals, pushing them to new forms of trance. There is first of all the passage from the community, with its more egalitarian characteristics, its more intimate solidarity, the relative homogeneity of its beliefs and its values, to a society which weakens the ties, deepens the void, ends in individual solitude, lost in the indifferent crowd. The nuclear family, which for a long time had helped such individuals to bear the burden of solitude, is undergoing a crisis where competition between the sexes takes the place of complementarity, where the young people find themselves isolated from adults, not so much, as has been repeatedly said, because the young have rebelled against their elders, but rather because they have felt themselves to be abandoned by their Fathers. Then there is the fracture between the mechanical, artificial, world of machines and of houses made out of reinforced concrete, and the living world of nature; . . . the union between mankind and the sky, water, plants, birds, is no longer possible, and one has to be satisfied with artificial ties. . . . In short, as Max Weber has shown, our entire culture is a culture of reason, of science, of progress, which leaves no part of our life beyond its scope, no possible freedom. And yet the laws of reason, if they are commanding, postulate the prior commitment of the intellect, submitting itself to a certain number of values that justify them in our view. These values can be contested even if the rules that are based on them cannot. But if they are challenged, the social law no longer takes the form of an instrument of oppression, an arbitrary constraint or, if you wish, the final threat of castration of the sons by those who exercise power, in the name of the Father. It is not without impunity that the awakening of the sacredness of the wild has been preceded historically by the triumph of the philosophy of the absurd that only served to translate into scientific terms these traits of anomie . . . ; mankind's solitude which incites him to seek a new "otherness" capable of quenching a thirst which it is impossible to eliminate—the severing of ties with the living world of nature which serves to awaken, deep within his heart the nostalgia of a cosmic experience—the triumph of Reason can only serve to make new chains, albeit gold, which will imprison his youthful Liberty, only just born with the crisis of adolescence. (Bastide 1975, 228–229)

These themes were to resurface constantly in the remarks and discourse of Jean-Marie in the years to come, for they confirmed the legitimacy of Melanesian culture and society and the pertinence of its contribution to mankind as a whole. He had found precisely what he needed to nourish his own reflection in Roger Bastide's intellectual and moral concern to identify the roots of racism and to determine the bases on which peoples and civilizations can interact without recourse to domination and assimilation.

A thesis project on "the problems of Kanak cultural identity" took form under the direction of Bastide and Guiart. A young French student, Patrice Godin, was there when Jean-Marie presented it to an ethnology class at the Sorbonne, and he recalled that it was to focus on Jean-Marie's own people at Hienghène, giving particular attention to the following issues:

> The Melanesian of New Caledonia is presently in search of his identity.
> 1. What is his reference framework and how authentic is it? What are the dynamic forces of this society, the constituting elements of Kanak personality at the end of the nineteenth century?
> 2. Does the primary cohesion of the system still exist today? In other words, is this system the bearer of an authentically Melanesian dynamic?
> 3. What are the new cultural elements in the present system? To what kind of new society is one moving, to what kind of Melanesian by the year 2000? (Godin 1989, 22)

On that particular occasion, as was often the case during his anthropological studies in Paris, Jean-Marie was condemned by fellow students and professors to be a mere informant, an object of scholarly interest. As Alban Bensa observed almost thirty years later, "there was not an embryo of a reflection by anthropologists at that time as to the trajectory these people were embarked on" (pers comm, 26 Nov 1996).[6] Jean-Marie tolerated this informant role, but he also periodically turned it to his own advantage with an astute mix of gravity and humor.

> The first day we met also revealed Jean-Marie's sense of humor. Pushed by a few students and an old ethnologist to elaborate on the cult of Thunder in the Hienghène area, he was hesitant, saying he couldn't disclose secrets without the risk of provoking a calamity. This response generated a few incredulous smiles. "Speaking when I am not authorized," Jean-Marie added, "means, in Kanak society, exposing oneself to the anger of Thunder." The rationalist students didn't have time to smile again. A thunderbolt struck outside and a gust of wind burst open the windows of the classroom. I recall lowering my head. The old ethnologist was completely white. And Jean-Marie burst into laughter, delighted at the trick he had played on us. (Godin 1989, 23)

Laughter . . . It was both an individual and a collective cultural trait that Jean-Marie carried until his death, a safety valve that enabled him to bear with and also to momentarily step aside from far more serious challenges and crises.

For all Melanesian students and soldiers in Paris, one door was always open—for rest, for company, and for counsel beyond the narrow boundaries of their professional lives. It was that of the apartment of Roch Pidjot, who represented New Caledonia as deputy at the National Assembly from 1964 to 1986. The first Kanak to occupy a seat in the French parliament, he came from La Conception (near Nouméa) and was a member of a tribe whose origins lay in the region of Pouébo, but who had followed the Catholic missionaries to Nouméa on their withdrawal from Balade early in the colonial period. Roch Pidjot was known as *grand-père* (grandfather) to a whole generation of Melanesians. This mark of respect could be explained by his being a minor chief, the founding president of UICALO, and one of the cofounders and the first elected president of the Union Calédonienne. He was a public figure deeply committed to the defense and promotion of the rights of his people, and a pioneer in the crucial areas of education and land reform. He had the reputation of being a totally honest man, motivated by a profound sense of service, and with no interest whatsoever in personal gain. He was also someone who, despite long absences in Paris, remained loyal to his tribal roots. "Apart from his parliamentary stays in Paris, Roch Pidjot spent all his time on his local land, between his yam plantations and the parish church at La Conception, the two foundations of his life as a countryman. In effect all those who knew Roch understand that he was above all a peasant, a man of the land" (Lenormand 1990–1991, 10).

In other words, Roch Pidjot was an exceptional elder statesman who exercised not power but authority, an authority that derived from his status and, more particularly, his chiefly responsibilities. As well, he demonstrated, in his words and in his acts, the crucial importance of the presence of the past; but he never sought refuge in it. Almost thirty years older than Jean-Marie, this Melanesian elder immediately became extremely important to him, in terms of his origins, his beliefs, his personality, and his commitment. His geographical and cultural foundations were similar to those of Jean-Marie, in the sense of their being unequivocally rooted in the tribe and the land. At the same time Roch Pidjot's actions were characterized by a progressive transition from custom—culture—into politics, a transition that marked a merging, not a break. The *petit chef* and the *grand-père* both acted in the name of an entire people—first, the local tribe, and second, the whole nation. Finally, his political commitment, which subsequently took the form of active promotion of Melanesian independence, was never made at the expense of the well-being of the other inhabitants of New Caledonia. It was made in the spirit of the Union Calédonienne, "Two colors, a single people," and with the conviction that the best interests of France lay in the European metropolis having free and friendly allies in the Pacific. These, too, were values that would guide Jean-Marie when he later entered the political arena.

Of considerable significance to him while he was in Paris, Roch Pidjot and his wife, Scholastique, were also to play a vital role in Jean-Marie's reentry into New Caledonia. His stay in the French capital was a critical influence on his change of vocation, despite being relatively short. Already Father Rouel had died in May 1969, thereby freeing him of a very personal obligation to the institution of the Catholic Church and to his place within it as a priest. Then, the following year, he learned that his father was dying and he left Paris in haste, only to arrive two days after the burial. Jean-Marie stayed on in New Caledonia for a while, to participate in a socioeconomic study of school-leavers in the north of the Grande Terre, including the Hienghène area. Then he returned to Paris to pursue his studies in anthropology. Before leaving, he met with fellow Melanesian priests to discuss the problems they were having with the local Catholic Church.[7] On this occasion he proposed that they collectively resign. "A political undertaking, one couldn't do it from within without committing the institution, hence without upsetting the . . . all the grandmothers, the nuns" (Tjibaou 1989c, 21).

Jean-Marie took the initiative during this return trip because, after an absence of only two years, he could now see an increasingly desperate Melanesian world that was no longer confined to the streets of Nouméa. It had become patently clear in his mind that he had to find a new way of serving his own people, the ordinary people and the poorest. "It was at that time too that alcohol was making inroads in the tribes. It was the first time I saw so much . . . because there was a lot of money around on account of the [nickel] boom. People were offering cartons of wine, cheap wine, beer . . . there wasn't any before, people drunk, but it was not a part of customary exchanges. There they were offering by carton loads. For me it was a . . . painful experience" (Tjibaou 1989c, 21).

Jean-Marie no doubt returned to Paris with a heavy heart and the conviction that more urgent matters needed his attention than an academic thesis. By the middle of 1971 he was back in New Caledonia, ostensibly to pursue his research. However, he had no income, he was in an ambiguous position with respect to the Church, and he needed to find work in an area where it mattered and where he could be of service. In reality the project had been shelved and his student days were over. He would never return to the academic world, or to the field of scholarly anthropology. It wasn't necessary, because he had learned by now how to better read his own world.

Jean-Marie Tjibaou never wrote his thesis, but the rest of his life bears witness to the fact that he found an answer to these questions [formulated above]. On that day [the occasion of his conference at the Sorbonne], he evoked in particular the fundamental links between the totemic ancestor of a clan in the valley, the stone that was in the possession of his priest, medicinal grasses and leaves, the words that are recited on the occasion of a healing ritual. He demonstrated that they were different aspects of a single reality; with words that were simple and profound, he stressed the coherence of the thought of his ancestors, permeated by the omnipresence within the community of the living and the dead. From my first meeting with Jean-Marie Tjibaou he taught me that social life is infused with meaning and ethnology is of value only if it constitutes a rigorous attempt at translation and mutual understanding. (Godin 1989, 22–23)

"Ethnology is only of worth if it is a rigorous attempt at translation and mutual comprehension." Jean-Marie had delved deep into the discipline (and also touched on sociology, economics, law, political science . . .) in order to find the analytical tools that would help him understand the struggles of his people and determine the path they should take into the future. His relationship to the Church was of a similar nature. "He went away asking himself whether he was a priest or a Kanak. He returned a priest and a Kanak. Totally priest, totally Kanak. And in the future he would only be both at the same time. So long as the Church didn't force him to choose. . . . For he had discovered his inner truth: he could be a Kanak and a priest, but he would never again be a priest without first being Kanak" (Rollat 1989b, 124). Jean-Marie was unequivocally a Melanesian, and soon to proclaim the name Kanak. Because of the Catholic Church's profound ambivalence toward the collective aspirations of the Melanesian inhabitants of New Caledonia, he had no choice but to abandon the priesthood, a step he finally took in 1972. If the Church had provided him with an education and enriched the notion of service, it had also progressively isolated him from his own people and threatened his very roots.

His approach to anthropology was analogous in the sense that it was motivated exclusively by the transcending needs and interests of his own people. Jean-Marie had entered it in order to acquire a better understanding of his own culture, with a view, first, to being able to describe and explain it to others, and second, to identifying a way forward for his people, to a future that they would choose for themselves and exercise control over. In this respect his anthropological journey to Lyon and on to Paris differed radically from his Catholic passage from Tiendanite to Nouméa. The earlier one had taken him away from his Melanesian roots, while the later one facilitated his return to them. Through his reading of Leenhardt and the counsel of Guiart, "he began to attend the school of his own culture" (Burck, pers comm, 22 Jan 1998); then the teaching of Bastide helped him to appreciate all that he felt in his guts and in his soul. Much more than a journey to and within metropolitan France, Jean-Marie's university experience was an intellectual trajectory that brought him into contact with anthropologists who were *passeurs de frontières*. The frontiers that Bastide and Leenhardt crossed were those of academic disciplines, religions, professions, institutions, languages, ideologies, cultures, and civilizations. Both were deeply religious people—Protestants—whose teachings and actions were directly nourished by their beliefs. One of the last courses Jean-Marie attended in Paris was at the Collège Coopératif, a college that provided an educational experience tributary to the ÉPHÉ and aimed at adults from developed and developing nations who were already active in the fields of economy and society. It was concerned with social movements, social economy, solidarity. . . . It was a world of committed Christians, and the course was offered by Roger Bastide.

Jean-Marie too was a *passeur de frontières.* In the company of his two most important Parisian mentors, Roger Bastide, the French scholar, and Roch Pidjot, the Melanesian politician, he came to appreciate why he could never confine himself to the Church or to the university, or renege on his debt to either. He now understood that his people were the inheritors and the bearers of a world without frontiers, and they had been unjustly condemned to living behind rigid boundaries imposed by uninvited occupants of their own land.

In Father Rouel, Jean-Marie had found a counselor and a priest to whom he had a deep spiritual and moral commitment. In Professor Bastide, he found a man who bridged the spiritual and intellectual worlds and who gave sense to his emotional experience of being a Melanesian. In the politician Roch Pidjot, he discovered *un homme sacré,* a Kanak pioneer in the secular world of French politics, and a symbol for himself and for a whole generation of young Kanak adults. Finally, in the writings of Maurice Leenhardt, a man he never knew, he found an ardent admirer and defender of his own people, a man who had journeyed into their hearts and souls.

It was time for Jean-Marie to move on, to return home and make use of his accumulated knowledge, skills, and understanding—of his own civilization, of the colonial experience, and of the modern world.

5 From Applied to Committed Anthropology
Social and Cultural Action in Nouméa

> In the name of the Faith and of "Civilization" the Kanak has
> had to practice self-denial. It is vital for him today, because the
> circumstances are different, to affirm his right to exist, and to exist
> culturally, in New Caledonia.
>
> If I can allow myself to say that, it is because I am convinced that
> we have erred, and that today, in the name of the glory of the Faith
> and the honor of "Civilization" the Kanak should be invited to the
> banquet of civilizations, not as a deculturated beggar but as a free
> person. His participation would simply constitute the affirmation of
> his personality through the rediscovered opportunity of being able
> to express himself in his own culture.

NEW CALEDONIA HAD changed radically between Jean-Marie's departure in 1968 and his return three years later. With its succession of right-wing governments France had continued to tighten its grip on the territory. The Billotte legislation, passed in January 1969, constituted the last step in the elimination of any semblance of autonomy. Local administrations—the *communes*—were brought under the direct control of the state, as was the mining sector of the economy. Nickel had been exploited since the last quarter of the nineteenth century. For long described as *Le roi nickel* (King Nickel), it was at the heart of the territory's economy and it was a mineral that placed New Caledonia close to the center of the global resource economy. Between 25 and 30 percent of the world's reserves of nickel are located on the Grande Terre. Moreover, by the onset of the First World War, its principal producer and sole refiner, Société le Nickel (SLN), was meeting one-third of global demand for the mineral. Following the discovery of major deposits elsewhere,[1] the territory's proportion of total world production has dropped significantly, to hover presently around 10 percent. However, demand, and therefore production, has continued to grow.

Nickel is widely used in arms manufacture as well as in a variety of other key industries, ranging from high technology to domestic consumer items. Like oil, it is considered a strategic resource and, as such, is stockpiled in the United States. France decided in 1969 that it too should exercise direct control over research and exploitation of the mineral and protect it from the risk of foreign takeovers, eventually becoming a major shareholder in a company (SLN) that had until then been controlled essentially by the Rothschild family. The shift to state ownership was motivated by de Gaulle's concern to restore France to its former status as a world power.

This increasing political stranglehold on New Caledonia was set against the larger background of what came to be known as the "nickel boom." In New Caledonia from 1967 to 1971, production of the mineral—both mining and refining—virtually tripled, while the territory's share of the world market increased even more. The boom was the result of rapid economic growth in the industrialized nations, together with the intense demand for armaments created by the Vietnam War. It was also aided by an extended strike at the Canadian mine of the principal global producer, INCO. The effects of the boom were felt throughout New Caledonian society and economy. The nickel refinery at Doniambo, just outside Nouméa, was expanded, the demand for labor exploded, and Nouméa took on the air of a boomtown where speculation was rife and consumer spending seemingly unlimited. For a time New Caledonia's gross domestic product far outstripped that of metropolitan France. Some fifteen thousand new immigrants arrived between 1969 and 1971, principally from France, but also from Wallis and Futuna, French Polynesia, Vanuatu, and even Australia. Among the metropolitan French were a significant number of Pieds Noirs[2] who had fled Algeria in the aftermath of national independence. There was an atmosphere of euphoria about the territory, and even "the official propaganda was saying 'Get rich in New Caledonia!'" (Rollat 1989b, 125).

However, the Melanesian population, residing dominantly on reservations, was not invited to participate in the boom, and few substantive benefits trickled down to them. More serious in the long term were the demographic implications for them of the intense economic activity. At 51.1 percent in 1956, the Melanesians had constituted a majority, albeit fragile, of the total population (34,969 out of 68,400).[3] By 1969 their proportion had dropped to 46 percent, and by 1974 to 40.8 percent, although actual numbers had increased, first to 46,200 and then to 53,725. During the same period (1956–1969) the European population had risen from 36.7 percent (25,160) to 41 percent (41,268), dropping slightly, in 1974, to 39.2 percent, while continuing to increase in absolute terms (to 51,582). For the same period, the group identified as "Others," consisting mostly of other Oceanians, had risen from 12.2 percent in 1956 to 20 percent in 1974 (8,351 to 26,358) (Christnacht 1987, 25). Immigration was focused essentially on Nouméa and its suburbs, with new employment opportunities occurring essentially in the secondary and tertiary sectors of the economy.

The bubble burst in 1972–1973, first as a result of the devaluation of the US dollar and the drop in world nickel prices, and then as a consequence of the global oil crisis. The frenzy that had gripped Nouméa disappeared almost as quickly as it had arrived, although nickel processing at the state-controlled Doniambo plant continued to expand for several more years. Brief though the boom was, its demographic implications for the Melanesian population were enduring, as were its political consequences.

The postwar political advance and then retreat in New Caledonia was paralleled by a major extension of the frontier of pioneer European settlement. If massive land alienation had occurred in the second half of the nineteenth century, with 250,000 hectares appropriated by settlers and the Melanesian population confined to reservations totaling half that amount, the situation remained more or less stable thereafter, for essentially demographic and sociological reasons. On the one hand European rural immigration effectively ended, and on the other, the severely demoralized Melanesian population first declined and then saw a slow demographic recovery. However, in 1945 a new, aggressive strategy of rural European settlement was initiated (Saussol 1986). Over the next thirty years, to 1975, the total land area attributed to European-owned estates rose from 270,000 to 390,000 hectares. During the same period an increasingly politicized and numerically expanding Melanesian population sought to extend the boundaries of its reservations. Further, as they became aware of the opportunities provided by the government, Melanesians started applying for individual land concessions. A rural crisis was inevitable and, for the first time since 1853, the Melanesians rather than the European settlers potentially held the initiative. Their population was being rejuvenated through accelerating growth, while their rural European counterpart was aging rapidly. In addition, the foundations of the Europeans' labor-intensive commercial agricultural economy had been severely damaged by the nickel boom, with many of their young people leaving to work in town. Simply put, the pioneer frontier and settler colony that had been at the heart of France's dream for New Caledonia was in a state of crisis. Nouméa, too, was in crisis with the collapse of the boom, but it had now unequivocally established its demographic and economic domination over the affairs of the territory. Together these shifts had the effect of accentuating the ethnic cleavage between the European city and the Melanesian bush.

Back in France, a right-wing government was still in power in the early seventies. That government's vision of the future of New Caledonia was clearly expressed in July 1972, in a letter that Prime Minister Pierre Mesmer wrote to Xavier Deniau, minister for overseas departments and territories (DOM-TOM) and ardent defender of *la francophonie mondiale* (the international French-speaking community).

New Caledonia, a settler colony, although dedicated to being a multiracial "salad bowl," is probably the last tropical non-independent territory in the world to which a developed nation is able to send its citizens.

It is vital, therefore, to take advantage of this ultimate opportunity to create another francophone country. The French presence in New Caledonia, a world war excepted, can only be threatened by nationalist claims on the part of indigenous populations supported by a few potential allies in other communities in the Pacific.

In the short and medium term, the mass immigration of French citizens from the metropolis or originating in the overseas *départements* (Réunion) should ensure that this risk is avoided, by virtue of maintaining or improving the demographic balance between communities.

In the long term, indigenous nationalist demands will only be avoided if the communities originating outside the Pacific constitute a demographic majority. It goes without saying that no long-term demographic effects will be achieved in the absence of the systematic immigration of women and of children.

In order to rectify the sexual imbalance within the non-indigenous population, it would no doubt be appropriate to set aside jobs for immigrants within the private sector. The ideal guiding principle would be for all positions that can be occupied by a woman be reserved for women (secretarial, commerce, administration). (quoted in Mathieu 1995, 34)

Widely quoted and reproduced in the years that followed, the letter must be placed in its larger setting—of France's reasserted status as a middle-range world power. If, in the context of the cold war, there was an easily identifiable place for France to occupy in the global arena, the situation was much more complex in Oceania. Samoa had acquired independence from New Zealand in 1962, Indonesia had pried West Papua from the hands of the Dutch by 1969, and Fiji had ceased to be a British colony in 1970. A wave of political change had taken form within a single decade and every indication was that it would sweep through the other Melanesian countries if not through the entire region, the French territories included.[4]

In this economic and political milieu, small groups of intellectuals of diverse origins began to publicly challenge the status quo—with respect to the French colonial presence, to land rights, and to discriminatory practices in public places in Nouméa. The two most important were the Groupe 1878 and the Foulards Rouges.[5] Foremost among their indigenous members, in terms of charisma and radical initiatives, was Nidoish Naisseline, the son of a high chief from Maré who had studied sociology at the Sorbonne. Yeiwéné Yeiwéné, Déwé Gorodey, and Elie Poigoune all experienced their political baptism in this arena. Some, like Nidoish, had participated in the uprising of May 1968 in France, while others, including Déwé Gorodey, were only to leave for Europe later on. Emerging in the late 1960s, these groups of young activists were ideologically driven by third world liberation movements, the class struggle, and Marxism. Influenced by debates and events in France, they were committed to raising public consciousness through direct action. They sought inspiration in emblematic revolutionary heroes and they found, in High Chief Ataï, the New Caledonian equivalent of Latin America's Che Guevara. The wearing of red headbands (*foulards rouges*), drawing graffiti, producing pamphlets and newsletters (*Canaque homme libre, Sikiss*), using Melanesian languages, occupying segregated restaurants, and seeking direct confrontation with the colonial authorities were among the strategies they adopted in order to gain attention.

Against this background, of radical and increasingly ethnic mobilization, the term *Canaque*—soon to be transformed into *Kanak*—began to be appropriated by the young Melanesian activists and used as a positive expression of collective indigenous identity. In turning the negative connotations of the name into positive ones, they were, of course, inspired by what Aimé Césaire had achieved with the term *Nègre* and descendants of slaves in the United States had done with *Black*.

These very public and provocative appeals for the recognition of Melanesian rights and political aspirations proved fatal for ties between the radical European (Caledonian) and Melanesian students and, more important, for the broad ethnic and national power base of the Union Calédonienne political party. Until 1970 the UC was very much a multiracial party displaying a clear consensus as to economic, social, and political goals. Provoked by the actions of the Foulards Rouges, conscious of the increasing economic marginalization of the Melanesian population, aware of growing demands for national autonomy if not independence—and of the emergence of distinct Melanesian political groupings as an expression of them—the UC started to fracture, with dramatic consequences. It was defeated in the 1972 territorial elections. The largely European right wing of the party left to join the Rassemblement pour la Calédonie dans la République (RPCR), while a variety of radical Melanesian splinter parties progressively emerged on the left, the first being the Union Multiraciale de la Nouvelle-Calédonie, led by Yann Céléné Uregeï, whose goal was self-government. Others included, notably, the Parti de Libération Kanak (PALIKA), the Libération Kanak Socialiste (LKS), and the Front Uni de Libération Kanak (FULK). In sum, the first half of the 1970s was marked by a high degree of volatility leading to the reformulation of political objectives and agendas, the emergence of new political actors, and the redrawing of boundaries, henceforth along increasingly ethnic lines.

For a new generation of tertiary and, increasingly, secularly educated Melanesians, postwar France had all the trappings of a "schizophrenic" country—enlightened and stimulating at its European heart, but dark and repressive on its distant Oceanic margins. Having been momentarily positioned at the vanguard of global decolonization movements, New Caledonia's indigenous population was now, in the early 1970s, drifting back into the state of anomie it had experienced prior to the Second World War. The nickel boom had served only to increase the pain, the mining frenzy having accelerated the degradation of the rural environment, and alcohol now fueling an explosive mix, on the reservations, of chronic despair and mounting frustration and anger.

This was the situation when Jean-Marie returned to New Caledonia, bringing with him a very different set of intellectual references and tools from those of Nidoish Naisseline and other members of the Foulards Rouges. The request to abandon the priesthood that he had submitted during his 1970 visit had been approved. It was not a decision he had taken lightly, nor was it a change of direction. As he explained to François Burck, also a priest at the time, "I'm not giving up, rather I'm committing myself. . . . I need to share the lives of those I claim to be committed to if I want to be credible" (quoted in Burck, 1989, 8). With the institution, and especially the constraints, of the Church now firmly behind him, he was in a position to seek a more effective way of serving his people, one that would proceed from both a recognition and a celebration of their Melanesian identity, for he was witness to the emergence of a new development: "During the boom years you saw people getting drunk, having wild parties, and then something new happened: people started to say things that they had never said before, to criticize the chief, society, customary leaders" (Tjibaou, quoted in Pitoiset 1999, 171–172).

The early 1970s was a period of hesitation and soul-searching, as much on the part of the government and the administration as on that of Jean-Marie and other European-educated Kanak. The crisis gripping Melanesian society could no longer be ignored by any of the major actors in the territory. Jean-Marie's spontaneous preferences were directed to social and cultural action at the base and to intercultural understanding, with a view to combating both the alienation and self-hatred of the vast majority of his people and the contempt in which they were held by a large part of the European community.

> To be worthy of being called a man
> in this new world
> one had to practice self-denial
> down to the base of one's roots.
>
> The rooftop totems
> bowed down
> in the sun
> and the clans were like the houses
> shredded after the hurricane.
>
> In the town
> we were like bums,

at the market, beggars selling their miserable harvest
and at school, second-rate students,
not with it,
eternal repeaters with 2000 years of history
to catch up on in extra classes.
    (TJIBAOU, AZAPUNIA, IEKAW, CITRE, AND MISSOTTE,
    Vers Mélanésia 2000, c21.)

For a while Jean-Marie offered seminars to "Europeans of goodwill," with the goal that they would "become acquainted with the Melanesian milieu" (Tjibaou 1996, 261). He also became active in the Comité territorial de lutte contre l'alcoolisme (Territorial Committee to Combat Alcoholism). However, those who probably played the most important role in assuring his reentry, helping him define his course of action over the four or five years following his return to New Caledonia, were Roch Pidjot and his wife Scholastique. First he joined the territorial government's Service de l'Éducation de base (Office of Grassroots Education), as a group leader. Established in the late 1950s by his future father-in-law, Doui Matayo Wetta, as a part of a range of new initiatives directed to the Melanesian population, it had been progressively emasculated in the following decade. Jean-Marie played a crucial role in its revival. Under his impetus, attention was directed to identifying the roots and breaking the ties of Melanesian psychological and material dependence. He established a Secrétariat mélanésien d'information et de recherches culturelles (Melanesian Secretariat for Information and Cultural Research) and he played a crucial role in the creation of two Melanesian associations. One, the Association mélanésienne pour le développement économique et social (Melanesian Association for Economic and Social Development), was directed to both customary and contemporary Melanesian leaders, with the aim of focusing attention on their people's aspirations as well as inciting the leaders to play an active role in satisfying them. It was a strategy aimed at promoting development from within. The second was the Mouvement féminin pour un souriant village mélanésien (Women's Movement for a Smiling Melanesian Village), created by Scholastique Pidjot in 1971. A chief herself, she was familiar with the reality of life in the tribe and was likewise motivated by an obligation to serve.

The movement rapidly established some eighteen local groups throughout the Grande Terre and the Loyalties. Its actions were directed to concrete issues of hygiene, alcoholism, and, in the broadest sense, improving the quality of village life.

[A]lcohol isn't an end in itself for the people who drink, and it is important not to aim at the wrong target. There is no point in forbidding alcohol, for the problem is elsewhere.
    Well then we fought to . . . improve living conditions, the houses . . . im-

proving kitchens, bathrooms, the living room, the house in short, and also the surroundings, with flowers.

We began with flowers, grassed areas, tidy villages. That's why we said "Smiling Melanesian Village."

But you know, between St. Louis and Conception tons of filth were removed from the village. Bottles . . . at St. Louis they filled up truckloads! Bottles and then old cars . . . Conception too.

Then it was time to say to the women, "There's no point in complaining if the men don't come home. You have to struggle in order for them to come of their own volition. You have to give them the means to do a bit of the work."

It is important too that the women dress up, attend to their hair, look good and the insides of their houses are comfortable, eh? The kids have to be clean too, so they don't work all day in dirty clothes. People who are tired from their work have no wish to see . . . to be depressed at home.

And that, that worked.

Then I said, "good, that's material, and now one has to try and do something which rallies people around the root of the problem, what. Around an image of themselves that is a source of pride. And what remains is the most specific, its culture." (Tjibaou 1989c, 24–26)

In May 1973 Jean-Marie married a colleague in the Service de l'Éducation de base, Marie-Claude Wetta. Her presence at his side was to be of vital importance in the years to follow, during his frequent absences as well as when he was at home. Theirs was a close-knit family, and Jean-Marie's increasingly public role meant that he needed strong emotional as well as material support. When overseas he was always concerned to know that "everything was going well," be it with his family, in the village at Tiendanite, or with his people in general. There were quite probably political actions that Marie-Claude did not always fully understand or sympathize with at the outset, for she came from a very different background. The Wetta were Protestants and loyalists, and both her father, Doui Matayo, and her brother, Henri, were to become active members of the RPCR, presided over by Jacques Lafleur. Here again, however, Jean-Marie's natural concern was to build bridges. The marriage itself was a highly symbolic act in three parts: a customary wedding; a religious wedding co-celebrated by François Burck (who was still a Catholic priest at the time) and a Protestant pastor, both taking place in his village, Tiendanite; and a civil union at the *mairie* (town hall) in Hienghène. As with so many of the gestures Jean-Marie made, it was a way of reaching out to all his people and expressing respect for them in their diversity of beliefs and practices.

The promotion of the rights and interests of Melanesians was the focus of attention of the emerging elite, who explored various avenues. For the young radicals, epitomized by Nidoish Naisseline, energy was directed toward the perpetration of "revolutionary" acts in Nouméa, through reference to external models. Their concerns were essentially political. A second group, clustered around André Gopéa and Edmond Nékiriaï, formally constituted in 1974 as the Union Progressiste Mélanésienne (Progressive Melanesian Union), directed its attention specifically to Melanesian social and economic development. Favoring relatively large-scale initiatives, it even explored the possibility of establishing a mining company. Neither the political nor the economic avenue proved particularly successful, in part because of the absence of a broadly based Melanesian identity in New Caledonia possessing a clear collective will. More serious, however, was the failure of both groups to directly address the vast majority of the population who lived on the reservations. This was the avenue that Jean-Marie chose to take, proposing a major cultural project with long-term economic and political goals. He was already convinced that initiatives imposed from above and from outside would never work. To be successful they had to be grounded in the rural Melanesian community. In initiating a cultural project from within he was also concerned to establish the foundations of a deep and sustained dialogue between the European and the indigenous communities.

Throughout the period 1972–1974 a flurry of organizations were created, some more enduring than others. In 1972 Jean-Marie had established, together with Marie-Claude, a Groupement mélanésien de développement social et culturel (Melanesian Group for Social and Cultural Development), with a view to coordinating development initiatives at the local (tribal) level. He went on, in 1974, to create a Comité pour le développement (Development Committee). He became active in a variety of spheres, all of which addressed spiritual and material poverty at the local level. During the same period he moved, within the territorial administration, from the Service de l'Éducation de base to the Direction de la Jeunesse et des Sports (Department of Youth and Sports). In both roles he acquired considerable experience of day-to-day life at the village level throughout the territory, and he came to the conclusion that his people were psychologically broken and economically marginalized, as well as being confronted with the very real risk of demographic extinction. As he was to repeat on many occasions in international arenas in the years to come, "We are living on borrowed time."

In the course of reflecting on the distress of his people, Jean-Marie met two metropolitan Frenchmen who would play crucial roles in elaborating his next step, both of them leaning strongly toward "the left-wing of Christian democracy." One was Philippe Missotte, and the other Michel Levallois. Philippe Missotte had been active for twelve years in the Scouts of France before coming to the territory, in 1971, with the explicit mandate of establishing a Centre de Formation d'Animateurs (CeFA, Center for the Training of Group Leaders) within the Direction de la Jeunesse et des Sports. A lay Catholic with "a calling for matters of concern to man and society," he was inspired by Pope Paul VI's March 1967 encyclical letter "On the Development of Peoples," which was addressed to "all men of good will." A firm believer in the promotion of development from within, the pope believed that grounded knowledge and experience could successfully project themselves onto the outside world. Inspired by the pope's values and by his own experience with adolescents in France, Philippe Missotte was also convinced that development initiatives should be centered on the group as distinct from the individual. It was the only possible way forward, the only "road to freedom," as far as he was concerned.

In Jean-Marie Tjibaou, Philippe Missotte found "a man that I loved, like a brother" (pers comm, 19 Nov 1996) and a close collaborator who revealed New Caledonia to him in a manner that made sense—in terms of his approach and his values, as well as of his earlier professional and moral engagements. "This arrival in New Caledonia, these discoveries and these actions are grounded in my earlier militant and/or professional career. This itinerary is more or less similar to the customary path, sparingly revealed through meeting the Kanak peoples: a complex web of relations and ancestral alliances, path of life, path of being. Without a certain knowledge of these networks, at least of their existence and of their function, neither Kanak history nor the Kanak person can be understood and apprehended" (Missotte 1985, 13–14).

Philippe Missotte had been to New Caledonia twice before taking up his position in the Direction de la Jeunesse et des Sports. On one occasion he had organized a gathering of francophone scouts of the Pacific and, on the other, had undertaken a study of the needs of the territory's young people. The recommendations of this study had led to his appointment. In addition to his religious beliefs and his professional experience, Philippe Missotte had lived through the Algerian war of independence. All this led him to be scandalized by what he found. It was the negation of everything he believed in, namely certain notions of justice and of human rights, and the founding principles of the modern, French republic.

The proposal to organize a major Melanesian cultural festival arose out of the joint concerns of the CeFA and the Mouvement féminin pour un souriant village mélanésien, the one inspired by Jean-Marie Tjibaou and Philippe Missotte, and the other by Scholastique Pidjot. Problems of alcoholism, self-denial, and self-destruction in the villages were at the heart of the preoccupations of both groups.

> Our hypothesis was that alcohol enabled the Canaques to avoid the conflict between two contradictory demands, one that denied their existence and the other that publicly enjoined them to adopt another, with the tacit resulting condition of ceasing to be Canaques, an obstacle sufficiently important that if they acquired the ambition, it would be in vain. As in other situations, close or distant—Maoris, Australian Aborigines, South Africans, American Indians, etc—the Canaques could not tolerate the absence of dignity resulting from the

refusal to acknowledge them as men, and to value their reason for living. These men drank in order to efface the shame of insignificance. (Missotte 1995, 61)

Michel Levallois made the project possible. A senior French civil servant, he was secretary-general for the territory in the early 1970s. Possessing a strong moral conscience, a sense of history, and fine judgment, he was the most influential representative of a small number of deeply concerned Europeans present in New Caledonia at the time. "[C]ivil servants and administrators, but also members of the Catholic and Protestant churches who had become aware of the very serious moral and political crisis the territory was experiencing, and in particular the Melanesian people. . . . We didn't have a very clear idea as to what should be done . . . but we were committed to moving forward, and to do it with the Melanesians, who for too long had been marginalized by administrative initiatives" (Levallois 1995, 126). Levallois was also no doubt something of a dreamer and an idealist, attracted by the utopian dimension of the project.

In early 1974 Jean-Marie Tjibaou and Scholastique Pidjot submitted to him a proposal to hold a Melanesian festival in Nouméa that would involve the participation of all the country's tribes. The aim was for the Melanesians—now called Canaques—to simultaneously reveal their own collective existence to themselves and to make themselves known to the other peoples of New Caledonia. It sought "to permit the Canaque to come face-to-face with himself, for him to discover himself and to redefine his identity as it stands in 1975 . . . to help him to regain confidence in himself and to find more dignity and pride . . . to rid him psychologically of his inferiority complex, linked in large part to the cultural insignificance to which he found himself reduced" (quoted in Levallois 1995, 126).

The administration, searching desperately for ways in which to promote the Melanesian community and, in particular, to respond to the aspirations of a new and radically different generation of young adults, seized on the proposal. Levallois convinced the high commissioner of the importance of the initiative. The deputy, Jacques Iékawé, took it under his wing, and it was incorporated in the "Promotion and Development" section of the Seventh Plan submission, which went on to obtain the unanimous approval of the Territorial Assembly. The support of the minister for DOM-TOM, in Paris, was then obtained, as well as that of the armed forces in New Caledonia. Thus, moral and material support for what would be called Mélanésia 2000 was readily forthcoming, and it was financed entirely by the French government and the territorial administration (apart from revenue generated by admission charges to the festival). Whether all supporting parties fully appreciated the nature of the project at the time is uncertain. However, for Michel Levallois and for others at the source of the initiative, it was clear. "It was essential, in effect, to recall [in 1995] that Mélanésia 2000 was not a cultural or folkloric event: it was an action, a political gesture for which the organizers, whether they were Melanesians or Europeans, politicians or civil servants, assumed full responsibility. We shared with Jean-Marie Tjibaou the conviction that culture, in lying at the heart of politics, gives it meaning and dignity, and we knew that the recognition of the Kanak people was a precondition for any sustaining political action in New Caledonia" (Levallois 1995, 127).

Organized by the CeFA and directed by Jean-Marie Tjibaou, the Mélanésia 2000 Festival took place in Nouméa in September 1975. In hindsight, it proved to be a crucial event in the formulation and expression of contemporary Kanak identity and the emergence of New Caledonia as we know it today. It was a historic moment that has since taken on mythical dimensions. In the circumstances it is hardly surprising that special issues of *Mwà Véé* (1995, no 10) and of the *Journal de la Société des Océanistes* (1995, vol 100–101), have been devoted to it, as well as a substantial *JSO* article by Jean Guiart (1996), written in response to them. Philippe Missotte also devoted a substantial part of his doctoral thesis to Mélanésia 2000 (1995), highlighting in his analysis how the festival had its roots in the larger developmental context of the Melanesian people of New Caledonia. Finally, the event generated its own publication, in French and English editions, *Kanaké, mélanésien de nouvelle calédonie* [*sic*], rapidly going out of print in the case of the original French edition (Tjibaou, Missotte, Folco, and Rives 1976, 1978). Together the various publications constitute a broad and often remarkably detailed mix of description, reflection, analysis, and evaluation, the last aimed at determining the long-term impact of the event on the people and on the country.

Jean-Marie's vision and objectives in conceiving the festival are set out in what Philippe Missotte called *le texte fondateur,* a document prepared by the development committee in May 1975 and used for promotional purposes. The introductory statement, written by Jean-Marie, affirmed at the outset that "the deep-seated motivation for this festival is that of faith in the possibility of establishing a richer and more sustained dialogue between European culture and indigenous culture." He evoked the dream of a fusing of the territory's diverse cultures where, in 2000, "the cultural profile of the Caledonian will be composed just as well of elements of European culture as of Melanesian culture. However, for this symbiosis to be achieved there is a necessary precondition, which is the reciprocal recognition[6] of the two cultures with regard to their specificities" (Tjibaou, quoted in Missotte 1995, 66–67).

He then identified four specific objectives for this Melanesian festival: first, the promotion of a new intercultural dialogue; second, the presentation of Kanak culture as it existed in 1975; third, Kanak rediscovery of their own identity, as a necessary condition for reacquiring self-esteem and dignity, and in order to be able to project themselves into the future; and, fourth, the opportunity for Europeans and the diverse ethnic groups in New Caledonia to observe, to become aware of and, it was hoped, recognize the legitimacy of the indigenous culture. It was an extremely ambitious project, in that it necessitated giving a sense of unity to Melanesian culture—making it possible to speak with one voice. It also required breaking through the geographical and psychological, if not indeed political, frontier between white (and ethnic) Nouméa and the Melanesian bush. In other words, while the ultimate goal was dialogue between the two dominant cultures, unity had first to be established across the diversity of tribes and regions of Melanesian New Caledonia. It was not that Jean-Marie believed a single, unified Melanesian culture existed. Rather, he recognized the strategic importance for Melanesians of being able to affirm their presence collectively and to speak with one voice, instead of remaining divided, turning against each other, and being exploited to the advantage of the colonizers, as had happened too often in the past. Jean Guiart was clear on this point: "His understanding of the culture was both global and local; however, tactically, he often chose to adopt the convenient theme of the unity of Kanak culture in order to make himself understood by the Whites" (1996, 94).

To achieve the goal of bringing all the territory's tribes together in Nouméa, several group leaders were given the task of using customary kinship and exchange networks in order to travel from tribe to tribe to present the festival project, collect information on material culture, songs, and dances, and prepare eight regional mini-festivals. These were held between February and August 1975, their purpose being to obtain support for the festival, create a certain momentum, and, more specifically, prepare dances, costumes, handicrafts, and other local expressions of Melanesian culture. A site was provided by the municipality of Nouméa at Plage 1000, on the edge of the town and close to the Tiga Peninsula where the Tjibaou Cultural Center would later be built. It was designed to receive participants and organize shows for up to five thousand spectators. The preparations were effective, and Mélanésia 2000 took place, as planned, on 3–7 September 1975.

If administration support for the initiative was unqualified, the journey to the festival was fraught with difficulties, in the form of doubts, criticism, and even outright opposition. Opposition came from across the political spectrum. The European right wing was hostile to any form of public celebration of Melanesian culture, while the various groups of young Kanak radicals and their Marxist allies in France considered it a "vast enterprise of folklorization of their culture" (Guidieri 1985, 34) and a sellout to liberal elements in the territorial administration. Student radicals also criticized the Melanesian organizers of the festival for their recourse to European collaborators and expertise if not, indeed, technology! Although neither of the extremes had any real influence on the course of events, more serious were the risks of divisions emanating from the Union Calédonienne and, notably, its European elements, who saw in Mélanésia 2000 an eminently political

act. They were right of course, and their preoccupations were simply another expression of the fractures that were developing in the party and that
would lead to most of its European members leaving to form the RPCR—
and to Jean-Marie Tjibaou taking over the leadership.

As a pragmatist and an astute strategist, Jean-Marie negotiated this
minefield and established many of the bridges that were so important to
him—between tribes, between the north and the south of the Grande Terre,
between the Grande Terre and the Loyalties, between Catholics and Protestants. If Mélanésia 2000 was an immense success, it was in large part because
of his capacity to bring people together and ensure that "the Word circu-
lated," but it was also because of his insistence that the event be technically
perfect (that is, professionally sophisticated). Some two thousand Melanesians participated in the festival, coming from close to half the communes
of New Caledonia—from Belep to La Conception and Hienghène to Tiga.
Even more important, it attracted an estimated fifty thousand spectators.
Services apart, the site was made up of nine *grandes cases* built by and cater-
ing for each regional delegation. Each *case* represented a distinctive culture
area, as formally expressed in a building made exclusively from local materials and built according to traditional methods (notably without recourse
to nails). A tenth *Grande Case du Sud* (chiefly conical house of the south)
represented the host clans, where the visiting delegations were received and
customary exchanges made.

For the Melanesian participants, the festival site was a place of inter-
action and exchange, of reactivating traditional networks, reinforcing old
ties and establishing new ones, as well as an opportunity to recognize and
celebrate a certain unity of cultural values and practices. For visitors of all
origins, it was an occasion to see public expressions of indigenous culture
and especially to hear Melanesian voices relating their interpretation of
their place and experience in the history of New Caledonia. In this respect
the climax of Mélanésia 2000 was the *jeu scénique* entitled *Kanaké,* a highly
ritualized play or "historical socio-drama" (Missotte 1995, 88), in three acts,
presented on the Friday and Saturday evenings in an amphitheater designed
to accommodate five thousand spectators. In fact it attracted between ten
and twelve thousand on each occasion. "Kanaké is one of the most powerful prototypes of the Melanesian world. He is the ancestor, the firstborn.
He is the ridge-pole, the centre post, the sanctuary of the great conical
house. He is the word at the source of man's existence. This same word establishes the organizational system that governs relations between men, and
their relations with the geographical and mythical environment" (Tjibaou
1978b, 5).

In three acts, or scenes, the play depicts the life, death, and resurrection of a people, summarizing the history and particularly the tribulations
of the Melanesian inhabitants of New Caledonia. The first scene, *Boénando,*
takes the form of a ceremony marking the end of mourning the death of

a high chief. Delegations representing six different clans from throughout New Caledonia—Canala, Goro, Hienghène, Maré, and two others—are received; they make their offerings, and then yams are shared. The scene ends with the clans dancing together in celebration of the ancestors and as an expression of joy and of a new beginning. Then, slowly, they become aware of the presence of soldiers, the incessant beating of their drums gradually infiltrating and then silencing the rhythm of the dancers and their musical instruments. The second scene, *La Conquête*, presents the coming of the Europeans. Thirty white-masked Melanesians, impersonating French soldiers, occupy the stage, bearing three enormous marionettes—the Soldier, the Trader, and the Missionary (figure 6). Each in its own manner imposes its order on the assembled clans: Christianity, trade goods, mission dresses, compulsory labor, alcohol. The banishment of a chief is portrayed, and the systematic and violent material, moral, and spiritual destruction of Melanesian society. The transition to the third scene is characterized by a long moment of hesitation, despair, and humiliation, with a long march through the night and over the ruins of their past. Then, in *Le partage des ignames* (The Sharing of the Yams), Kanaké, the firstborn, addresses a group of sandalwood traders:

White men, it is to you that I speak because it is your hands that have broken our past, like a shell that one crushes. . . .

You did not even honor us with your hatred, only your pity, and your pity, it was the doctor to treat the sicknesses that you brought. Your pity, it was the priest to make us love the God who had killed our Gods!

Your pity, it was your money to buy from you that made us crazy!

Your pity, it was your civilization!

Are you so sure of it today?

Are you sure that in a hundred years the planet that you dominate will be happier than our island was when you conquered it?

Are you sure that you are more worthy than us of the title of men, of true men?

[One of the traders steps forward. Representing The White Man, he engages a dialogue with Kanaké.]

[W]e ask you to make the peaceful rhythm of the Boénando, which erases grief and which calms anger, ring out anew. We ask you to receive us here, not as masters who impose their presence, but as brothers that one invites.

They then proceed to an exchange of gifts, each offering to the other the riches of their respective civilization. In Kanaké's *case*, three yams are designated, one evoking the spiritual wealth of Melanesian civilization, the second the beauty of the country, and the third "the treasures of our mines, whose wealth no one can yet calculate." The third yam had been buried, and it was the European who removed it from the earth.

Figure 6. Mélanésia 2000: "Thirty white-masked Melanesians, impersonating French soldiers occupy the stage, bearing three enormous marionettes." The marionette shown here is the Soldier. *(ADCK-Centre Culturel Tjibaou)*

The scene ends with the Kanak and the European dancers merging to form a single group, so that the festivities can recommence and the yams be shared. They gather in a circle around the master of ceremonies, who proceeds to address them:

> Our feasts are the movement of the needle that serves to attach the straw on the top of our house; so that all the strands come together to form one roof, as our words come together to form one Word.
>
> Here is the path that leads to our future. In the center the Karoti stands, the tree of mourning that denies access to it!
>
> May the sacred conch shells resound so that the spirits of our ancestors can be soothed!
>
> Now I pull out the Karoti so that no hatred, no bitterness bar the way of our future!
>
> May each one of us tear the tree of discord from his heart.
>
> Our ancestors threw the tree of mourning into the water, we will throw it into the fire; for the fire purifies, gives light and warmth. And it is our wish that hatred be burnt, the path to our future be clear, and the circle we open to all the other peoples be fraternal. Such is the call that I make! (Dobbelaere and Tjibaou 1975, 32)

The cycle of life, death, and resurrection is complete.

Mélanésia 2000 was, without a shadow of doubt, an immense success, and it was run by a Melanesian team. Confronted by a dubious and often cynical European population, they proved they were capable of mounting a highly complex event. Unequivocally at the helm, they turned to Europeans for specific professional skills that no one in the Melanesian community possessed at the time. If the young Kanak radicals were vehement in their criticism of this particular initiative, Jean-Marie's response was unequivocal.

> The festival as it was conceived . . . , no such thing exists traditionally: a gathering of such a kind, in a given period of time, precise, very short. If one questions it . . . one also has to question everything that is foreign to the Melanesian world: clothing, the houses one lives in, electricity, etc. The entire contribution of the Western world, if one is consistent, to the point of committing hara-kiri, even the manner in which one discusses has to be questioned, and the language one uses to discuss. In criticizing the presence of White technicians, it is the whole question of the contribution of the Western techniques, chosen to promote anew specifically what has been destroyed through colonization by the West, which is thrown into doubt. (Tjibaou 1996, 41–42)

Quality and sophistication were the leitmotifs—an Australian company for the sound, Alain Tartas from the Théâtre de la Ville de Paris as stage manager, Pierre Bernard from the French radio and television corporation (ORTF) for the background music, Georges Dobbelaere for the scenery, and marionettes directly inspired by the Bread and Puppet Theater of New York. At the same time the ideas and the content were placed firmly in Melanesian hands; Jean-Marie himself—the only member of the team with tertiary educational qualifications—Jacques Iékawé, Scholastique Pidjot, Doui Matayo Wetta, Marie-Claude Tjibaou. . . . In addition to the cultural contributions generated by the mini-festivals, substantial reference was made to the writings of Maurice Leenhardt, and notably his 1930 *Notes d'ethnologie néo-calédonienne* (Notes on the Ethnology of New Caledonia), to create Kanaké.

With respect to his own people, Jean-Marie's explicit aim in organizing the festival was for them to rediscover and be proud of themselves, to conduct a cultural inventory, and to share that knowledge *within the city*, thereby enabling them to become conscious of the underlying unity that transcends the diversity of specific cultural practices. As he wrote in the introduction to the festival program, "To be recognized [by oneself and by others] one must know oneself." It was an ambitious project because, in this public presentation of Melanesian civilization, he was principally concerned with spiritual matters, with revealing "what, in 1975, is the meaning of the indigenous way of life for people of our times" (Tjibaou 1975a, 5). With this in mind, the festival program ended with a three-page text on "myth in Kanak society," written by Jean-Marie. In it he recounted how the Melanesian world is conceptualized, in terms of its origins, its internal organization, the network of relations between individual members of tribes, and between clans. He emphasized the role of the spoken word in giving a sense to and providing cohesion within the group and connections to the cosmos, as well as in interweaving the social and natural landscapes to create what he called the "living archives" of a people. "The man from the tribe acquires a personality through his relationship to myth and his relationship to place" (Tjibaou 1975b, 36). This brief statement was to form the basis of a much longer article published in the *Journal de la Société des Océanistes* a year later. Entitled "Recherche d'identité mélanésienne et société traditionnelle," it was the first scholarly anthropological study of the Melanesian society of New Caledonia written by one of its own members (Tjibaou 1976).

Melanesians emerged from Mélanésia 2000 with a sense of a strong collective identity, of being from that point on Kanak, a single undivided people, rather than Melanesians separated into a multitude of distinct communities, cultures, and language groups. In holding what was an enormous customary ceremony on the outskirts of Nouméa, and embracing tribes coming from throughout New Caledonia, an entire people publicly affirmed their modernity and claimed their place in the city. In rendering their new collective name linguistically invariable they highlighted both this new-found unity and their Oceanian specificity. The people existed, and they demanded recognition and respect. It was a climactic moment in the emergence of modern Kanaky. As the man responsible for organizing the Païcî delegation said, "After Mélanésia 2000, the Kanak began to be respected, to be addressed as 'vous' for example, whereas before we were always spoken to with the familiar 'tu'" (Pwârâpwéwé 1995, 149).

The festival demonstrated astuteness in both its words and its actions. It was concerned to educate but not to alienate, to unify rather than divide. Alcohol was forbidden on the site, Ataï and the 1878 insurrection were not evoked, care was taken not to wound the religious sensitivities of many Kanak, and politics were never mentioned, even though the festival was an eminently political act, whose intentions were unequivocally long-term.

Jean-Marie's second goal, of promoting intercultural dialogue, proved much more elusive. Certainly the Kanak emerged from Mélanésia 2000 as a force to be reckoned with. As subsequent events would reveal, they moved rapidly to concerted political action and to the promotion first of self-government and then of independence for a country to be called Kanaky. It was the first step in a move toward seeking a new equilibrium in New Caledonia that was both ethnic and geographical in nature. But at the individual and group levels it was a very different matter. Europeans had been invited to participate, as actors, in the stage play, but only two responded, and Kanak ended up assuming the European roles. (Yet they no doubt portrayed their interpretation of the history of New Caledonia to much greater effect.)

In choosing Nouméa for the site of the festival, a key objective had been to reveal Kanak culture to Europeans. If many French of metropolitan origin attended, as well as what Jean Guiart described as "the ordinary people of Nouméa" (1996, 109), the Caldoche from the bush and the wealthy Caledonian families did not go. Their absence was significant in the sense that it implied either a failure to grasp the overall nature of Jean-Marie's vision of the future of New Caledonia, or an outright refusal to engage in the dialogue that he was proposing.

From the outset the idea was that a second festival, to be entitled Calédonia 2000, would be held in 1980 on the same site, with the Kanak as hosts, but where the European and other ethnic communities would present their cultures and so engage in the dialogue proposed by Mélanésia 2000. Although efforts were made to pursue the initiative in the aftermath of the 1975 festival, the leaders of the European community quickly made it clear that their interests were directed exclusively to the promotion of long-term investments in infrastructures for themselves: a museum devoted to deportation at the old Nouville prison, a museum of European popular arts and traditions in Nouméa, the reconstruction of the Bernheim Library, the creation of a cultural precinct in Pouembout.[7] Dialogue was not part of their agenda. "We did Mélanésia 2000 and opposite there was no wish to recognize us . . . it is not for want of seeking to explain. Whatever, we are there. . . . We exist!" (M-C Tjibaou 1995, 120). A festival committee was created, but it was dominated by Europeans and riddled with local, sectarian interests. In the meantime, the site at Plage 1000 was allowed to fall into disuse. "Politics took over and if Caledonia 2000 didn't take place, it is perhaps because we are not ready to carry out a joint project. . . . There never was any Caledonian festival" (M-C Tjibaou 1995, 121).

In contrast, for the Melanesian participants, the event was a transforming experience. "The many events were such an intense experience that the Canaques could not believe that the celebrations were truly over. It was only several days later, our eyes filled with tears, that we went our separate ways. Charles Attiti declared: 'At this time, we solemnly vow to gather again as soon as we hear the sound of the conch shell'" (Michel Degorce-Dumas, quoted in Missotte 1985, 533).

Precisely because Mélanésia 2000 was such a symbolically charged and moving experience, as well as a turning point in the destiny of the Kanak people, the fragility of its foundations was overlooked, both in its immediate aftermath and in the turmoil of the 1980s. Over half the communes of New Caledonia were not represented at the festival. Specifically, the Protestants of Ouvéa, including Goosana, had chosen not to participate. This reality, of voluntary nonparticipation on the part of certain tribes and regions, was a surface expression of a fundamental characteristic of Kanak and, indeed, all indigenous Pacific Island societies that Jean Guiart made a point of highlighting in his own assessment of Mélanésia 2000: "Oceanian societies are societies of confrontation and competition where the much-vaunted consensus is, on each occasion, a mere moment of history destined to be set aside" (1996, 110).

In conceiving and organizing Mélanésia 2000, was Jean-Marie misreading his own culture, or was he simply taking a calculated risk and, perhaps, adopting the only possible course his people could reasonably take into the future? His choices, on that occasion and later, were eminently pragmatic. They were determined by what he perceived as the foundations of Kanak identity and by the encompassing ethnic configuration of New Caledonia. In 1975, they were marked by a great deal of patience and a clear vision for the future. "We are not a people who have chosen to die. We want to live. We want to tell the European that we wish to live together and create the culture of tomorrow. We want to forge with them and with our children the fraternal bonds of the Caledonia of the future. It is with the old people that we must build the house, together, and unite the old and the young" (Tjibaou, quoted in Missotte 1995, 86).

Jean-Marie's speech, on the first evening of the festival, "was exactly what was required, and it had signaled the birth of a leader suddenly raising himself above the greyness of the moment" (J Guiart 1996, 107).

6 Contrasting but Complementary Civilizations
The Search for Mutual Understanding

Westerners are a little bit victims; they are colonized by this Judaeo-Christian philosophy which has succeeded in inculcating them with the notion that man is soul and body, that he is alone. This is a myth, like any other, but it is a dangerous myth, dangerous for the planet. Calvinism has been studied in terms of its links with capitalism; succeed on earth is the sign that one is saved, but saved individually. . . . if someone is in my way I must, if not eliminate him, at least overshadow him so that my star is the only one that shines in the firmament. . . .

With us, it's the other system; the universe, and above all the earth, must be viewed as a mother, as the spatial, sociological, psychological and everlasting place, where man exists through those that are dead, those that are alive today, and through those who are yet to come.

MÉLANÉSIA 2000 PROJECTED Jean-Marie into the public arena. It endowed him with credibility and authority, as much with the French and the territorial administration as with his own people. He was no longer the obscure defrocked priest or student seeking to reinsert himself into the fabric of his country. It was a defining experience. His actions since returning had brought him into close contact with women's groups, chiefs, and young people. He now had confidence, vision, and a greatly enriched understanding of both Kanak and European societies. He was always a chief who traveled far beyond the boundaries of his tribe; in a certain sense he was still very much a priest who navigated beyond the limits of the Church, and he continued to be an anthropologist, constantly seeking to enrich his knowledge and understanding of his own civilization. He was also progressively adopting the habits of a philosopher, searching for the spiritual wealth that lies at the roots of the human condition: myth, beauty, dignity, generosity, the omnipresence of the past and of the ancestors. As he would say to Philippe Missotte, "When a person flouts custom on this earth, it disturbs the dead."

In an interview published in the *Journal Calédonien* immediately after the festival, Jean-Marie was portrayed as *l'homme de demain* (the man of tomorrow), leading inevitably to the question, "Who are you, Jean-Marie? Are you thinking about assuming a political role in New Caledonia?" His response was revealing.

> Let's say I'm waiting. At a certain point I was contacted to engage in politics, but I did not respond favorably. We try and work in a different way from the others. Too many people are active in this area for me to be able to agree with anyone on political matters.
>
> One always talks of politics. And one always stumbles over the same words, isolating oneself in the same flaws of thinking, Autonomy, Independence, French Caledonia. . . . It seems to me that if one thought about the future of New Caledonia in terms of culture, it would be possible to talk about the territory's institutions without reference to the political arena. In politics, one is not allowed to dream, one is expected to propose practical solutions. In the creative realm it is much simpler. But it is not without interest, for it enables you to avoid certain constraints, it gives you full scope to invent tomorrow's world.
>
> To come back to my political allegiance, I can tell you that I only mount a horse I know. (1975c, 5)

In Mélanésia 2000 Jean-Marie had revealed his commitment to inventing tomorrow's world, a world in which the voices of all peoples and all cultures would be heard, however small and seemingly insignificant. In this utopian vision, culture stood clearly before politics, and he needed to fully possess the first before rising to the challenge of the second. Motivated by the experience and by his involvement in the Mouvement féminin pour un souriant village mélanésien, he was now firmly convinced that, irrespective of local practices, there existed a common weave of values and concerns among all individual Kanak cultures. In creating Mélanésia 2000 he had drawn heavily on the teachings and writings of Roger Bastide, whose influence would be apparent in actions that were to follow. The paths of Jean-Marie Tjibaou and Roger Bastide had crossed in Paris at a stage in which the teacher and mentor was drawing the threads of a lifetime's observations and meditations together. *Les Amériques noires* was published in 1967, *Le prochain et le lointain* in 1970, and *Anthropologie appliquée* in 1971.[1] Enveloped in Bastide's thoughts and writings on the sacred, on myths and origins, on warm, vibrant, and timeless expressions of human needs and desires, and on syncretism, fraternity, and peace, Jean-Marie's experience, knowledge, and intuitive understanding of his own civilization took on a new dimension. He could place it in the larger context of the dislocation of peoples and of the brutal clash of civilizations that were provoked by colonialism and empire. His anthropological studies had also served to reinforce his childhood experience, his Catholic education, and his role as a priest where, in a world dominated by reason and by cultural incomprehension, it was vital to explore and give full expression to the spiritual and irrational foundations of human experience.

Kanaké itself lived on, in the sense that the first scene, *Boénando,* was presented at the Second Pacific Arts Festival, held in Rotorua (New Zealand) in 1976, Jean-Marie accompanying the New Caledonian delegation on that occasion. That event apart, he continued to work for the Centre de Formation d'Animateurs for two more years, running (together with Philippe Missotte) seminars on Melanesian culture and on intercultural relations for the Société le Nickel, the École des Infirmières, the École Normale, and FR3 (radio-television) attended by managers, employees, teachers, and nurses of predominantly European and Kanak ethnic origins. Held over the best part of a week, the seminars devoted the first day to determining what the participants (and, by extension, non-Kanak in general) thought and said about Kanak, the second and third days to a presentation of Kanak civilization, and the fourth to questions, followed by group reflection on ways of constructing bridges between Kanak and European civilizations. The first day revealed the extent of negative stereotyping of Kanak. Missotte detailed them in his thesis: irresponsible, lazy, passive, no sense of time, unreliable, alcoholics, timid, ignorant, unintelligent, without culture, incapable of adapting to the modern world; in short, insignificant and without hope, unless forcibly removed from the dead weight of their past and the ruins of their culture (Missotte 1985, 204–224). It was a revelation, because the Kanak participants invariably confirmed the reality of the stereotypes to which they were victim, while the Europeans never doubted them. In the following days, Jean-Marie gave a detailed presentation of Kanak culture. The key he used to highlight cultural practices and identity was what he characterized as the "three warm elements of socialized time": birth, mourning, and marriage. "At the beginning and at the end, they are inscribed in time, but between the two they are warmth, fervor, comfort and the experience of proven fraternity. In experiencing these worldly events, the Canaque attains that global reality whereby he exists and he exists wholeheartedly" (Tjibaou 1976, 292).

In his presentations, Jean-Marie sought to dispel caricature and prejudice by revealing the nature of Kanak spirituality and the importance of the social bonds that are inscribed in both space and time. There is no record of the final day's exchange at these seminars, notably as to whether European participants responded positively to his portrait and whether they were able to propose bridges between the two civilizations. Regardless, these repeated experiences rendered Jean-Marie increasingly articulate in his presentation of his own civilization and increasingly lucid in his critique of Western civilization. In his mind, explaining Kanak culture and values to Europeans was no longer simply a question of seeking recognition, but more and more an exercise in comparing the two civilizations and highlighting what Kanak civilization had to offer of value to the West and for the future of mankind as a whole. This growing conviction of the importance of a Kanak voice being heard at the "banquet of civilizations" became an integral part of his reasoning in the late 1970s and 1980s, despite his energies then being directed almost exclusively to political action.

In March 1981 Jean-Marie gave a talk at the Université de Genève. The invitation came from Marie-Joëlle Dardelin, in the Faculté des Sciences de l'Éducation. In the mid-to-late 1970s Mme Dardelin had investigated the reasons for the poor academic performance of Kanak students in the New Caledonia school system (Dardelin 1984) and had participated, at the start of her research, in one of Jean-Marie's seminars. Jean-Marie was in Geneva to participate in a workshop on political issues in developing countries, offered by the World Council of Churches. This connection with a broad-based ecumenical movement dedicated to Christian unity would become very important in the late 1980s.

There were not many people at the conference and, as was his habit, Jean-Marie spoke freely, without the least hesitation, on what it means to be Melanesian in the modern world, occasionally consulting a small notebook in which he had scribbled a few points. The lecture was recorded, a literal transcription made of it, and it was published in the journal *Esprit* later that year, in spite of overt skepticism on the part of the editorial board and certain Oceanian scholars. The board members had doubts as to whether the topic would interest their readers—hence their insistence that Jean-Marie write an introductory statement—while the scholars expressed their disbelief as to the authenticity of the text, at least one of them affirming, "He doesn't have any ideas of his own. He was only repeating Leenhardt"![2] Of course, Jean-Marie fully recognized his personal debt, and that of the Kanak in general, to the missionary scholar who, essentially alone, had ensured that so much cultural knowledge survived the hecatomb of the first half of the twentieth century. As to the academic culture and preoccupations of the Oceanian scholars, Leenhardt had quickly learned what Jean-Marie of course knew, that the spoken word was not the "property" of any single person. Rather it was the voice of the firstborn, it was the founding myth, and it gave sense and meaning to collective existence.

Jean-Marie expressed Melanesian identity and worldview in clear and simple language, translating both into terms that were meaningful to his audience. The Protestants and the Protestant ministers present were greatly moved by his presentation. His discourse made sense to them because it had deep spiritual foundations, it drew analogies with their own beliefs, and it was an all-embracing vision. Subsequently, in the introduction to the published transcription of his address, he insisted on the importance of tradition—in the sense of the past and of accumulated experience—in providing references to guide his people into the future. Only in this way, he affirmed, could they creatively innovate. In this same short statement he highlighted the nature of his people's *parole sur le monde* (worldview).

> It does not operate on the basis of hypotheses followed by proofs according to a demonstrated linear trajectory. On the contrary it has the habit of considering the object to be merged into the life of the cosmos in the same way as the subject itself is. The most important consequence of all that is, without a shadow of a doubt insofar as we are concerned, death is simply passing from the back to the front side or, if you wish, from light to shadow within one and the same life. Our efforts are directed toward recovering our way of experiencing life and being responsible for the future. (Tjibaou 1981, 82)

Several years later, he elaborated on his sense and explanation of this *parole kanak* to the journalist Jean-Paul Besset. "The Kanak discourse is not conceived in terms of thesis, antithesis, synthesis. It consists in repeating in order to convince, with a view to permeating the guts of the Word, for the Word to invest the entire body" (quoted in Besset 1989, 21). In his address, Jean-Marie spoke of the nature and meaning of Kanak existence, its origins, its raison d'être, its sense of time and of place, the place of the individual in society, of service, of the rhythm of nature and of life, all the while comparing his own Melanesian with his audience's European experience.

Someone at the university had chosen the title "Mélanésiens d'hier et d'aujourd'hui" (Melanesians of Yesterday and Today) for his talk, and Jean-Marie began by expressing dismay with regard to a distinction that his people did not make. He explained that the life of a Melanesian community is a continuously unfolding experience where time past, time present, and time future are all part of a distinctive whole. Some elements from the past serve as essential references and do not change through time, while others are set aside in order to negotiate the reality of a constantly changing world. "Tradition" is part of the present, it is cultural capital, and it is expressed in ties, interactions, and relationships. The Melanesian world is a vibrant one that is the product of a particular past and is designed to address the reality of a particular place.

> [T]he Melanesian man is perhaps another way of expressing the human condition, but it is an expression of the same thing, the same reality. And that reality is expressed in a manner that must take into account the environment, history. One might say, in a manner that is quite trite, that man produces society, and society in turn *manufactures* man. And, thrust into the world of the living, the simple man is a sum of needs and aspirations, the need for food, for shelter, to feel secure, to dress, to speak, to exchange, and to perpetuate himself through

creating, and procreating; and the society which embraces him proposes a mass of answers related to the environment: ecological, geographic, climatic, historic. (Tjibaou 1981, 83; emphasis in original here and in following quotations)

This notion of being welcomed into a society at birth, and of being molded by it, thus of recognizing the role of the ancestors in guiding that society, was dear to Jean-Marie. In his political speeches in the 1980s he would invariably begin by thanking them for being present, for their presence would help the group move forward and ensure that decisions were grounded in local reality, experience, desires, and expectations—that they responded to deeply felt collective needs. And the presence of the ancestors would ensure that the people of today be heard.

To help his Geneva audience grasp the meaning of his words, Jean-Marie explained that he had felt insecure that morning at seeing, through his window, the falling snow, because "[t]he group that welcomed me into its midst at my birth didn't provide me with the reflexes, the habits, the *culture* adapted to this phenomenon. . . . I'm not used to it" (1981, 83). He then proceeded to explain how Melanesians are linked to their past, to the world that lies "behind the mirror," while stressing that the questions they ask of themselves are common to all mankind: "Where do we come from? Who are we? Where are we going?" (1981, 84). For his people, the answers are found in a specific clan and in a local earth, with, at the source, a sacred totem—the spirits, which command respect and veneration. "[W]e find, in the end, a tree, or an animal, or a stone, or thunder. It is the bond with the earth, with the environment, with the land, with the local place. *We are not men from elsewhere. We are men who are born of this earth*" (1981, 84). This time, rather than contrasting, he drew a parallel for the benefit of his audience. "I refer to the Bible because it is also a writing that has emerged from the rural world and you find the same patterns there: the people from such and such a place, they have such and such as sons, and, as in any traditional society, the firstborn, those who were the first to see the sun, it is they who have the right to speak" (1981, 84).

If genealogies traced the route back to the firstborn and to the origin, within nature, of each clan, they also gave sense and direction to actions in the world of the living.

And life unfolds through this genealogy and this genealogy, it is my father's, but it is also the clan that gave my mother, and which, in giving my mother, gives me life. The principle of life, we say it is the mother who gives life. The father gives the personality, the social status, the land. . . . Life is provided by the blood. The blood, it is my mother who gives it. She is the proprietor of the blood; it is her, her brothers, her fathers. So I am always *dual*. I am never an individual. *I cannot be an individual.* (1981, 86)

This concept of the newborn being at the intersection of two clans and of two networks has major implications in terms of both decision making and aspirations in life.

> I am always someone *in relation to.* . . . So we are always consulting, advising, engaged in endless discussions. . . . It is important, because this relationship which exists at the level of the individual, of the person, also exists in society. One only exists *in relation to.* . . . Always. In such a context I would say that the successful man is the man who takes good care of his alliances, on one side and on the other. . . .
>
> The man who attains saintliness, harmony, perfection, is the one who looks after both these relationships. (Tjibaou 1981, 86–87)

Again, in helping his audience grasp the implications of such cultural values and practices, Jean-Marie evoked the frustrations Europeans experienced on account of the time it took for Melanesians to reach decisions, or because of their seemingly infinite number of close kin and kinship obligations.

Kanak existence, as Jean-Marie described it, is characterized by a *flux vital*—constant movement and circulation, with kin and with the ancestors—resulting in a totally different view of success in life. "In the Melanesian system, to be a man of prestige, one must of course 'have,' as everywhere. Therefore you have to work in order to have a big family, which in turn ensures you *have* a great deal: assets that are replenished through work. But to *have* does not confer prestige. *Prestige comes from giving, giving a great deal, and giving everywhere*" (1981, 87). Inevitably he drew a direct contrast with the West.

> It is the exact opposite of the capitalist world! Here [in Europe] one says, one teaches children to economize, to accumulate, then when one has a few savings, one has to provide returns on this saving. After, one says one is loaded [bricks] if one has a million . . . and with money [bricks] you build your castle, you create your own status as a man and you become "someone." The more money you have, the more you climb, the bigger you are, even if there is nothing inside! It is really important. And what do you do with the money you have beneath your feet? You have to gather it up, capitalize it. In our system, if you do that . . . you become small, because you don't have social relations. You are obliged to cut yourself off from the community. You cannot honor your uncles if you possess a lot and you don't give. The more you have, the more you have to give. And since communities are small, people know what you have! There isn't the anonymity of big cities, so you can't escape. (1981, 87–88)

Relations are inscribed, at least in part, in genealogies. Plants and animals, as totems, are a part of genealogies. And genealogies link Melanesians to the earth. For these reasons Jean-Marie proceeded, in his talk, to describe the nature and importance of ties to the *terroir,* or local earth. He explained that, for his people, the land is not a commodity to give or to be sold. Rather, "the earth, the ancestors are in the earth. Genealogies are rooted in the earth. Genealogies have no meaning if they are not inscribed in space, in a specific place" (1981, 89).

He drew his audience's attention to the fact that he had jotted down in a notebook some points for his address and that, later on, his children would be able to read it and learn what he had talked about in Geneva. The point made sense to Europeans, of course. However he went on to stress that, in the case of Melanesians, the land is the notebook. "On the land of my country, in my tribe, the genealogy . . . , the earth is the notebook; it is such and such a stone, with such and such an origin. And at a given place which bears a given name, that's where history begins. You go on, you go on, until the water, and you have roots, a spatiality, and one has a history, in relation to this place. Otherwise, one has no history. One is a citizen of the world and of nowhere" (1981, 89).

Jean-Marie completed his overview of Melanesian culture by relating the manner in which time is perceived and experienced.

> And that . . . I would say for members of society, in the tribes, it's not a preoccupation. . . . One doesn't talk about time. Sure, one talks of seasons. But not of the time of day. . . . The time of day, that's a modern phenomenon and it's precisely because of the time of day that one is obliged to talk about the manner in which people experience time. . . . Time, it's the rhythm of nature. The rhythm of the seasons . . . it is what plays the role of the hand, of the clock, it is the plants . . . that grow and that die. . . .
>
> For people, in traditional Melanesian society, yams determine the calendar as a whole and create the entire year's cycle. It is calculated in terms of moons. And all celebrations are based on that, all planned gatherings. The occasion for the enthronement of a chief, or afterwards, when food is abundant. House construction is planned for the end of the year, before the cyclones, when everything is dry, the time when the straw is ready. . . . this rhythm of nature, it's that which determines the rhythm of society and, when all is said and done, that of man. (1981, 90–91)

Again, Jean-Marie was concerned to draw parallels with the European world—the seasonal cycle of the vine, the rhythm of peasant life—and also to highlight the fracture lines separating civilizations. If Melanesians inhabit time, Europeans are driven by it. The former is "long" and warm; the latter is "short," febrile, ephemeral, and cold. It is not simply the rhythm that accelerates, but the system of values is transformed, and time is broken into smaller and smaller segments. If Melanesian time is grounded in the "time beyond time" of the great myths, European time is driven by strictly material

considerations, of productivity. "And that, it's something new. It's a new phenomenon with regard to the rhythm of work, but also in the rhythm of life,
in the rhythm of thought. It obliges us to rethink the world. One projects,
and one might say that one is going to submit the world to its rhythm. . . . It
is day and night with respect to the traditional world" (1981, 91).

The themes of the relations between people and between clans, the
bond with the cosmos, the attachment to place, and the experience of time
were all addressed in a more scholarly manner in Jean-Marie's earlier paper
in the *Journal de la Société des Océanistes* (1976). More descriptive in nature
and tightly bound to the topic of the functioning (both traditional and contemporary) of his own society, it is nevertheless marked by several generous
envolées (lyrical flights) illustrative of the degree to which he was *un homme de
parole*—a man of honor and of words that came from afar, were measured,
and were pregnant with meaning. "[C]anaque time is above all an experience determined by the rhythm of nature, of warmth and coolness, of yams,
of old age and youth, and the event that renews alliances, reinvigorates the
community, and makes it grow in stature" (1976, 285).

Jean-Marie would say that he spoke *comme les idées me viennent* (as the
ideas come to me) (Besset 1989, 21). It was a part of his charisma and of his
chiefly stature, but the expression also highlighted that he was constantly
nourished by the ideas of his people and of his ancestors. This sense of
waiting, of poise and expectation gave a particular tone to his manner of
speaking. Jacques Violette was acutely conscious of it, in transcribing his
long interview with him that was published posthumously as "Le message de
Jean-Marie Tjibaou." "Even harder (than developing the photos and seeing
the face of Jean-Marie appear in the red laboratory light) was the transcription of the tape recording, of listening several times over to these three
hours of recording. Of hearing the sound of this voice again, the intona-
tions, the sound which rises and falls, the elocution, the articulation, the
hesitations . . . the silences. I regret not being able to accompany each line
of text with a line of a music score" (Violette 1989, 6).

Because the circumstances of Jean-Marie's Geneva talk were amicable, he
was able to make analogies and draw parallels between the Bible and Christianity on the one hand, and Melanesian civilization on the other, as well as
to evoke, in passing, Europe's peasant roots. It was an avenue of reflection
that led him to formulate, by way of conclusion, the question, Must one follow you? As a man who possessed to a remarkable degree both his own and
French cultures the interrogation was a vital one, central to his preoccupations, regardless of—or perhaps precisely because of—the several professions
he had assumed in the course of his life to that point. He was attracted by
the modern world, he was conscious of its absolute power and that his people
were committed to negotiating it, but he was also aware of its very considerable limitations. At the same time, like virtually all Kanak of his generation,
he was born on a reservation and knew the value of his own culture.

Jean-Marie conceived of Kanak culture as a constantly evolving reality, "a culture on the move [where there are] things to be invented, things to keep and things to be respected according to tradition (secrets)" (Gilbert Tein, pers comm, 3 May 1997). In one of his most widely cited observations, made in the course of an interview conducted several years later and published in a special issue of the journal *Les temps modernes* dedicated to New Caledonia, Jean-Marie affirmed:

> The return to tradition is a myth; I insist on saying it and I repeat it. It is a myth. No people have ever experienced it. Insofar as I am concerned, the search for identity, the model, lies before us, never behind. It is being constantly reformulated. And I will say that the challenge right now is to include the maximum number of elements belonging to our past, to our culture, in the model of mankind and society that we aspire to for the creation of the city. Others, perhaps, propose different analyses, but that is how I see things. Our identity is in front of us. Finally, when we die, people will take our image and they will put it in niches, and it will help them to construct their own identity. Otherwise, one will never succeed in killing one's father, and we are done for. (1985a, 1601)

However, if Kanak culture was condemned to change in order to survive and flourish, it was also anchored in "custom," a term which he disliked, because it had been imposed by Europeans, but which he was obliged constantly to defend and to justify. "[I]t is a generic term that Europeans give to a group of things that they don't understand, which are Kanak ways. . . . For us . . . it is our right, our way of life, the set of institutions which govern us" (Tjibaou 1996, 202).

If Jean-Marie was critical of Western civilization, it was not simply because of its inability to recognize and to respect Kanak ways and values, to admit that Kanak *exist;* it was also because he was acutely aware of its many shortcomings. He was able to read and judge it through Kanak eyes. So, in Geneva, he spoke of the dangers of following a civilization, now of global dimensions, which was itself uncertain as to the direction it should take, which lacked bearings, and was in an evident state of disarray.

> [N]ow we see that you have been to the moon, that you are unsatisfied, and that one is searching. . . . And since it is difficult to follow someone who is looking for their way, there is a sort of movement of return to the roots. . . .
>
> So, that world, one has no idea *where it is.* One doesn't know where its roots are, and one can't identify with it. So one is lost. . . . When you are swept away by a current, you look for rocks to cling to. This reality, I think it is a worldwide phenomenon. . . .
>
> for us, there is a return movement . . . to a kind of environment, a kind of universe where, culturally, at the group level, at the level of associations, one

can find oneself, have the sentiment of being *"among humans,"* of there being a human dimension. (Tjibaou 1981, 93)

In the final analysis, his questioning at the close of a Geneva winter transcended issues of kinship and sharing. It was concerned with belonging, where scale was a crucial variable, with local societies offering intimacy and warmth in what was an increasingly disenchanted world. To illustrate his point Jean-Marie would often recount an experience he had during one of his many visits to Paris in the 1980s. He and his wife Marie-Claude were crossing over one of the many bridges on the Seine in order to go to Église Notre-Dame, where they went to pray whenever they were in the capital. Suddenly he was struck by the thousands of people weaving down the footpaths around them, and by the fact that he knew nobody, that nobody knew anyone, that it was simply a sea of individuals, each alone. He realized then that, in the space of a few minutes, he had seen more people than he would meet in a whole year in his country . . . and that in his country he knew everyone. It led him to the conviction that individual freedom is cold, that Kanak society is a warm society while European society is, in contrast, a cold, clinical one.[3]

This sense of intimacy, of intuitive understanding, he extended to Oceanian civilization as a whole. "I don't know why, but among Oceanians we always kind of understand each other, when we meet in a group where there are Westerners or Asians. There is a bit of complicity, because there is a common cultural base which results in the concepts used to explain the world, the relations between people within society, the sense of the earth, the relationship with the gods, or the sense of destiny, all being shared concepts. There is not the same complicity with Westerners; with them, you always have to explain" (Tjibaou 1996, 198).

Jean-Marie's concerns about Western civilization were not, of course, only social or spiritual, for he knew the city and Europe well. They were also material. If he was preoccupied with the future of his people for their own sake, he also placed them in the perspective of his concerns about the future of all peoples. In a long exchange with Jean Chesneaux that took place in 1981, when Jean-Marie was only beginning to be politically active at the national level, he remarked on how the two destinies—the local and the global—were closely interwoven, and how Kanak interrogations and values might contribute to the edification of a better world for all.

> [I]t is not in Paris that one is going to learn how to survive. We are well-placed in Oceania to understand that we are heading toward a reckless world. We are well-placed to give soul to our social life. We only have limited monetary means, but for us, being is much more important than having. We have to succeed in expressing at the institutional level the Kanak system of production. . . .

When those who went to the French school come to the tribe, they are use-less, they are like loafers. School only teaches them to be workers for the Com-mon Market; its only objective is to standardize people. The unemployment that plagues us is a consequence of the way the world is currently organized. Poten-tial capabilities are stifled by the race for riches, production, and armaments. The school teaches you that you have to go to Nouméa; it doesn't teach you how to live in the tribe. However in Nouméa, people have no sense of life. . . .

Around the city, around Nouméa, people become crazy; nature there is filthy and dead. Once again, we are not at a stage where it is necessary to turn around and go back, rather we are at a stage where we need to take our bearings. . . .

The only alternative that the West offers us is industrialization, and we are on a tightrope. But the SOS is coming from the West itself, with its fear of war and of [everything] nuclear. The West is like a machine out of control; people are using their feet to try and brake. It hasn't invented other forms of social organization yet. That's why we need to reconsider the very way life is organized. (Tjibaou 1996, 118–119)

Jean-Marie saw the West as being committed to growth without devel-opment, material wealth without human understanding, power without hu-mility. It was, he believed, philosophically and spiritually impoverished. To evoke an image he had first formulated in preparing Mélanésia 2000, it was a drifting world, locked into the present and ill equipped to address the dangers taking form on the horizon.

A man who has no culture
is like a coconut that falls into the sea,
he wanders, sterile, in the grip of the oceans
tossed from shore to shore
(Tjibaou, Azapunia, Iekaw, Citre, and Missotte 1975, 11)

The Kanak, on the other hand, by virtue of the constant presence of and references to the past, had not lost sight of the fundamental question:

Where are we going? That means: what is there after, after the grave? The an-swers given by each of the world's peoples take one back to a specific geographi-cal environment. For us, what is abiding is the reference to ancestors, to totems, who come from the earth, from the sea. On the land these totems are rocks, animals, lizards, serpents, stones too, thunder, and in the ocean, sharks or other fish. . . .

    face to the ocean and on these small islands, there is something unchanging and significant: a kind of, not fatalism, but let's say for us, faced with life, there is nothing that is irreparable; because life, that is what is fundamental, it is what endures and what is always there, irrespective of whether the members of the group are living or are already with the ancestors. (Tjibaou 1996, 193)

In an address to the Second Forum of Pacific Trade Unions, held in Nouméa some eighteen months later (September 1982), Jean-Marie spoke of nine increasingly serious dangers confronting the peoples of the Pacific: (1) Denial of the existence of indigenous peoples and of their cultural heritage; (2) Negation of the essential dignity allowing people to take charge of their own lives and destiny; (3) Blind industrialization that coats the earth in asphalt and cement, preventing it from breathing; (4) Tentacular multinational corporations that suck out the substance of our lands for stomachs and brains located elsewhere; (5) Sociological distortions related to the rapid evolution of modern technology, and its slow assimilation by the peoples of the Pacific; (6) Nuclear weapons; (7) Biological weapons; (8) Genetic engineering; and (9) Struggles for political hegemony over the region. He concluded his speech to the assembled trade unionists with an appeal. "We are condemned, ladies and gentlemen, to solidarity, to structuring this solidarity, so that the Pacific continues to be a paradise for life on our planet" (1982, 15).

In the political combat that he led throughout the 1980s he was to repeatedly express the same sentiments with respect to the non-Kanak inhabitants of New Caledonia and the French government. The Kanak people were condemned to collaborate, *as partners and as equals,* as they were condemned to innovate. They were not adrift or lost, it was simply that they had no political recognition; they were denied the right to exist, to flourish, and to share. Those who stood face to face with the Kanak were also condemned to collaborate, but they had first to recognize that obligation. Once assumed and the dialogue engaged in, it would be possible to adopt an approach to decolonization that respected Kanak identity and values, and would in turn ensure his people acquired, as Kanak, the necessary tools to engage in the modern world.

> [I]t is impossible for us to consider as values that which constitutes the foundation of your societies, because that conceptual knowledge is destructive for us. In order to adapt to the world we are obliged to consider the economy not as an end in itself but as a technique. Accumulation, savings, capitalization, investment, expansion, growth, and their corollaries, efficiency, profitability . . . we can only utilize them as techniques. We are conscious of the fact that we come from elsewhere and that we are pursued by this elsewhere which constitutes the sum of our references. (Tjibaou 1989f, 78)

These references were the tribe, the ancestors, and the land, in other words an identity anchored in a clearly recognizable and shared space-time. Jean-Marie was certain that his was a rich and meaningful system in comparison to the "primitive" alternative proposed by the colonial order, where people were reduced to individuals and judged according to the purely economic criteria of productivity and consumption.

7   *New Caledonia or Kanaky*
The Inexorable Drift from Political Negotiation to Violent Confrontation

Political parties are nothing more than crutches that enable the guts of the Earth to express themselves.

"FIRST GIVE YE the political kingdom and all else will follow": such was the message that swept across the African continent in the wake of the Second World War. It was a euphoric era of national independence movements that embraced Asia as well as Africa. Notably it gave birth to a third world that sought to carve a distinctive path between the communist and capitalist blocs, with a view to promoting global peace and cooperation and breaking the economic stranglehold the metropolitan powers exercised over their distant empires. The Bandung Conference, held in Indonesia in April 1955, was the first major manifestation of this new and distinctive expression of solidarity. Organized by the host nation, together with Egypt, Burma, Sri Lanka, and Pakistan, it brought together twenty-nine countries and thirty national liberation movements representing over 50 percent of the world's population. The Nonaligned Movement, created in 1961, gave formal expression to the sentiments expressed in Bandung. Again, Indonesia was one of its architects, along with Egypt, Yugoslavia, and India. The movement was totally opposed to colonialism in all its forms, and Algeria's long and bloody war of independence, then drawing to a close, served as a powerful symbol for its founding member countries.

No Pacific country was present at the 1955 or 1961 meetings, for the simple reason that the first to achieve independence, Samoa, only did so in 1962, to be followed by Nauru six years later, Fiji in 1970, and then by a surge of new nations between 1974 and 1980. Pacific Island peoples developed a global consciousness and articulated their desire for independence in a more complex, postcolonial era. By the early 1980s new forces were starting to obscure the simple cold war dialectic. The hegemony of the state was being challenged by the unquenchable thirst of the corporation; a regional consciousness had emerged and was spawning its own institutions; and an array of new Pacific Basin actors made it more problematic to read the world exclusively in terms of relations between the colonizer and the colonized. Vanuatu, the last Pacific nation to become independent, strove more or less alone, and with very limited means, to adopt the discourse and engage in some of the practices of the Nonaligned Movement.

Despite the ending of the cold war the Nonaligned Movement still exists as a forum for discussion in the context of the United Nations. With over one hundred members it still represents more than 50 percent of the world's population, yet even today the only two Pacific countries inscribed on its lists are Papua New Guinea and, once again, Vanuatu. The first has leaned consciously toward Asia for several decades now. The second was deeply marked, in the years immediately following independence, by a secular and ideologically driven leadership concerned to impose a distinctive personality on a country that had been shared by two colonial powers, where the British had departed voluntarily and the French had, to all intents and purposes, been ejected.

In most cases far removed from the vicissitudes of the cold war and less directly concerned by international debates and agendas, several prominent members of the first generation of Pacific Island leaders made a plea for a distinctively Oceanian pathway into the future. Ratu Mara, in Fiji, spoke of the Pacific Way (Fortune 2000), and Bernard Narakobi, in Papua New Guinea, of the Melanesian Way (1980). Both were no doubt inspired by the fact that the social fabric of their societies was largely intact in the 1970s and early 1980s, the populations of their countries were still predominantly rural and, in many cases, rich and diverse subsistence economies continued to thrive. Their own and neighboring countries were not yet scarred by abject poverty, large squatter settlements, or massive dislocations of populations. Both personalities insisted on the importance of cultural references and values for ensuring the successful entry of their countries into the modern world and, at the same time, countering its unforgiving economic logic. Culture was seen as a powerful vector that would enable Oceanians to invest in the future on their own terms. It was cause for pride and celebration, and the guarantee of a better life for all.

It can be argued that for both Ratu Mara and Bernard Narakobi the evocation of culture was, to a significant degree, an act of faith. For Jean-Marie Tjibaou, however, it was a very different matter. His cultural discourse was firmly grounded in events that had marked his own personal life and the collective experience of his people. By the time he entered the political arena, in the mid-1970s, the world's newly independent nations, together with their observers and analysts, were already in a position to measure the extent to which they had realized their initial goals and satisfied their dreams of liberation. The portrait was, to say the least, an equivocal one. Jean-Marie had learned in his university courses in France about the nature and practice of neocolonialism, about unequal terms of exchange, and about the birth, in many countries, of a new political class of compradors. His fellow students from Africa, Latin America, and Asia had described their deceptions, while his lecturers had analyzed and conceptualized a reality that was at once new and unchanged. He had walked the streets of Nouméa as a priest, and those of Lyon and Paris as a student. Born on a contested island, he had undergone the very personal experience of being severed from his family and tribe, through loss of language and vows of celibacy. He had seen his own people adrift in town and had been witness to the drama of North African immigrants condemned to living on the margins of the city in France. In both time and place, his experience was very different from that of his friend Ratu Mara, who had come from the aristocratic and sheltered Lau Islands and whose European academic experience had been restricted to the cloistered quadrangles of Oxford.

It was hardly surprising, in the circumstances, that Jean-Marie equated his own personal tribulations with those of the entire Kanak people. Culture was not an abstract concept for him, but variously an anchor, a lifebelt, potentially a prison, but also the only realistic way forward. Philippe Missotte described this interpretation of the Kanak condition as the key that Jean-Marie gave him to undertake his own New Caledonian journey at the dawn of the 1970s: "I found myself constantly in the presence of the Kanak man, his dynamism destroyed, each time he was cut from his roots and enslaved to an exclusively exogenous truth" (1985, 33). This fracture was at the origin of the Kanak affirmation, "In Custom I am someone, in town I am nothing" (Tjibaou 1989a, 77), and custom, or the memory of custom, had become a refuge for many, for it stood outside the modern world, both sheltered and excluded from it.

The tension between the tribe and the city determined Jean-Marie's approach to the realm of political action. Culture, for him, preceded and transcended politics for, in order to act collectively, responsibly, and creatively, it was first necessary to provide a sense and a direction to people's lives. Their lives must be integrated, whole, rather than split into conflicting parts. This overriding concern lay at the heart of his political actions and explains why he was convinced that the foundations on which to construct the future of his people and his country were vested in the tribe. The pursuit of cultural goals was a direction few twentieth-century politicians anywhere in the world chose to take, and it was the source of much criticism and doubt, even among fellow Kanak intellectuals and political activists.

Just as the Pacific as a region had stood, for historical reasons, outside the third world movement, so its nascent elites were less marked by radical and, notably, Marxist discourse. Distance, scale, and rurality were contributing factors. Most came from small, locally organized societies and were traditional leaders who had been trained and assumed roles within the institution of the Church. Massive settler, plantation, and primary re-source–based economies were for long the exception rather than the rule in the islands. Yet in precisely this respect New Caledonia stood apart from its neighbors. Conceived almost from the outset as a settler colony, its econ-omy was rapidly dominated by nickel and by the interests of a small group of settler families.

This distinctive situation meant that, despite being nineteen thousand kilometers from France, the colony was always closely linked to an intellectu-ally and politically turbulent metropolitan power, but never more so than in the aftermath of the Second World War. Several young Kanak who engaged in tertiary studies there in the late 1960s and 1970s were markedly influ-enced by and adopted the radical discourse and revolutionary ideals of the epoch, using them to address the flagrant colonial injustices that prevailed in the territory. Nidoish Naisseline was the most prominent among them, but the movement also attracted other personalities that are well known today, notably Déwé Gorodey and Fote Trolue. It was an intellectual climate that gave birth to the Foulards Rouges and the Groupe 1878. Essentially the creation of a small number of highly educated Kanak, both groups also appealed to young men from the reservations who had briefly found paid employment in the context of the nickel boom, only to be laid off following its collapse and drift on the margins of Nouméa or return disillusioned to their tribes.

These new, highly vocal groups condemned any political initiative they judged to be "culturalist." For them, an approach to politics that was grounded in culture was both naively Christian (and an assimilation of mis-sionary discourse) and profoundly misleading in that it refused to recog-nize the plurality of local Kanak identities. It was a discourse that sought to fabricate a single people defined exclusively in terms of their precolo-nial experience. In addition to being false representation, such a culturalist strategy served, in their view, to focus attention on relatively esoteric issues of identity rather than on the much more pressing and fundamental po-litical struggle against colonialism. Even more serious, the approach could be construed as an act of blatant folklorization of Kanak culture, thereby playing directly into the hands of the European community and the French authorities, namely the colonizer and the objective enemies of the Kanak people. These dialectically opposed perspectives, characterized by the con-fronting of the *experience* of one group, epitomized by Jean-Marie Tjibaou, with the *ideas* of the other, epitomized by Nidoish Naisseline, crystallized in 1975, in the debate surrounding Mélanésia 2000.

The radical critique, together with Jean-Marie's response to it, can be summarized in this exchange:

Foulards Rouges: "You reduce Kanak metaphysics to folklore."
Jean-Marie Tjibaou: "There is no Kanak metaphysics. There are only myths.

Nothing beyond. The past, the present, the future. Everything is there." (Missotte, pers comm, 19 Nov 1996)

If Jean-Marie's vision of culture was a contested one, his judgment of the Foulards Rouges' position and of radical discourse in general was uncompromising. He considered both to be driven by ideology and, as such, inherently disembodied in nature. Political radicalism was what he called a kind of "reverse colonialism," that is, a discourse imposed from outside and used by intelligent people who had become prisoners of "a different thinking." He saw such people as constantly changing direction, both as the debate evolved and in response to their own particular interests, if not their personal quest for political power. Jean-Marie insisted, "It's a doctrine that doesn't fill one's guts," by which he undoubtedly meant both physical and spiritual nourishment. His reaction to what he considered a strictly ideological approach to decolonization was unequivocal: "I can't take my people to the wall."

This confrontation with transplanted discourse would haunt Jean-Marie throughout his political career, for it was also espoused by those Kanak linked to radical forces in the English-speaking Oceanian world, notably in Vanuatu and Fiji. At the same time, it was central to the convictions of many of the metropolitan French militants who allied themselves with the independence movement, in both Europe and New Caledonia. He did his best to shield himself and his people from them, with varying degrees of success. But when pragmatism failed and dialogue proved impossible, even Jean-Marie swung to outright confrontation and formal condemnation of the very principles on which the French Republic was based. Then, when he returned to dialogue in the last year of his life, the divisive force of ideology came to haunt him once again, and it was a determining factor in his violent death on Ouvéa in May 1989.

As has been revealed in the previous chapter, Jean-Marie was a severe critic of the West, but his criticism was not ideological, it was civilizational. If, in leaving the reservation, the Kanak was obliged to renounce his identity, so it was, in turn, the reservation that defined it. With this in mind—and from this perspective—Jean-Marie was concerned to address, first and foremost, issues of dignity, self-respect, and recognition. It was essential, in his view, to read the world from a local, Kanak perspective, for the tribe—and not the university classroom—was the depository of the body of references necessary to address the material conditions of life and to elaborate the foundations for political action.

For Jean-Marie, identity was vested in land, hence the reservation, for that is the place of origin of the firstborn, who is linked to the cosmos through a totem and whose origins are recounted in founding myth. There the ancestors are buried and so live on, there is the source of the spoken word, the place around which social relations are organized and from which exchange networks and alliances are developed that structure the Kanak world, and there the food crops that mark the passage of time are grown. Kanak life is ordered, establishes its rhythm, and acquires meaning within the tribe and on the land. That is also the place where strangers are welcomed into their midst. This particular point was central to Jean-Marie's reasoning with regard to how, in the future, New Caledonia, would become a shared land.

Finally, it is within the tribe and on its land that identity is modeled and values are transferred from generation to generation. Jean-Marie made this point clear to his people in one of his earliest political speeches, at the Union Calédonienne congress on Maré in 1978.

> The principles of the reservation, we are attached to them, because it is there that we live our cultural lives. . . . it is the one *space,* the one *place* where tradition is authorized. . . . Neither school, nor television, nor radio, nor literature, nor theater, nor cinema offers us an image of ourselves. There is only the tribe. And our kids, who are brought up in the educational system, the cultural system, good as it is, our young people are made into strangers in relation to our society, strangers to us. We are no longer the fathers of our children. They, they are illegitimate in relation to us. Because they are the sons of others, the sons of those who *give* them the cultural models which they will henceforth live. And us, what do we have to offer to them? (quoted in Mokaddem 2005, 353; emphasis in original)

Furthermore, while the imported models are locked essentially into the present and the immediate future, those of the reservation invite the Kanak to enter into communion with nature and with the cosmos. It is a place of great spiritual wealth where mortal beings experience eternity through simple ceremonial acts. There the Kanak people can communicate with the world beyond.

> He breaks open the yam. He invokes the ancestor. The people seek, on the one hand, to bring the ancestor—who has become a god—into the present, and on the other, to project themselves into the ancestor's present, which in effect means projecting themselves into the past. He gives a piece to each person. Steam escapes from it, for the yam has come out of the embers. The priest gives his blessing. Everyone listens, is affected. At that moment one seeks to transcend everyday life in order to be united with something else . . . with the ancestors. This experience engenders a certain way of perceiving time. In effect the group is engaged in restoring mythical time to the level of day-to-day life as a kind of sharing of the sacraments (Eucharist). One can hypothesize that they are experiencing a certain dimension of existence that is wary of time. It

is interesting to know that people experience this at certain times of year, that this experience unites them and transports them into another time. (Tjibaou, quoted in Missotte 1985, 70)

Jean-Marie was convinced that such customary acts gave sense to people's lives, drew individuals together to form a single, cohesive group, inscribed them in history, and projected them into a future that would be of their own configuration. "Landscape, village layout, society, the deceased and mythical beings constitute a whole that is not only indivisible but still practically undifferentiated. . . . The space of the tribe appears in this way like the immense stage of a perpetual theater where each person plays his role at an assigned place" (Tjibaou 1976, 284–285). It was an enchanted, poetized world animated by great beauty and unlimited desire.

The portrait Jean-Marie drew at the time of his entry into the political arena was perhaps a utopian one. It even had mystical qualities, of the kind he denounced in the case of the Church, because they were alienating. His, by contrast, were unequivocally Kanak. Yet it was a portrait motivated by clear strategic and practical considerations, which he expressed to fellow Oceanians on the occasion of the 1980 Waigani Conference in Papua New Guinea. He summarized them in the introduction he wrote to explain his paper, "Etre Mélanésien aujourd'hui" (On Being Melanesian Today) to readers of the journal Esprit. "Our aim is to affirm the richness of our own models and (at the same time) to leave wide open the range of cultural choices that allow people to create a personality. It is in tradition that the contemporary development models must draw their inspiration, instead of their being artificially imposed and always coming from elsewhere" (Tjibaou 1981, 81).

His vision of development was global; it was human, social, and economic as well as political. It also stood in clear opposition to the arbitrary distinction between tradition and modernity that was invariably made by Europeans in New Caledonia and by many scholars. Tradition, or custom, was perceived by these Western observers as something that belonged to the past and was static. For many of these outsiders it was, at best, irrelevant to the contemporary world and, at worst, an impediment to change. Variously judged as impenetrable, "sad," and in tatters, Kanak tradition was a mere anachronism. But for Jean-Marie no such line could be drawn between his people's past and their present for, as he said time and again, at home and abroad, "traditional man: it is he who comes from the earth, from the humus, from the tribe, who circulates in town but who is not a product of the university, who is a product of the earth, a product of the tribe" (1981, 84). He embraced modernity—the coming world—but always from the standpoint of the tribe and from the perspective of his own people and culture, thus on his own terms. Given this very different perspective, Jean-Marie's political strategy and actions were dictated by the need to project the past into the present, and the present into the future. He was concerned to maintain unbroken the "long thread of desire," rather than accept the alternative, that his people advance naked and vulnerable into the modern world, only to be remodeled and consumed by it.

Two of the most striking ways in which he expressed his distinctive approach to politics were in his frequent references to ideas and to the ancestors. As he pointed out on the occasion of an interview by Marguerite Duras, "I was lucky enough not to know the discourse. . . . How would you say it? I'll say prefabricated, 'accepted,' organized. I speak as the ideas come to me" (Tjibaou 1986, 12).

If the pathway into the future was necessarily grounded in the reservation, it also had to be constructed piece by piece. As Jean-Marie would repeatedly say, "It is not the day that independence is declared which is important, but the day after," and it was vital to ensure a certain osmosis "between the country claimed in theory and the country one puts in place in order to become independent" (1989c, 46). It had to be simultaneously a victory of an idea, a victory over oneself, and a victory over the land that is rendered independent.

However, his was a generous and all-embracing vision that had to be enacted in the real world of a distant French colony and of a land shared with a broad array of immigrant peoples and dominated by one—the European settler community. Without doubt this was a severely constraining factor, and it meant that Jean-Marie was obliged constantly to accommodate and respond to forces that lay outside the immediate Kanak universe. More often than not, these forces were overtly hostile to his people's aspirations, and invariably incoherent in their failure (or unwillingness?) to understand them and to recognize the Melanesian values of good faith and generosity in which they were grounded. The situation was further complicated because the "front line" in the political battle lay in New Caledonia, while the overarching confrontation was with metropolitan France. And in France, the position with respect to its most distant colony was typically dictated by internal political considerations rather than by the objective reality of a small and little-known overseas territory. Finally, the local political agenda was driven by major demographic considerations. Following their rapid proportional decline in the late 1960s and early 1970s, the Melanesian component of the territory's total population had stabilized at around 41 to 42 percent, while their total number scarcely exceeded that of the European population: 53,725 and 51,582 respectively in 1974. It was an extremely vulnerable situation for the Kanak, for the only realistic political strategy they could adopt was one of compromise and of seeking to build bridges between communities. Yet it was also vital for the Kanak people to set the terms of any partnership, to be the senior partner, to occupy the moral and political high ground, rather than be condemned to the fate of a "first nation" struggling for a limited degree of recognition within a country that could never again be theirs. However, from a Caldoche, an immigrant, and a metropolitan French perspective this same demographic reality could be read very differently. Given time and patience, the Kanak percentage of the total population might reasonably start to decline again to the point where they would, effectively, cease to be the dominant ethnic group in New Caledonia. For the Kanak, time was running out and it was urgent to change the course of colonial history, while for the Caldoche and the immigrant communities it was vital to maintain the existing trajectory and play for time.

With hindsight, 1975 proved to be a turning point in the modern history of the Melanesian people of New Caledonia. In that year they moved from the margins, to which they had been rejected by colonial history, back onto center stage as key actors in an island nation that no longer had any choice but to redefine the very bases of its political and cultural identity. They became Kanak—a single, undifferentiated people with, potentially, a unity of purpose. And they made their presence felt in the city. If Jean-Marie Tjibaou had been the architect of Mélanésia 2000 in September of that year, Nidoish Naisseline and his Foulards Rouges had, in the preceding months, started calling for national independence, and Déwé Gorodey had publicly burned the French flag. While undoubtedly provocative, all these essentially symbolic acts were overshadowed by a political meeting held in June.

That meeting directly followed French President Giscard d'Estaing's refusal to meet Yann Céléné Uregeï on the occasion of a trip to Paris, or even deign to respond to his open letter requesting that New Caledonia's right to internal self-government—a status that had been removed in 1963 *(lois Jacquinot)* and in 1969 *(lois Billotte)*—be the object of a referendum. At the time Uregeï was president of the Territorial Assembly. He was deeply angered by this expression of presidential indifference, as was Roch Pidjot, the long-suffering solitary Kanak deputy in the French National Assembly. Pidjot immediately took the initiative of inviting Uregeï, together with the leaders of all the existing Kanak political movements, to a meeting on his tribal reservation at La Conception.[1] It resulted in the first formal declaration in favor of Kanak independence and a demand for a referendum on the question, and it also raised the possibilities of creating a single Kanak political party and of sending a delegation to New York to address the United Nations. The declaration was signed by all the elected Kanak members of the Territorial Assembly.

On 27 December of the same year a Marxist political party, PALIKA (Parti de Libération Kanak), was created out of the Foulards Rouges and the Groupe 1878, while on the same night a young Kanak was shot and killed by a gendarme on the Place des Cocotiers, in the center of Nouméa. The wind had changed, and the Kanak people were no longer willing to suffer in silence, but the territory's other communities and the French authorities were at a loss to know how to respond to the new situation. Repression was beginning to rear its ugly head. In the meantime the newly independent countries of the Pacific, together with neighboring Australia and New Zealand, were becoming increasingly aware of what was happening in New Caledonia.

Nineteen seventy-five was also the year in which the territorial administration adopted, for the first time, more direct and radical means to address what they recognized as a rapidly growing crisis within the Melanesian community. Following its active support of Mélanésia 2000 and of a number of smaller social and cultural initiatives, the administration shifted its attention to the economic realm, creating the Fonds d'aide au développement des îles et de l'intérieur (FADIL). This program was concerned to promote land redistribution and facilitate the access of Melanesians to the mining sector, favoring, however, individual as distinct from group initiatives in order to reduce disparities between communities. If the administration finally recognized that there was a major problem to be addressed, the solution proposed did not appeal to the vast majority of Kanak. It simply served to nourish their growing frustrations and expectations, in that it ignored the nascent demands for (political) liberation.

Roch Pidjot was president of the Union Calédonienne as well as parliamentary deputy in Paris, but the UC was not present as such at the meeting he had organized at La Conception. The one party that had successfully embraced the Kanak and the diverse settler communities and had benefited from the active support of the churches was in disarray, and its leadership was finding itself less and less capable of addressing ethnically polarized political agendas. No national congress had been held since 1971, and by 1975 the party had the air of a sinking ship, with Kanak leaving it to join the independence movement and Europeans gravitating toward groups favoring the status quo. The poor settler communities, from which it had for long drawn much of its support, were experiencing a serious economic crisis and were by this time quite simply struggling to survive. As a result a dangerous political vacuum was in the process of being created. In this atmosphere Roch Pidjot delivered his explosive analysis of the situation in New Caledonia, in an article published in *Le Monde* in June 1976.

> New Caledonia is still waiting to be decolonized. All the other countries of the Pacific have become independent or self-governing: Fiji, Samoa, Tonga, Nauru, New Guinea [*sic*], Cook Islands. There is only France which retains, under new names, true colonies, with supervising ministers in Paris and, on the ground, governors or administrators. It is patently obvious that no colonial structure in New Caledonia has changed since the beginning of the century.
>
> It is important to know that the situation of Melanesians is more and more intolerable. . . .
>
> The Union Calédonienne will soon be holding its Congress. Created a quarter of a century ago, this political movement, of which I am the president, will determine how much time is left until the year 2000 in order to achieve a de-

colonization that is both indispensable and unavoidable. It is the precondition for any advancement of the Melanesians, any real institutional progress, any development carried out first and foremost for the benefits of the inhabitants of New Caledonia, regardless of whether they be black or white.

We have always . . . tirelessly demanded, over the last twenty-five years, a self-governing status as assured by the preamble to the Constitution. We are all in favor of maintaining ties with France, which is achieved through self-government. But if the status of a territory is not open to self-government in the short term—and before 1978—there is a strong possibility that Caledonians will consider, in order to ensure the survival of their collectivity, turning to independence, out of desperation. (Pidjot 1976)

The portrait Roch Pidjot drew of the situation in New Caledonia was no doubt a crucial factor in determining the timing and the avenue Jean-Marie chose to enter the political arena.

Jean-Marie had come from a Union Calédonienne background, his father having been active in the party at Hienghène, and in the same year as Roch Pidjot's public warning to the French people he decided to join the local branch of the party. It was a natural expression of his logic of working from the base and of using traditional Kanak networks and alliances, both to create a climate of confidence and solidarity and to take over the institutions of the modern state. In March 1977 he was elected mayor of Hienghène, but not on the Union Calédonienne list. Jean-Marie described to the journalist Lionel Duroy the process that had led to his selection and election.

We had been celebrating following a good yam harvest, and a speech was made proposing that I be candidate for the position of mayor. No one wanted the UC, which was headed at Hienghène by Bob Alquier, the grocer, a dead loss. Maurice Lenormand's [one of the founders and principal European driving force behind the UC] connections were with the rich merchants. It didn't serve the interests of the tribes, only the Europeans. Whence the idea of creating the *Maxha* movement, which means "hold your head up" [in Pijé, the language spoken at Tiendanite], as in the slave's revolutionary gesture. Our campaign was well planned and eight of us were elected, the UC five, plus Devillelongue, the outgoing mayor, making six. Hienghène was a catastrophe for them and they all went away to weep. All the Whites came to the first Town Council meeting, to see whether we were capable of preparing a budget. That was in March 1977. Some called for me to be expelled from the UC, then things calmed down. (Tjibaou 1996, 263)

The immediate reason for the decision to enter local politics was the European-dominated municipal council's patent lack of interest in the surrounding Kanak communities and, in particular, in their pressing claims for the restitution of tribal land abandoned by departing Asian settlers. The request to participate in the elections came from his own tribe at Tiendanite and he was able to exploit traditional networks in order to gain support and take control of the municipal council by democratic means, a situation that confirmed, in Jean-Marie's mind, the importance of using culture as the foundation for political action. This first experience of politics also demonstrated that, while his ultimate goal was to build bridges between communities, if the Europeans continued to act exclusively in their own interests and ignore his invitations to collaborate—as had been the case with Mélanésia 2000—he was prepared to "go it alone." The control of the municipal council of Hienghène also provided another essential opportunity in the exercise of power, in demonstrating to the Kanak themselves and to the administration (and so to Europeans) that they possessed the skills to govern.

The next move, from the local to the national (New Caledonia) level, followed quickly. The Union Calédonienne decided to hold a congress at Bourail, an important Caldoche community, in May 1977. Already a number of Europeans had abandoned ship, as had Yann Céléné Urugeï, the most radical of Kanak militants, and there was every indication that the party would become the next victim of the accelerating ethnic and political polarization process. But again the Kanak elder statesman Roch Pidjot, together with his long-standing associate Maurice Lenormand, came to the rescue, ensuring that a new Kanak-dominated leadership would take over. Jean-Marie was elected vice president, under the ongoing presidency of Roch Pidjot. Surrounding him was a team made up of François Burck and Eloï Machoro, all three (including Jean-Marie) products of the Saint-Léon seminary at Païta, where the idea of political independence had first taken form; Yeiwéné Yeiwéné, from the Loyalty Islands; and a metropolitan Frenchman, Pierre Declercq, who was a Jeunesse Ouvrière Chrétienne militant. Prior to their being installed at the helm of the UC, however, the congress addressed the question of the party's position with regard to the political destiny of New Caledonia. The response was clear—it was henceforth to be independence, although not yet a specifically Kanak independence.

From this point on, Jean-Marie's destiny was sealed. Within twenty months of having organized Mélanésia 2000 he had become a national leader and, in a very real sense, the spiritual heir to Roch Pidjot, who was no longer pleading alone in the desert of the French National Assembly, but was now buttressed by an increasingly powerful movement at home. Events in New Caledonia accelerated in rapid succession. First, in September 1977, Jean-Marie and the new UC team were all elected as deputies to the Territorial Assembly, in a context where three-quarters of the Kanak electorate voted for political parties favoring independence. Then, on the metropolitan front in the following year, the new secretary of state for the DOM-TOM, Paul Dijoud, recognized the distinctive character of Melanesian culture and that the Kanak were the "first occupants of the land." In February 1979 the minister submitted a major plan for the future of New Caledonia that covered topics ranging from the economy to culture and land rights to the tax regime, all with a view to respecting the historic rights and promoting the distinctive interests of the Melanesian community while favoring inter-ethnic harmony. However, the burning question of the political future of New Caledonia was skirted, the plan's goal being to integrate Melanesians into the larger society and economy. Because of this the independentists rejected it. The plan was implemented, nevertheless.

The emergence of specifically Kanak political parties and the radicalization of the Union Calédonienne on the one hand, and the implementation of the Plan Dijoud on the other, had a traumatizing effect on the Caldoche community, for they saw themselves as trapped between a resurgent Melanesian community and an ill-informed (albeit right-wing) French government. The risk of a major transfer of power from one ethnic community to another was very real, and the inevitable result was that the Europeans began to mobilize, as loyalists, under the leadership of their principal economic stakeholders, notably Jacques Lafleur. In April 1977 Lafleur created the Rassemblement pour la Calédonie which, a little over a year later, became the Rassemblement pour la Calédonie dans la République (RPCR), at the incitation of none other than Jacques Chirac. He had already set his sights on the French presidency and saw in the RPCR a valuable ally and instrument for his own metropolitan party, Rassemblement pour la République. The new Caldoche-led party, dominated by powerful economic interests, had no difficulty in capturing the support of two vulnerable minority communities—one, the recent immigrants, made up primarily of Pieds Noirs and Polynesians, and the other, the poor settlers who were variously of European, mixed-race, Javanese, and Japanese origins.

Another major development in 1977 was the creation of a second seat for New Caledonia in France's National Assembly. In an electorate dominated by Nouméa, Jacques Lafleur was immediately elected and his presence had the designed effect of creating a Caldoche and loyalist voice to counter the Kanak and now independentist voice of Roch Pidjot. This mobilization of the loyalists, together with the strengthening of their visibility and credibility in France, took place in a local political arena where the Union Calédonienne, after having dominated a relatively powerful Territorial Assembly and the Conseil de gouvernement (Government Council) in the late 1950s, then experienced the emasculation of its powers in the 1960s, and since 1972, had been condemned to the opposition. Meanwhile, the Kanak, having exercised significant local political power under the colony's status as an Overseas Territory, were, by the late 1970s, experiencing both increasing political marginalization and overt hostility on the part of the European and immigrant communities. At the same time, in becoming increasingly articulate and radical in their political demands, the Kanak opposition was also fragmenting. In response to this crisis the various Kanak independentist political parties regrouped their forces in June 1979 to create their own coalition, the Front Indépendantiste (FI), with Jean-Marie as president. Despite this move, the party lost the territorial elections the following month—to an RPCR-dominated coalition.

Strategically, between 1975 and 1977, Jean-Marie had shifted from the cultural to the political arena and, between 1977 and 1979, had moved from local to national (territorial) politics, working to regroup the various political "identities" that had emerged in the preceding years. The strategy closely resembled the one he had adopted in the early 1970s with respect to culture. It was dominated by considerations of pragmatism rather than of ideology, the overriding concern being to unite the Kanak and to maintain open lines of communication with the territory's other communities. They hoped that they could enter into dialogue and achieve consensus with respect to the territory's political future. The goal was necessarily independence and, by 1979, it had become clear that it had to be Kanak independence. "Before the sun, before the world, the indigenous Kanak people are the sole legitimate inhabitants of the 'Rock.' Europeans who campaign for the same cause are legitimized by this struggle for independence that they undertake with the Kanak" (Tjibaou, quoted in Rollat 1989b, 173). The language had changed, in terms of vocabulary and tone, as had the intentions that lay behind it. Henceforth it was a matter of the first occupants of the land's inalienable right to independence, of their "right to choose the interdependencies" (Tjibaou 1996, 93) and of their intention to fight for that right:

> [W]e are weary of shedding tears; our eyes are dry from crying over our lot. Today, we are turning to fighting, and we will fight until the end. I believe that the Kanak people's awareness of their condition will continue to grow. Tension is mounting. People are taking up arms. The Kanak, however, are still not arming themselves; first because it is difficult to obtain weapons, and then because it is not part of our ways to go into the street with guns to assert our rights. But if the pressure continues, if the tensions cannot be expressed through the normal demonstrations—which are safety valves for the people—it is impossible to say what the future holds for us or for our country. The fact is that people are increasingly mobilized and many today are unfortunately ready—and I say unfortunately in relation to the pressure of colonialism—to die for their country. (Tjibaou 1996, 96–97)

If there was a climate of increased confidence it was no doubt because, in August of the same year, the Protestant Church *(Église évangélique)* formally took a position in favor of independence for the Melanesian people. Further, at a meeting of the Front Indépendantiste and the French Parti Socialiste, held in Paris in November, the latter, "expressed its entire solidarity with the Front Indépendantiste in the struggle that it is conducting against the political Right, and reaffirmed its intention to support and to guarantee the right of the Kanak people to decide freely as to their future."[2]

The declaration was made during the campaign for the French presidential elections, to take place in May 1981. François Mitterrand, who would be the socialist candidate, stated less than two weeks later, in a speech to the National Assembly, "We have had sufficient experience, over the last quarter of a century, of the problems of decolonization to know the degree of despair, then anger, of populations who no longer know who to turn to, or although knowing who, do not find in their interlocutor, the French government, either attention, or vigilance, or benevolence, or understanding. Then one arrives at the state of despair that precedes, I can assure you, a state of confrontation. . . . To what extent must one accept the demands of the Front Indépendantiste? *You will appreciate that we, the Parti Socialiste, have already taken a stand*" (23 Nov 1979, quoted in Rollat 1989b, 176–177; my italics).

While the situation was blocked in the territory, and was "on hold" but promising in France, it was now possible to envisage new initiatives at the regional and global levels, with a view to gaining support for the Kanak cause. In keeping with the logic, already expressed in 1978, that "we belong to the peoples of the Pacific and not to the Mediterranean" (Tjibaou 1996, 91), the first step was to send a delegation to the Pacific Forum annual meeting, held in Honiara in July 1979, thereby bringing their case to the attention of Australia and New Zealand as well as the island countries. On this occasion, Jean-Marie was accompanied by Nidoish Naisseline and Yann Céléné Urugeï. With the support of the newly independent Pacific Island countries it would in turn be possible to address the United Nations Committee on Decolonization.

Dates started to be advanced. Already Roch Pidjot had spoken of 1978 as the last chance for France to restore political autonomy and, if that was not achieved, the goal would inevitably become independence. Following the creation of the Front Indépendantiste, 1980 was put forward as the critical year; then 1982; then 1984, always with 24 September as the specific date on which independence would be declared.

The last major factor in setting the political scene for New Caledonia was the circumstances surrounding the birth, on 30 July 1980, of the neighboring nation of Vanuatu. A few hundred kilometers from the territory, the New Hebrides, as it was then called, had been administered for over seventy years as a joint Anglo-French condominium. In many respects the condominium had served as an extension of New Caledonia. On the one hand it assumed the role of the northern frontier of European pioneer settlement and, on the other, a significant number of its Melanesians had journeyed south to further their education, with others coming as migrants to a country where "the streets were paved in gold." Finally, there were significant New Caledonian commercial interests and investments in the New Hebrides.

The colony had experienced a troubled and, from the New Caledonian perspective, troubling lead-up to independence. While the British were intent on leaving, the French were not, and this fracture was reflected within the colony's Melanesian population. The independence leadership was composed essentially of English-educated Protestants who, as time passed, revealed that they had little sympathy for their French-educated counterparts. Pioneer settlement meant there were French-speaking mixed-race as well as European settlers. Immediately prior to independence, violence erupted, notably on the islands of Tanna and Espiritu Santo. In the days and weeks following the event, threats of secession were voiced and troops were called in from Papua New Guinea to quash the disturbances. Some French passport holders were expelled and others left voluntarily, virtually all for New Caledonia. They were seen, and considered themselves to be, political refugees, victims of a Melanesian-inspired independence movement. It was a regional drama that fueled the fears and the hostility of loyalists toward Kanak independentists, and it was another factor to be taken into account by their strategists, for in the minds of some it evoked the specter of Algeria.

In assuming the leadership of the independence movement, Jean-Marie was concerned as much to develop a strategy as to define its spirit and its values. It took on three dimensions: political, militant, and diplomatic. While the three would be practiced more or less simultaneously, emphasis would shift from one to another, depending on the prevailing circumstances, the constraints, and the opportunities. In the event of an impasse in the political and militant arenas, initiatives would be called to a temporary halt. However, the door was never closed on diplomacy.

With regard to politics, Jean-Marie was concerned to use the democratic institutions of the French state to promote the inalienable right of the Kanak people to independence. Given that those institutions were based on the principles of one person one vote and majority rule, more often than not they were used as a platform to signal the particular problem confronting the first occupants, who had become, in numerical terms, a minority in their own land. With respect to militantism, Jean-Marie was increasingly conscious that, given the formal opposition of other groups and interests in New Caledonia to Kanak political aspirations, it was necessary to engage in combat, to make radical gestures, and to defend and occupy land, all in order to attract attention and to modify the balance of power within the territory. Finally, through diplomacy, Jean-Marie was concerned to keep the lines of communication open, even with opponents, and to seek new allies in the Pacific, in France, and in international forums, with a view to appealing to reason, obtaining counsel, and assuring support.

With the benefit of hindsight 1977 to 1981 can be seen as a period of crystallization of the forces in play in New Caledonia, where political parties came to be defined primarily in ethnic terms, where each party sought to place its pawns on the local chessboard and to search, at the same time, for allies and support beyond the immediate geographical boundaries of the territory. It was a transitional phase of preparation and of waiting where, as far as the Kanak independentists were concerned, time was fast running out, because a cycle of growing awareness–manifestation–physical repression had commenced on the streets of Nouméa and in the small towns and villages of the Grande Terre—Bourail, Canala, Bouloupari. . . . For Jean-Marie it outlined that there had been a fundamental shift in thinking, on his own part and that of his people. "[T]hese are not spiritual beings that are walking in the streets, but men in flesh and blood who are trapped by material, physical, economic, and political constraints" (1996, 98).

If the cultural foundations of political change had been laid in previous years, it had now become urgent to focus on the building blocks of a soon-to-be-independent nation and to highlight the multiple dimensions of the struggle. In the same text, dated 11 September 1979 and written "following the suppression by force of a demonstration" (Bensa and Wittersheim 1996, 93), Jean-Marie pointed to the growing sense of insecurity among his people. "This insecurity that we experience is linked to our struggle for freedom, our struggle for the nation, for Kanak citizenship; it follows above all from the feeling of insecurity expressed by people who are frightened by this growth of Kanak consciousness, and who are perhaps afraid for their possessions. . . . The most hostile, the most scared, are the big investors, the people who have the mines, the banks, the major capital investments in the country" (Tjibaou 1996, 98). In radicalizing his discourse and, particularly, in speaking of social class and the economy, Jean-Marie inevitably started to describe the whole of New Caledonia not simply in terms of a heritage but also as "a wreck to be looted" (1996, 90), again pointing his finger at a small group of capitalists. "The exploiters are those who must be made to feel insecure. They ought to keep their insecurity for themselves but they share it with the ordinary people, so that these latter will support them in their shameless exploitation of our patrimony, of our country" (1996, 98–99).

In the course of the four years of Kanak mobilization, the anniversary of France's "taking possession" of New Caledonia (24 September) had developed into a source of public confrontation. If, for the loyalists and the French authorities, it was an occasion for celebration, for the independentists it had become a day of national mourning, increasingly marked by acts of provocation and violence. Here again, Jean-Marie's tone had started to change, for in speaking of combat he necessarily spoke of confrontation, and of the memory and consequences of violence. "The majority of militants . . . are ready to confront the anniversary. The problem is one of strategy, of tactics, and of means; I wouldn't say armed means because experience—history—has taught us that in 1878, with the few arms that we possessed, we, the Kanak, were crushed. In 1917, the Northern rebellion (and I am well placed to talk about it because my paternal grandmother was killed by the soldiers engaged in its repression) was crushed too" (1996, 95).

Written in September 1979 for the Catholic Commission on Justice and Peace's enquiry into demands for independence in the French Pacific territories, it was probably one of the first public admissions that he was conscious of the probability, if not indeed of the inevitability of violence, and of its implications for the Kanak people.

In May 1981 François Mitterrand, member of the Parti Socialiste, was elected president of France. For the next eight years, until Jean-Marie's own violent death in May 1989, events accelerated, actors multiplied, and New Caledonia, the Kanak, and Jean-Marie himself were projected onto the global stage. People were listening and watching elsewhere in the Pacific, in Australia and New Zealand, in francophone Africa, throughout France's DOM-TOMs, in Paris, New York, and Geneva, as events unfolded in New Caledonia. For many of them, amid the mounting clamor for independence, there was something different about Jean-Marie's *parole*, because he spoke of dignity and of the rights of dispossessed peoples. It was a clear message, not clothed in "the language of wood, or of stone," simply expressed, and appealing simultaneously to both reason and emotion. Insistent and demanding, it was also characterized by the hand extended as a gesture of friendship and of a willingness to share. It was by nature nonviolent and it offered a generous vision of the future.

For eight years Jean-Marie was at the helm of the independence movement, navigating between a variety of roles and spheres of action. He made little distinction between the personal and the public realms, both by choice and by circumstance. Rapid decisions had to be made, opponents identified, and allies sought, in an incredibly fluid world where the Kanak were numerically weak, politically vulnerable, militarily powerless, and marked by a fragile unity that only held in times of extreme crisis, when there was a clearly identified common enemy. A succession of such crises began with the first political assassination, of Pierre Declercq, the UC secretary-general, in September 1981, and ended with the military assault on the cave at Goosana in May 1988. Jean-Marie passed through a panoply of mental states, beginning with a high degree of serenity and conviction following the election of Mitterrand and terminating in periods of extreme doubt, if not outright despair, following the signing of the Matignon Accords in June 1988. Between these two temporal and emotional extremes, he shifted progressively from tenacity, shrouded in anger and even bitterness, to what was probably a profound fatigue when all communication between the Kanak and the other peoples of New Caledonia—backed by an inflexible political leadership in France—effectively ceased.

As the leader of the independence movement, Jean-Marie also needed to stand above the succession of dramas on the ground. He had to keep the movement on course and faithful to the guiding principles he had elaborated prior to entering the political arena. One of these was the conviction that identity, Kanak identity, is something that is constantly unfolding, always being constructed. Another was that in a concrete sense, in terms of economics, institutions, and skills, independence had to be prepared with care and discipline. The counsel of his ni-Vanuatu friend, Gérard Leymang, rang in his ears. "We bungled our independence because we didn't know how to prepare it. Don't do like us" (Leymang, quoted in Rollat 1989b, 267). Vanuatu was not only New Caledonia's closest neighbor, its people were fellow Melanesians.

In a letter he addressed to François Mitterrand within two months of his accession to the presidency, Roch Pidjot stated, "The [pre-electoral] proposition that you made to us, to jointly investigate as quickly as possible the political actions which must be taken, aroused tremendous hope among the Kanak people at the time of your election." He went on to say, "We ask that the right of nations to self-determination, presented as being in line with your political position, be effectively recognized for the Kanak, a people with regard to whom France has a direct responsibility" (Pidjot, quoted in Lenormand 1991, 146).

Already in August 1980 the Union Calédonienne had announced, at its annual congress, the intention of declaring independence on 24 September 1982. The movement in favor of the Kanak independentists gained momentum in June 1982 following a shift in alliances within the Territorial Assembly. The moderate Fédération pour la Nouvelle Société Calédonienne (FNSC), a minority party composed essentially of European and affiliated former members of the UC, joined with the UC to create a new government, which thereby obtained the majority in the Territorial Assembly. A new Conseil de gouvernement was formed where Jean-Marie was elected vice president (the president being the French government's high commissioner). The following three years saw the exercise of power by a group of seven elected ministers, four of whom were members of the UC and a fifth was Marie-Claude's brother, Henri Wetta. Henri was a Protestant and, above all, a loyalist. He had hesitated a long time before accepting the invitation, but as an expression of openness and generosity on the part of his brother-in-law, it was a proposition he could scarcely refuse. This UC-FNSC coalition government proved to be an exceptional one that demonstrated itself in full possession of the political and managerial skills necessary for the effective running of a country. "This Tjibaou government . . . at the end of three years in charge had a budget surplus of one billion, and had reduced the rate of inflation to 7 percent, whereas it stood at 14 percent in Tahiti and in metropolitan France. A state convention, where all the professional groups shared their experience and their knowledge, resulted in a three-year development plan being drawn up" (Lenormand 1991, 148).

The Kanak independence movement sensed it was moving rapidly forward over the entire period from May 1981 to November 1984. The Parti Socialiste was in power in France, with François Mitterrand as president, the UC had gained power in New Caledonia, Jean-Marie was vice president of the Government Council, the territory was well managed, the Pacific Region was taking a keen interest in the local political situation, and dates for the momentous event were being fixed. Jean-Marie envisaged the future with qualified confidence.

> We agree to play the institutional game [in New Caledonia], but if that should translate into the negation of our fundamental political demands, we would draw conclusions on the basis of it. Our presence within the institutions provides security, but it is security which is a little dangerous: there is always the risk of getting bogged down, whereas remaining in the opposition results in progress. . . .
>
> Simultaneously, we treat the metropolitan Parti Socialiste as a partner, even if we are not on the same wave-length as the government we support. There is a kind of moral contract between us: if they don't make headway with our fundamental demand, they are morally obliged to ensure it does not regress. We are committing ourselves to this "clear-vague" or this "vague-clear" avenue. However we would not have made the same commitment prior to 1981. (Tjibaou 1996, 128)

It was a calculated risk that was undermined from the very outset, for Mitterrand's opponent, Valéry Giscard d'Estaing, had been the overwhelming choice of the New Caledonian electorate, obtaining almost two-thirds of the votes in the presidential elections compared with one-third for the incoming president. The Caldoches were angry losers in an election where independence and, more specifically, Kanak independence was, if not yet on the agenda, certainly in the air. The new government in France rapidly undertook a variety of initiatives to improve the material conditions of the Kanak, notably with regard to land reform (Office foncier) and regional development (Office de développement de l'intérieur et des îles). An Office culturel was also established. These initiatives pointed to the beginnings of a major shift of power from one community to the other and they generated fear, on the part of Europeans, as to their progressive isolation. The European reaction was to express outright hostility to the independentists and to initiate a campaign of intimidation and violence. The Pieds Noirs and the poor, often mixed-race, settlers were particularly sensitive to a discourse that drew parallels with Algeria, the former often making clear they had no intention of becoming political refugees for a second time. Pieds Noirs were all too familiar with interethnic violence, New Caledonia had a violent colonial history, and, the political wind having changed, loyalist elements had no hesitation about resurrecting old practices. The first victim was Pierre Declercq, secretary-general of the UC, who was assassinated on 23 September 1981, less than two months after his return from France, where he had been a member of a UC delegation that informed President Mitterrand that the Kanak people intended to declare independence for New Caledonia on 24 September of the following year, 1982.

Right-wing groups, with armed branches, were constituted in the territory, acting outside the law and calling for open confrontation with the independentists. At the November 1981 UC congress it was asserted that these groups of Ultras had established a list of leaders to be eliminated, one by one: Pierre Declercq, Eloï Machoro, Maurice Lenormand, Jean-Marie Tjibaou, Yeiwéné Yeiwéné, and Roch Pidjot. A spiral of violence had started, initiated by the opponents to independence and finding political encouragement in the extreme right-wing Front National of Jean-Marie Le Pen, which was by now investing the political scene in metropolitan France and would quickly establish itself in New Caledonia as well. The Kanak had no choice but to react on the ground, and their response to Pierre Declercq's assassination was to set up roadblocks at different points around the territory, the objective being as much to defend themselves as to claim possession of the land. Blood had started to flow, and a pattern had been established whereby the political process was at once circumvented and directly influenced through systematic recourse to violence.

The reaction of the French socialist government was to advance . . . and then retreat, with respect to Kanak demands and in the face of the systematic opposition of the European community, opting for development at the expense of decolonization. While the social and economic reforms of the first secretary of state for the DOM-TOM, Henri Emmanuelli, had been implemented with little difficulty, largely because the RPCR controlled the Territorial Assembly, those of his successor in 1983, Georges Lemoine, proved much more problematic, precisely because they sought to address political issues. Immediately following Pierre Declercq's assassination, Roch Pidjot led another UC delegation, which included Jean-Marie Tjibaou, to meet the president (figure 7). They made it clear to him that reforms without political independence as an outcome were of no interest to the Front Indépendantiste. In the hope of reconciling the two political options and ethnic communities, and willing to envisage all political options, Lemoine organized a meeting of the FI, the FNSC, and the RPCR, together with a representative of the high chiefs, at Nainville-les-Roches, near Paris, in July 1983. The communiqué issued at the end of the meeting, and overseen by the minister, called for the end of colonialism and recognized the existence of the Kanak people, as well as their innate and active right to independence. It also stated that this right should be extended to those non-Kanak recognized to be "Victims of History," defined as settlers of at least two generations' standing. All parties present signed the communiqué, with the exception of Jacques Lafleur's RPCR, which withdrew at the last minute.

This moment of hope—of the real possibility of an electoral victory should the agreement be implemented—was set against a backdrop of increasing mobilization and violence on the ground, together with growing disenchantment with respect to the political process. If Georges Lemoine had at the outset envisaged the possibility of independence, when subsequently

Figure 7. Jean-Marie being received by President Mitterrand in Paris, with Roch Pidjot in the background, January 1986. *(ADCK-Centre Culturel Tjibaou/ Rémy Moyen)*

confronted by the complexities of a settler colony and growing right-wing anger, he limited his recommendations principally to immediate economic and administrative reforms. At the same time, he advanced the notion of an "evolving and transitional" political status leading, after five years, to a referendum on the political future of the territory that would include independence as one of the options. Approved by the French National Assembly in May 1984, the *statut Lemoine* was boycotted by the independentists in New Caledonia, for it offered little more, in terms of powers, than the territory had possessed for a brief period in the late 1950s to early 1960s under the *loi Defferre,* it failed to address the delicate question of definition of the electoral body, and it further delayed the date for independence. Although innovative and radical from a metropolitan perspective, it was too little, too late for the Kanak, in a context where their expectations—and their frustrations—were high, hostility on the part of the loyalists, the authorities, and their executants on the ground was growing day by day, and the right wing, with Chirac as presidential candidate, was preparing for a return to power in France.

In the course of the debate on the *statut Lemoine,* Roch Pidjot, then aged 77, gave his last speech to the National Assembly in Paris.

Throughout the debate on this project I have sought dialogue. I have not been heard. The legitimacy of the Kanak people, their right to independence, is scorned. The Kanak people, the first occupants of the Territory, will continue to be strangers in their own land, for it is the colonizer, through this status, who exercises his rights to self-government and to independence. France's sole preoccupation is to maintain its presence in the Pacific. In order to do this, it privileges the interests of Europeans and of other immigrants. It also flouts the promise made prior to 1981 by the PS [Parti Socialiste] and the PC [Parti Communiste], and the Nainville-les-Roches declaration on the inherent and active right of the Kanak people to independence.

I am ashamed for you, for the contempt, the smearing attitude that you have shown in speaking of my people. How can the colonizing power claim to be the guarantor of everything that it has itself flouted for one hundred and thirty years? What allows it to assert that those it has colonized will be equally intolerant? It points to a very poor understanding of our civilization. . . .

Convinced that New Caledonia must be governed at the center, you play into the hands of the most reactionary elements in this country and those of small political groups, thereby providing an unexpected chance for them to appear much more important than they are in reality. You have adopted a strategy that you have yourself termed "watershed."

We want nothing to do with this strategy of so-called decolonization.

It is a classic strategy: you divide to rule. . . . The Front Indépendantiste refuses to play your game.

I solemnly warn you of the risks of destabilization that you will yourselves have engendered. Our human dignity is profoundly wounded by declarations to the effect that Kanak independence would be racist. . . .

[T]his project does not take into account the aspirations of the Kanak. You know how determined we are. Our wish is that the referendum be held and that New Caledonia becomes independent in the course of this presidential term of office. You have hurt us too many times. So we have become skeptical, and we will judge the Government not on its declarations but on its actions. (Pidjot, quoted in *L'Avenir Calédonien* 1990, 2)

While a mere eight deputies were there to hear his words, Eloï Machoro was seated in the Public Gallery.

Significantly, as of mid-June 1984, Roch Pidjot, *un homme sacré* in the eyes of his people, ceased to be associated with the Parti Socialiste in the National Assembly.

This deep sense of skepticism with regard to the French government, regardless of the political party in power, was now shared by Jean-Marie. He could no longer place his trust in the president, the Parti Socialiste, or the democratic institutions of the French state. Shortly before attending the meeting at Nainville-les-Roches he had visited Algeria at the invitation of the FLN, to see what he might learn from their experience. Their warning to him was unequivocal. "The French don't keep their word. Like all West-

erners, they only understand relationships of power" (Tjibaou, quoted in
Rollat 1989b, 206).

Jean-Marie was beginning to discover what realpolitik meant. In a sense
that was the nature of Roch Pidjot's final counsel and political message, a
message that found expression in a series of organizational and strategic
changes made in late 1984, and also in a warning. At the closure of the Fif-
teenth Congress of the Union Calédonienne, held at Touho at the beginning of November, the *grand-père* spoke of the need for the Kanak people
to mobilize and to combat the *statut Lemoine* and he warned that "we will go
through a stormy period where all the elements will rage against us" (Pidjot,
quoted in *L'Avenir Calédonien* 1990, 3) (figure 8). He ended his speech with
the affirmation, "A people only possesses what it struggles for." It was a different vocabulary and another way forward, albeit to be used in association
with those more familiar ones practiced within the institutions of the state.
The battle lines were being drawn, and a second front had to be opened in
the struggle for independence. This new front, elaborated at a number of
political meetings held between September and December 1984, marked
another major step in the intellectual and strategic progression of Jean-
Marie Tjibaou, for it required moving forward from party politics to people's
struggle, again without abandoning the sphere of ideas, of convictions, and
of action that had progressively taken form.

On 24 September of that year, the various Kanak independence movements issued a joint communiqué announcing the creation of a much
broader-based independence group to replace the Front Indépendantiste
(figure 9). It was to be called Front de Libération Nationale Kanak Socialiste (FLNKS). The name of the future country was Kanaky, its flag consisting of three colored horizontal bands, green for the land, red as a symbol
of struggle and for the blood that unites people, and blue for sovereignty,
set in the wider context of the Pacific Ocean. A yellow circle occupied the
center of the flag—the sun—and, placed within it, a *flêche faîtière* or central
rooftop totem, evoking the home, its occupants, and their link to the ancestors and the cosmos (see figure 10). The new movement stated its intention
to establish a Provisional Government of Kanaky, with local *comités de lutte*
(mobilization or combat committees), and to turn to the UN Committee on
Decolonization and to a variety of international organizations, including
the World Council of Churches, Amnesty International, and Justice and
Peace for support. The decision was made, at the same time, to actively
boycott the territorial elections planned for 18 November 1984. Active boycott meant the putting up of roadblocks on election day and, in the case of
Eloï Machoro, Pierre Declercq's successor as secretary-general of the UC,
the symbolic but much publicized shattering of a ballot box with an axe at
Canala. On 20 November 1984 the Provisional Government of Kanaky was
established, Jean-Marie was appointed president, and Eloï minister of security.

Jean-Marie formally raised the flag and announced the creation of the

FIGURE 8. Political mobilization: The UC congress at Arama in November 1985. *(ADCK-Centre Culturel Tjibaou)*

FIGURE 9. With New Caledonia hovering on the verge of civil war, the FLNKS leadership had to constantly explain and justify its actions to journalists. Jean-Marie is speaking into the microphone, while Yeiwéné Yeiwéné, with a bandanna on his head, stands in the background, May 1985. *(ADCK-Centre Culturel Tjibaou/ Gamma)*

FIGURE 10. The mid-1980s were marked by youthful dreams of an independent Kanaky. *(ADCK-Centre Culturel Tjibaou)*

Provisional Government on 1 December 1984 at La Conception, on Roch Pidjot's tribal land. The event was steeped in symbolism, revealing the dreams and values as well as the determination of a people. In his speech, Jean-Marie thanked the ancestors for being present, remembered those who had died in the struggle for freedom and respect, spoke of alienation and of determination, and demanded the pardon of his opponents. "And allow me to request that together we may pardon those men in whom we install hatred because of our logic, this commitment for our people's sovereignty to be reinstated in Kanaky" (1996, 170–171).

A pattern was set in the latter part of 1984 that prevailed until mid-1988, of sometimes participating in and sometimes boycotting elections based on the principle of universal suffrage. The reason for it was simple: the Kanak had come to appreciate that democratic institutions served, and were even repeatedly used, to thwart rather than to promote their interests as a people in the context of postwar New Caledonia. This reality led them to create a specifically Kanak government.

> The problem is that when we constituted a majority, there was no taking account of the democratic majority. . . . Today one invokes democracy when the Kanaks are a minority. But it was only invoked from the point at which immigration from French overseas territories or from France was set in process, with a view to reversing the numerical relationship between the indigenous population and the immigrant population. . . .
>
> We are opposed to this democracy installed colonially with the political intention of opposing Kanak demands for independence, which are in the first instance a demand for self-government. The Kanak presence must be treated seriously. Such is the present reality. This denial of our reality has been typical of most governments, with the exception of the socialists who, I believe, really tried to do something. But institutions are difficult to handle. With them, and

in the absence of experience on our part, we were unable to meet our objective. Inexperienced, but also without any real political commitment on the part of the socialist government, at a point at which, on our part, we were at the height of our mobilization. (Tjibaou 1996, 247–248)

This particular assessment of the political reality was made by Jean-Marie in the days following the military assault on the cave at Goosana, in 1988. In presenting the transcription of the interview, Alban Bensa and Éric Wittersheim pointed out that Jean-Marie "is giving free expression to his bitterness, to his weariness here, after four years of struggle on the ground and of negotiations" (1996, 243). Those four years were characterized, from the law and order perspective, as a *situation insurrectionnelle,* but are referred to more euphemistically by the Caldoche and immigrant communities in New Caledonia, even today, as the *événements.* Roch Pidjot had insisted that it was necessary to take this course in order to influence political decision making in France, and the consequences were as he predicted. It was a tragic period marked by manifestations that all too frequently ended in violence, hostage taking, barrages, the occupation of land, police posts, and the towns of Thio and Canala, the killing of Kanak and of Caldoche, and the sending of over six thousand French troops to New Caledonia, to patrol the territory. The arena—the center of action—shifted from the National Assembly in Paris to the Grande Terre, and to where Jean-Marie Tjibaou took over the helm from Roch Pidjot. Two events set the tone of a period during which France gave the impression of moving inexorably toward a colonial war in New Caledonia. The first was the massacre that took place on the road leading from Hienghène to Tiendanite, on 5 December 1984. The second was the killing, on 12 January 1985, of the secretary-general of the UC and the military strategist of the Provisional Government, Éloï Machoro, and of his assistant, Marcel Nonnaro, by police (GIGN) sharpshooters. Éloï Machoro was the second on the list of Kanak independence leaders to be eliminated, according to the document that had been revealed a few weeks earlier at the UC congress. His death resulted in a state of emergency being called for the first time in the territory.

Éloï was another charismatic figure, particularly for young Kanak. Conscious of the limited ability of his people to negotiate with the French government and of their extreme vulnerability with regard to armed militia elements within the local European community, he proposed a strategy of progressive occupation of the interior of New Caledonia, advancing commune by commune. "[H]e would go right to the end. He came to invite us to fight with him, until the final victory or until death if necessary. It was a compelling discourse. He recounted his experience at Thio. We all listened in silence and with respect for he who was speaking. He was going to conquer New Caledonia" (R Guiart 1991, 130).

In Thio on 20 November he had masterminded the occupation of the

Figure 11. Confrontation in Houaïlou, June 1985. *(ADCK-Centre Culturel Tjibaou/ Rémy Moyen)*

Figure 12. Military intervention to remove roadblocks in Saint-Louis, November 1987. *(ADCK-Centre Culturel Tjibaou/ Rémy Moyen)*

FIGURE 13. Loyalist demonstrations in Nouméa, September 1987. *(ADCK-Centre Culturel Tjibaou/ Rémy Moyen)*

police post, disarmed the Caldoche settlers, and left with the weapons of both. La Foa was to be the next objective, then Bouloupari. As the Kanak advanced, so the Europeans would withdraw from the countryside and seek refuge in the Greater Nouméa area. If Eloï Machoro's analysis made strategic sense, it suffered from the reality that he possessed neither the numbers nor the weapons to carry it through. Further, it alienated the poor white and métis settlers who had long occupied the middle ground between the Kanak and the much wealthier Caldoche and French communities. His actions, together with the reactions to them, served only to fuel antagonism and hatred and to harden the boundaries between communities, pushing the country in the direction of civil war and nourishing the French government's fears of being embroiled in a second Algeria. By the end of 1984, given the nature of New Caledonia's economy, with the alliance of the interests of the European community and the nickel industry, it was inevitable that if a choice were to be made, even on the part of a socialist government, it would have to be at the expense of the Kanak. "Eloï Machoro's analysis was based on the observation that constant deceit had too often been the substance of French policy with regard to the Kanaks, that they had been consistently divested of their possessions and their freedom in the name of a certain social progress of which they would be the ultimate beneficiaries" (R Guiart 1991, 138).

Eloï was undoubtedly another dreamer, another idealist, like Jean-Marie Tjibaou, and like Djubelly Wéa as well. Perhaps in a sense he resembled Djubelly more than Jean-Marie, for he was concerned not only to accelerate history, but also to modify its trajectory—and to give no quarter.

> Eloï was . . . an uncompromising man, devoid of any theoretical grounding or perspective, not in the least bit Marxist and still profoundly Christian, permanently stretched to the breaking point, perhaps conscious of the fact that he was destined to be different, much more preoccupied as he was than others with the need for true reconciliation in struggle and in action between the descendants of the 1878 insurgents and the grandsons of those who had made, at the time, the mistake of turning to the Whites. His choice of La Foa to pursue the struggle—a tactical error that was evident given the imbalance between the forces on the ground, in a large gently undulating plain, and in the final analysis his voluntary sacrifice—seems to bear witness to this. (R Guiart 1991, 138–139)

René Guiart and other militants have suggested that the FLNKS leadership, including Jean-Marie himself, was "comforted" by Eloï's elimination. It was a cruel judgment on their part that ignored how, being extremely limited in resources, the leaders were often simply overcome by events. It also ignored a crucial observation that they had themselves arrived at: "Eloï Machoro was right, but seventy thousand Kanak aren't enough in an armed struggle" (R Guiart 1991, 138). It was even a grave illusion on the part of radicals to affirm that seventy thousand Kanak stood behind the heroic figure. Rather, "Eloï found himself alone, face to face with his word, face to face with his sole intent. We were very few capable of following him, above all if it was only going to be a gallant last stand. Too many factors stood against him, too many factors which could have stood in his favor" (R Guiart 1991, 130).

There on 12 January 1985, in the half-light at La Bachèlerie near La Foa, Eloï Machoro, together with his close friend and fellow minister, Marcel Nonnaro, found themselves encircled by French gendarmes and marksmen, with no place to go other than their certain death. Eloï turned to the thirty or so militants sheltering with him on the abandoned Caldoche property and offered his last words. "'We will show them that Kanaks know how to die'" (Machoro, quoted in R Guiart 1991, 136). In some tragic way it was a foretaste of things to come on Ouvéa, first in 1988, when Alphonse Dianou and companions were encircled and killed by the military, and then in 1989, when Djubelly Wéa also "found himself alone, face to face with his word, face to face with his sole intent," choosing—if, indeed, any real choice remained—to take Jean-Marie Tjibaou and Yeiwéné Yeiwéné with him "on the journey to the other side of the mirror."

If Jean-Marie was deeply wounded and embittered by Machoro's death, and by the accusations that he was in some perverse way party to it, the massacre at Hienghène would mark him personally and define him as a leader. In its immediate aftermath, he unequivocally demonstrated to allies and opponents that, while he was prepared to act outside the law and engage in violent confrontation, he would also seek, time and again, to set aside hatred. On this second occasion, more than any other, he demonstrated the path he was intent on following.

On the evening of 5 December 1984 seventeen men from Tiendanite were returning to the village from a local FLNKS *comité de lutte* meeting that had been held at the Cultural Center in Hienghène. Jean-Marie was expected to have been among them but at the last minute he had agreed to stay in Nouméa in order to meet Edgard Pisani, who had just been appointed *délégué du gouvernement en Nouvelle-Calédonie* (government delegate), his mandate being to find a satisfactory solution for the political future of its two principal ethnic communities. Winding up the Hienghène valley, the militants suddenly found their way blocked by a tree that had been placed across the track. Their assassins were waiting: poor white and mixed-race settlers who had lived close to the river for several generations. Without warning they opened fire, killing ten of the Kanak on the spot, including two of Jean-Marie's brothers, and wounding four others. Only three men, including a third brother, escaped unscathed. Such was the anger of the assassins at discovering that Jean-Marie was not among the group that they immediately went up to Tiendanite and burned his house down. Then they disappeared.

The poor settlers have long gone from the valley, but the charred remains of two pickup trucks are still there today, a silent monument on the edge of the road, marked with names and dates, an inscribed plaque, and tattered pieces of *manou* knotted to poles, all witness to a lost generation, this time from the tribe at Tiendanite (figures 14, 15). It had undoubtedly been a crime, if not directly conceived, almost certainly fomented by extreme rightwing elements in Nouméa, the executants being themselves truly "victims of history," economically marginalized occupants of land that the local Kanak were waiting impatiently to have restored to them. They were trapped in a spiraling confrontation between Caldoche and Kanak communities, participating in both but belonging to neither. It was another final, desperate

FIGURE 14 (*opposite, top*). The memorial in the Hienghène valley to the ten militants from Tiendanite killed in ambush on 5 December 1984. The charred and rusted remains of the two pickup trucks in which they were traveling are draped in cloth, with a banner above. (*ADCK-Centre Culturel Tjibaou/ Gérard del Rio*)

FIGURE 15 (*opposite, bottom*). Between the trucks is a plaque inscribed with the names of those killed and the words, "Fils de Kanaky, souviens-toi." (*ADCK-Centre Culturel Tjibaou/ Gérard del Rio*)

gesture of despair, similar in many respects to that of Eloï Machoro or of Djubelly Wéa, with a singular difference: the assassins — Maurice Mitride, Raoul Lapetite and his four sons, and Robert Sineimene — occupied a social and economic space that was visibly shrinking under their feet. The vast majority of the European residents of the township of Hienghène were being evacuated to Nouméa at the time, by helicopter or by road, and the houses of the poor settlers were being burned, one by one, torched by Kanak or by themselves. It was the end of an era, a last violent parting gesture before Hienghène and the valleys around it were restored by default to the first occupants of the land.

It was not the first attempt to eliminate Jean-Marie Tjibaou, who was now condemned to live with bodyguards provided by the French government. It was also not the first time since 1853 that the tribe at Tiendanite had counted its dead. But it was the most tragic. Within the space of a few minutes it lost ten out of a total of twenty-six adult males. The village was decimated, Jean-Marie's own family included (figures 16, 17). The massacre had been precipitated by Kanak requests to the European and métis communities of the Hienghène area not to vote in the 18 November elections. Such a demand for solidarity with their cause was linked with the promise of being able to stay in the region and on the land once independence was achieved. However, the settlers chose to brave the barricades and vote (massively for Jacques Lafleur's RPCR), thereby provoking the anger of their Kanak neighbors and, inevitably, retaliation.

Within a few short weeks New Caledonia had moved to the verge of civil war. With anger and demands for retribution multiplying on both sides, along with clear attempts being made to geographically delimit the territories of the Kanak and Caldoche communities and to control access to them, there were only two possible avenues to take on the ground. One was to consciously pursue the spiral of violence; the other was to step back, refusing to respond to the provocations of the European extremists, in a situation where there was a sense that "Kanaky is being born." Jean-Marie chose, without hesitation, the avenue of nonviolence, not perhaps for reasons of principle, but because he believed it was the only possible way to achieve the goal of independence. "[W]e have to appear in the eyes of the world to be a movement of dignity and of freedom. . . . Otherwise, we will lose all credibility. We can't at one and the same time justify and obtain international support in the name of freedom and then loudly proclaim that we also have to advance at gunpoint on the ground" (Tjibaou 1989a, 39).

At this crucial moment, Jean-Marie demonstrated to his fellow Kanak that he possessed the qualities of a statesman. Rather than match violence with violence and seek retribution, he decided to maintain the dialogue commenced with Edgard Pisani and remove the roadblocks.

"For us, we understood then that he had the ability to govern a country. He was a true statesman, capable of putting the interests of his country be-

FIGURE 16. Jean-Marie officiating at the ceremony to mark the end of mourning the death of the Tiendanite militants. *(ADCK-Centre Culturel Tjibaou/ Philippe Huneau)*

FIGURE 17. The graves of the ten militants at Tiendanite. *(ADCK-Centre Culturel Tjibaou/ Henri Wedoye)*

fore his personal interests" (François Burck, pers com, 22 Jan 1998). It was an act of courage, one of many he would be called on to make, essentially alone, in the following years. His objective was to find a way to break the vicious circle of hostility and violence on the part of the local European community and of incoherence on the part of the French state, toward the demands of the Kanak people. The task was a massive one, for it simultaneously involved addressing the situation on the ground on an almost day-to-day basis, negotiating with the French government, appealing to the international community, and preparing for independence.

For Jean-Marie, the period from early 1985 until the crisis on Ouvéa in April 1988 was marked by a mixture of tenacity and anger, but also of increasing bitterness and despair. In the case of the European community in New Caledonia it had become evident that the boundary had hardened and communication was impossible. Jacques Lafleur had failed to sign the Nainville-les-Roches communiqué and had not engaged in any dialogue thereafter, while extreme right-wing groups—both violent and nonviolent— flourished. Both were nourished by the progression of the Front National in France. Already, in late 1983, the FN had played a key role in winning the Dreux municipal election, while in 1985 its visibility at the national level had increased following the introduction of a system of proportional representation. Then, in March 1986, the right-wing RPR won the National Assembly elections.

For the next two years France experienced a political regime characterized as cohabitation, with a socialist president, François Mitterrand, and a right-wing prime minister, Jacques Chirac. It was a period marked by conflict between the two leaders, notably with respect to New Caledonia. Already, prior to cohabitation, Pisani's and then Fabius's offer of independence with association (with elections to be held in December 1987) had failed to meet with the approval of the FLNKS because it contained no assurance of independence. Moreover, the proposed date for elections was after the next National Assembly elections in France, when it was expected (and subsequently confirmed) that the right wing would return to power and the offer would be withdrawn. On the other hand, the Pisani-Fabius reforms did propose a decentralization of government in New Caledonia, with the creation of four regions, thus a certain degree of federalism. Approved by the National Assembly in August 1985, they became the organizational basis for the territorial elections held a month later. The FLNKS participated in them, gaining three of the four regions. Jean-Marie was appointed president of the Northern Region, thereby acquiring six months' grace during which there was a sense of constructing, region by region, an independent country.

However, following the elections in France in March 1986, Chirac replaced Fabius as prime minister and Bernard Pons took over from Edgard Pisani as minister for DOM-TOM. The immediate consequences in New

Caledonia of these transfers of power were to stop land redistribution, radically reduce the spheres of jurisdiction of the regions, and put an end to the political aspirations of the Melanesian "people," for, in Chirac's and Pons's eyes, no such people existed. In short, Chirac's arrival announced a new period of centralization of power and active repression of the Kanak independence movement. It was a bitter bill to swallow and it had come on top of François Mitterrand's question to Jean-Marie Tjibaou, expressed on the occasion of his brief visit to Nouméa immediately after the killing of Eloï Machoro. "Let us imagine that I am capable of granting you independence. . . . With what army will you take Nouméa?" (Mitterrand, quoted in Rollat 1989b, 225).

It was a question he posed to Jean-Marie and to other independence leaders on a number of occasions thereafter, asking them at the same time "what they intended to do with the people that didn't share their ideas" (François Burck, pers comm, 22 Jan 1998). For a man like Jean-Marie, who believed that the very raison d'être of a people was to share, they were brutal questions, given that he had not once experienced a willingness on the part of the Caldoche community to open to the Kanak people or to manifest any desire to respect their aspirations. Already, in the aftermath of Mélanésia 2000, when he had unsuccessfully advanced the project of a second festival, reuniting Caldoche and Kanak, he had expressed, sadly, to the then DOM-TOM minister, Olivier Stirn, "The Whites here haven't understood anything. They want nothing to do with us. Why?" (quoted in Rollat 1989b, 167).

Ever a statesman, he was able to handle the worst insults with dignity, as in January 1985 when, seated in the public gallery at the National Assembly in Paris in order to follow a debate on New Caledonia, "He was violently set on there, insulted and finally ordered by the opposition deputies to leave the premises. The *Quotidien de Paris* editorialist, Dominique Jamet, saw fit to agree, in writing on 24 January: 'In Clemenceau's time, six bullets would have been sufficient for this half-priest'" (Bensa and Wittersheim 1996, 174). In alluding to the occasion, in an interview published in a special issue of *Les Temps modernes* dedicated to New Caledonia, Jean-Marie simply remarked, "It was the verbal aggression at the National Assembly that surprised me, when I am of no consequence. It was rather a question of the people disclosing their sense of helplessness" (1996, 174).

When Georges Lemoine first visited New Caledonia, prior to the Nainville-les-Roches meeting, simultaneous demonstrations were held at the Place des Cocotiers by loyalists and independentists, with thirty thousand Europeans on one side and three thousand Kanak on the other, separated by a few riot police (CRS). Even then, Jean-Marie chose to address both groups, affirming, "We are all equals." Confronted by prejudice he could only respond in terms of values, even if in private he did let escape on the same occasion his only known verbal faux pas: "I'm weary of the smell

. . . (of the White man)." The slip was scarcely surprising given the context (Patrice Godin, pers comm, 29 April 1997).

Jean-Marie's anger and real sense of despair effectively surfaced in 1987, during the reign of Jacques Chirac and Bernard Pons. Their avowed goal was to neutralize the FLNKS and to intimidate the population. Six thousand five hundred troops had been sent to New Caledonia and were scattered across the territory, in a strategy of *nomadisation*. Jacques Lafleur had demanded that the FLNKS be dissolved, and participants in a sit-in on the Place des Cocotiers had been beaten violently by the riot police. Pons's and Chirac's objective of bringing New Caledonia back to the status quo ante and of "putting an end to the illusions" proffered by Mitterrand, Pisani, Fabius, and others, had simply served to accentuate interethnic violence and further provoke Kanak militants. It was October 1987. The FLNKS decision to boycott the previous month's territorial elections (which were designed to facilitate the implementation of Pons's plans) had proved successful, an estimated 83.5 percent of the Kanak electorate having refrained from voting. The retrial (after an earlier dismissal) of the seven settlers held responsible for the bloody Hienghène ambush was underway in Nouméa, and was inevitably highly political, as was Jean-Marie's wish. On trial on this occasion was either France or the Kanak people, and French justice, in acquitting the accused on the grounds of "legitimate defense," dictated that the Kanak people were at fault, not the perpetrators of the crime.

Jean-Marie had been called as a witness, and he had ended his statement with the observation, "I have come in order that the memory of our dead not be confined uniquely to the page of trivial news items. . . . But judgment has already been passed: we are in a state of rebellion; it's logical that you kill us" (quoted in Duroy 1988, 317). A few days later, as the dialogue of the deaf pursued its course and the trial progressed inexorably toward the acquittal of the accused, Jean-Marie turned to the European loyalists present in the courtroom and asked, "Do we have anything left to say to each other?" (quoted in Duroy 1988, 319).

In December, relating to the journalist Alain Rollat the succession of killings his tribe had been subject to since the beginning of the colony, Jean-Marie announced, "We are weary of this fate which has turned us into victims for the past century" (quoted in Rollat 1989b, 245–246).

Stupefaction and anger at the announcement of the acquittal of the authors of the Hienghène massacre, certainly, but especially frustration and fatigue. The battle lines had been drawn in no uncertain way, and the only logic known to Chirac and Pons was that of open confrontation, with the aim of crushing the Kanak independence movement. Cohabitation in Paris, the progression of the Front National throughout the country, and the announcement in October 1987 that its leader, Jean-Marie Le Pen, intended to stand for president in the upcoming elections, meant that Kanak initiatives on the ground had shifted from *construct* (an independent country) to *resist* (as a people). Ironically, this was a period when all eyes were on New

Caledonia, and there was much sympathy for the Kanak cause, notably in the Pacific Region—the member states of the Forum, the Melanesian Spearhead Group, Australia, and New Zealand—but also in the larger international community. On 6 September 1986 the Eighth Nonaligned Movement Summit, held in Harare (Zimbabwe) admitted the FLNKS to official observer status, while on 2 December 1986 the United Nations General Assembly reinscribed New Caledonia on its list of Non-Self-Governing Territories (admittedly without the support, this time, of the members of the European Union), thereby recognizing "the inalienable right of the people in New Caledonia to self-determination and to independence." Jean-Marie was instrumental in achieving both goals and was present on each occasion. Nevertheless, for him, both were qualified successes. "For the time being, we have this diplomatic support, *but insofar as material aid is concerned, it's hopeless*" (Tjibaou 1996, 254; my italics).

By 1987–1988 it was as if, in the context of France and of the European community in New Caledonia, there was no longer any hope of appealing to reason, no longer any margin for maneuver. "The fact that there are French socialists in power changes nothing with regard to France's foreign policy. France looks at itself and, through itself, looks at the world" (Tjibaou 1996, 210). As an Overseas Territory, New Caledonia was condemned to being at once an overseas extension of the French state and a witness to the fact that France was a middle-range world power. Kanak inability to maneuver was dictated by another terrible reality on the ground, of which the carefully orchestrated military assault on the cave in Goosana on 5 May 1988 was the ultimate expression. "I don't know whether you are aware of it, but the day the nineteen Ouvéa militants were slaughtered, there were people who applauded, as they had applauded when Eloï Machoro and his companion Marcel Nonnaro were assassinated, when the Hienghène and Ougéo ten were killed, and the other Kanak militants. Everytime a Kanak has fallen the Whites have applauded. For them, the fewer the Kanaks the less the danger" (Tjibaou 1996, 246).

It was a frightening situation for a people who had affirmed, time and again, "We are at home here, we have no other native land but this country" (Tjibaou 1996, 245) and for a man who repeatedly asserted, "We are such a small people that we run the risk at any moment of disappearing." Jean-Marie Le Pen and his Front National would have desired nothing better, and they made their presence felt in no uncertain terms in the context of the 1988 presidential elections in France. "The absolute peak and crowning achievement of this contempt was the Ouvéa affair and the bloodbath that followed. It was a gratuitous bloodbath, motivated by the electoral goal of winning the Le Pen votes. Concerning Ouvéa, Le Pen had declared a few days before the second round that it was a case of 'submission or extermination.' The survivors can bear witness to it today, and I hope the truth will be heard about this carnage, this massacre orchestrated by Chirac, Pons, Pasqua, and Lafleur in order to get the right-wing votes" (Tjibaou 1996, 251).

In the course of a few short years the Kanak independence project, led by Jean-Marie Tjibaou, had swung from a euphoric state of *fol espoir* (insane hope) to a somber condition of *légitime défense*. As Jean-Marie had said in the days following the acquittal of the perpetrators of the Hienghène massacre:

> The hunting of Kanak is permitted; we said it on the evening of the verdict. The Whites have permits to hunt and hence to massacre Kanak.
>
> The Kanak must become conscious of this situation and recognize that no one will come to help them.
>
> They have to get organized, to defend themselves, to prevent these dogs from coming into the tribes and massacring anyone, any way and under any pretext. From now on, from that point at which justice vindicates the murdering of Kanak. The people have to get organized, to ensure their own security and their self-defense. (1987a, 12)

In 1985 and 1986, the threat came from armed and uniformed militia, generally Wallisians supervised by Europeans. By 1987 it was the French military itself. In October 1987 justice had sided against the Kanak, while in June 1988 the state had authorized the massacre. Ouvéa evoked a future without hope. It had the makings of a "big black hole" into which all of Jean-Marie's people were being inexorably drawn. Perhaps it was time to step back, for Jean-Marie had no intention of taking his people to extinction, physical or political.

*   *   *

> There were times when I saw tears of grief in Jean-Marie Tjibaou's eyes, but never tears of despair. So I will never forget the afternoon of Monday, 7 December 1987, when he appeared before us in the salle Colbert at the Palais-Bourbon, totally distraught, to the point of ending his press conference with a voice choked by emotion. He was appealing to the whole world for help, and the echo that came back to him was, yet again, the sniggering of death. Perhaps he already sensed that there was nothing more to be done in the face of the infernal, unrelenting machine that had been set off by the blindness of a government that despised his people. . . . He had reached the bottom of the abyss that he had himself sunk into, by virtue of repeatedly relying on reason, on this obsessive quest for peace. (Rollat 1989b, 245)

8   *The One Remaining Hope*
Appealing to the French People

> [E]ach being that enters the world "breaks" things in coming. To
> come out of his egg the chick is obliged to break the shell, the child
> hurts his mother, and every living being, in order to exist, in order
> to awaken to life, must shake off the dust, must shake off everything
> that covers him in order to appear like someone who has an identity,
> a name, which is what defines him.

THERE IS NO doubt that key figures during President Mitterrand's first term
of office from 1981 to 1988—Henri Emmanuelli, Georges Lemoine, Edgard
Pisani, and François Mitterrand himself—were fully conscious of the social
and economic discrimination to which the Kanak people were subject and
were very sympathetic to their political aspirations. They were likewise impressed by the personality of Jean-Marie Tjibaou—his charisma, his intelligence, his sincerity, and his lucidity. They were even determined to right
the wrongs of one and a half centuries of French colonial history. However,
they all too quickly learned that they were constrained in their actions by
the reality of sectarian violence on the ground in New Caledonia and the
dictates of the Constitution at home. Further, when called on to address the
question, they discovered that, like the vast majority of their compatriots,
they knew precious little about a small colony that was nineteen thousand
kilometers from Paris. While espousing the principles of self-determination
for colonized peoples, they had failed to realize the size and determination
of the territory's settler community, and the important (and essentially self-
serving) political relationships that existed between that community and
right-wing political parties in metropolitan France. In the final analysis, the
specter that came to haunt them in the case of New Caledonia was not that
of Algeria, but of Northern Ireland, hence of a potentially insoluble crisis.

In acquiring political power in France, the socialists rapidly came to appreciate that they had long-standing interests to protect and promote that
were not necessarily compatible with the demands of the Kanak indepen-

dentists. These were the interests and obligations of a middle-range world power, of a permanent member of the UN Security Council, of a country possessing nuclear weapons and still engaged in nuclear testing, of a state with a global reach and presence, and of a nation that possessed, in New Caledonia, a very substantial percentage of the world's nickel resources. France also felt itself particularly vulnerable, having been invaded and at least partly occupied on several occasions in recent history, notably during the Second World War. Against this perspective, overseas territories were perceived to play a crucial role in the reinforcement of a potentially fragile edifice. When Charles Pasqua, minister of the Interior in the Chirac government, came up with the formula, on his first visit to New Caledonia in 1986, that "La défense de Bastia commence à Nouméa" (The defense of Bastia[1] begins in Nouméa), he knew precisely what emotional chord he was striking. The same Charles Pasqua, in the same capacity (of being in charge of law enforcement), gave the order to storm the cave at Goosana on 5 May 1988.

In the real world of politics, the search for intermediate solutions, for compromise, is always possible. Such was Edgard Pisani's objective when, in January 1985, he proposed a model of self-government in free association, that is, of independence in association with France. It was a visionary model that was violently contested by loyalists in the territory, opposed in metropolitan France, and almost immediately rejected by President Mitterrand himself. Personal considerations apart—as to his "inscrutability"—the president, like the FLNKS, was conscious of the mounting pressure of the right wing in France; there was every possibility that it would win the legislative elections due the following year and install Jacques Chirac as prime minister. Already in November 1984 five former RPR prime ministers had addressed a "solemn appeal to the president of the Republic to avoid embarking on a process that would flout the wish of the majority in New Caledonia . . . and that would be contrary to the interests of France in the world and to its international vocation" (quoted in Mathieu 1995, 48). In the circumstances, Pisani's project came too late to satisfy either party. The battle lines had been drawn, suspicion was rife, and the window of political opportunity was closing. For the Kanak, independence had to be "now," and the political outcome of any negotiations must be achieved before March 1986. For the Caldoche it must be "never" or had at least to be delayed until after that date. It was a no-win situation.

Mitterrand and his various ministers' position with respect to the FLNKS was also determined by the French Constitution and, in a broader sense, by contemporary conceptions of citizenship and democracy as superior systems of government. Article One of the 1958 Constitution states:

> France is a Republic, undivided, secular, democratic and social. It ensures equality before the law of all its citizens without regard to origin, to race or to religion. . . .

[Article Two states:] The Republic's motto is Liberty, Equality, Fraternity.

Its principle is: government of the people, by the people, and for the people.

[Article Three specifies:] National sovereignty belongs to the people, who exercise it through their representatives and by referendum.

No group of people, no individual can attribute to itself this task.

Suffrage . . . is always universal, equal, and secret.

It is a model of society and of polity that recognizes individual civil rights and places everyone on an equal footing in the eyes of the state. Such is the nature of citizenship, a citizenship that recognizes only a single, undifferentiated, and undivided people—the French people. Having acquired French citizenship in the aftermath of the Second World War, the Kanak were recognized to be an integral part of the French people.

Viewed through the prism of the French Constitution and notably in the eyes of the political Right, "Il n'y a pas de peuple kanak" (There is no [such thing as a] Kanak people) and, perhaps even more dramatic, there is no possible Kanak view of the world, no Kanak reality, no Kanak legitimacy. The repeated insistence on this point by Bernard Pons, minister of DOM-TOM in the Chirac government, was both unqualified provocation to Jean-Marie and overtly discriminatory.

According to Pons and his friends . . . , we do not exist. Consequently we don't have our own claims, we are only reasoning on the basis of a pedantic or French leftist discourse. So we had this discussion. We said to Pons: "You treat us as ideologists, but it is according to your ideology that you say it. Why wouldn't we be capable of thinking? You only recognize the existence of those who conceive the world on the basis of your frame of thought, on the basis of technical superiority, on the basis of the fact that Europe went out into the world to conquer it with guns and boats and all that; and that what comes out of your mouth is the truth, which we, we are obliged to accept and to consider as being something fantastic." (Tjibaou 1996, 219–220)

To condemn the Constitution as being an ideological statement was inconceivable in the eyes of the Right, the possessors of power and the arbiters of progress and modernity. The French Constitution, like the American one, is widely considered to be a political, social, and cultural model for all of mankind. It is morally superior, just, and universally applicable. But from a Kanak perspective, it was a most effective means of condemning an entire people to minority status and political emasculation. It was also, as Jean-Marie repeatedly stressed, a cultural condemnation in that it struck at the foundations of Kanak identity. "Man is never an individual; he is immersed in a group. He is the center of relations and he has a role to play in a given center of relations" (Tjibaou 1996, 200). How then could a Kanak be called on to act politically as an individual if he were expected culturally to be integrated into a group?

In the eyes of Jean-Marie and the FLNKS, the Kanak people had an intrinsic right to exist, a right to be different, a right to be independent, and a right to choose what he called the "interdependencies" once nationhood was achieved. As early as 1979, Jean-Marie had expressed this view to a representative of the Catholic Justice and Peace movement that had been investigating the situation in New Caledonia. "[T]he Kanak people's struggle for freedom is a tough one, despite the sunshine. I would say that it's David against Goliath, and David has to seek the path in the bush in order to try and overcome a Goliath who has the means, who has the helicopters, who has the guns, who has everything. However we, we have the right. I hope that you will be able to share these ideas with your entourage, in France, so that right prevails, the right of the Kanak people, obviously, but it's a matter of right, quite simply" (1996, 99). Tragically, however, the Constitution did not recognize such a right, and French politicians' and civil servants' actions were dictated by the Constitution. For some this was by design, to consciously and systematically thwart and crush Kanak aspirations. For others it was by default, and they sought ways if not to circumvent it at least to limit its damaging effects.

Jean-Marie's repeated affirmation that "Injustice equals Inequality" was not lost on the Socialists. For that reason, to counter the mounting opposition of the right wing in both New Caledonia and France in 1984–1985, the Socialist government transformed the political organization of the territory, replacing the Territorial Assembly with four largely self-governing regions: North, Center, South, and Loyalties. The elected members of the four regional councils were in turn members of a Territorial Congress. The presidents of these five bodies formed the Executive Council, presided over by the French high commissioner in New Caledonia. In other words, the *statut Pisani-Fabius,* adopted in April 1985, resulted in the creation of a federal political and administrative structure, marked at once by a significant increase in power at the regional level and the loss of territorial autonomy in favor of the French governing authorities.

Elections were held in September 1985 and actively supported by the FLNKS; participation was massive, with 80 percent of the Kanak voting for one or other of the FLNKS parties. They obtained control of three of the four regions. Only the South, consisting essentially of Greater Nouméa, fell into the hands of the loyalists. Thus, through a strategy of political devolution, the Republican principle of majority rule was respected, but at the cost of the geographical separation of the two principal ethnic communities. Provisional satisfaction was thereby given to Kanak independentists, in that they acquired the opportunity to exercise power over the majority of the territory's land area, and assurance was given that efforts would be directed to a better redistribution of wealth within New Caledonia as a whole. The promise was also made that a referendum would be held on "independence, in association with France" by 31 December 1987—long after the elections in France and the expected return to power of the Right. This adroit political move of the Socialist government also satisfied the Caldoche loyalists in the short term, but their leader, Jacques Lafleur, was quick to remark that the Socialists had "given the majority to a minority" (quoted in Rollat 1989b, 235).

In the long run the impasse remained, insofar as the independentists were dedicated to the liberation of Kanaky and they were also fully aware that effective power was concentrated in Nouméa. For its part, the Socialist government remained sensitive to the issue of decolonization. Jean-Marie was advised in the highest places to circumvent the institutions of the state in order to plead his case. "It was François Mitterrand in person who had counseled him to address French public opinion directly, in order to convince it of his good faith, his moderation, and his spirit of reconciliation with respect to the Caldoches" (Rollat 1989b, 225). That was in January 1985, on the occasion of a visit to Paris in the aftermath of the Hienghène massacre, and in the wake of a brief visit of Mitterrand to Nouméa, loyalist riots in the city, the killing of Eloï Machoro, the declaration of a state of emergency throughout New Caledonia, and of Mitterrand's rejection of Edgard Pisani's self-government in free association project. Sentiment was growing that the territory was edging toward civil war and that the French president had stepped back. In inviting Jean-Marie Tjibaou, as the president of the Provisional Government of Kanaky, to directly address his own political constituency, President Mitterrand made a remarkable gesture that was in keeping with the Kanak leader's own political philosophy and values.

Jean-Marie did not seize on the opportunity until April 1987, halfway through the period of tense cohabitation between a socialist president and a right-wing prime minister. By this time he had decided how he would address the French people.[2] His model was that of the French president himself, as was the practice, of penning an open letter. Jean-Marie Tjibaou was also a president, of Kanaky, and he spoke on behalf of his own people, the Kanak, his words being directed to another people, the French, with whom their destinies were interwoven. The structure was purposely symmetrical. The tone was dignified, at once distant and familiar, while the message itself was pedagogical, generous, and pressing. In style and references, it evoked a fine knowledge of the underpinnings of French civilization and a deep concern to reveal to the French people the injustices to which his own people had been subjected, the nature of their values, and the legitimacy of their expectations. He sought to draw a distinction, in his "Lettre ouverte aux Français,"[3] between an intelligent and generous people and a government and political class that consciously and constantly misled them. "I have confidence in the people of France, those of the Declaration of Human Rights, of opposition to the Fascists, of decolonization in the 1960s. But is this people conscious of the simple fact that the Kanak—my people—have been and are still colonized, this being officially recognized by the United Nations?" (Tjibaou, reproduced in Milne 1996, 230).

The dialogue was based on mutual respect and comprehension and on principles of human rights that were vested in the Constitution itself. It also aimed at subverting the partisan actions of governments.

> The government wants to make us believe that its policy is a generous one. Its policy is a hoax: it's not France's policy but the policy of RPCR extremists. . . .
>
> The French people are too intelligent and too kind-hearted to fail to say to their elected representatives that they are being misled. Colonialism disfigures and weakens a people, in spite of first appearances. It is decolonization that makes them grow in stature and fortifies them. Don't spoil, don't let us spoil the chance for solidarity and friendship between the Kanak and French peoples. You know full well that only independence is capable of preserving both. For it alone will make it possible to define with you, with your country, new ties, no longer based on dependence and submission, but on dignity and cooperation between two sovereign and friendly states. Although successive governments of yours have betrayed us, today we possess, in your country, a network of solidarity and a certain current of sympathy at the level of public opinion which still allows us to dare to hope that your government will in time understand that in excluding us from its constitutional process, it assumes full responsibility for present and future provocations as well as for the tensions and troubles, the seeds of which are vested in its project. (Tjibaou, reproduced in Milne 1996, 230–231)

Jean-Marie terminated his letter by quoting Charles de Gaulle, possibly the sole postwar political figure who had sought to speak for the French people and the French nation, and at the same time to distance himself from the shallow arena of partisan politics. "De Gaulle said with regard to Tunisia, 'We must never insult the future'" (Tjibaou, reproduced in Milne 1996, 231).

Jean-Marie wrote as a statesman, seeking to inform and to counsel, explicitly inviting the French people to distance themselves from their political leaders. The letter contained a degree of confidence, even though the larger political context was a dramatic one.

A year later, in April 1988, Jean-Marie wrote directly to the French president. The election campaign was in full swing in France; Jacques Chirac was a candidate, as was the leader of the Front National, Jean-Marie Le Pen. The situation in New Caledonia was, to say the least, dramatic, with Bernard Pons, the minister of DOM-TOM, seeking to crush, both through the ballot box and by force, the Kanak independence movement. The tone of this second letter was significantly graver. "What future do you have in store for us, Mr President? Are we to be the last of the Mohicans for the Pacific region, like there were the last Tasmanians? You know that the Kanak people have always refused to be considered as some kind of archaeological relic in world history. They will be even more adamantly opposed to being the same in French colonial history" (Tjibaou 1996, 238). He went on to express his hope that François Mitterrand would be reelected because he had personally been a source of hope for the Kanak people, despite the Socialist government's failure to resolve the prevailing colonial situation. Under Chirac, it had considerably deteriorated and was likely to worsen in the days leading up to the territorial elections, to be held on 24 April — the same date as the first round of the presidential elections in France.

> Mr President, I am hoping for the return of liberties, the return to normal, in France as well as in New Caledonia. That is why I hope you will be reelected president, forming a different government that will not systematically imprison Kanak, like the present one does.
>
> Mr President, I trust that the message I am sending you will not be in vain. Our people are incurring greater and greater risks for their physical safety. I would like you to be able to confront French public opinion with its responsibilities, to solicit it during this electoral campaign, for it to realize that, within its midst, justice is being denied. Is it willing to tolerate at home practices that it denounces elsewhere, in South Africa or in the Occupied Territories? (Tjibaou 1996, 238–239)

It was still one president addressing another, but the tone was graver and there was a distinct air of skepticism about it. Bernard Pons was intending to crush the FLNKS, and more armed soldiers were being brought into New Caledonia. This time it was as if Mitterrand represented the last chance for the Kanak people.

The French president was on the point of penning his own "Lettre à tous les Français," outlining his electoral program, when he received Jean-Marie's plea and responded to him. François Mitterrand's sympathy for the cause, his respect for Jean-Marie Tjibaou as a person, his distant reading of the political and ethnic situation prevailing in New Caledonia, and his commitment to Republican principles are all revealed in a classic sibylline manner.

> [A]s I write these words, a message from M. Tjibaou is placed on my table. It is a cry for help and, at the same time, a reminder of the principles that inspire him. He is fighting for the independence of New Caledonia and, for him, New Caledonia is above all the Canaque people. I'm summarizing a little quickly, perhaps, his thinking. M. Tjibaou and his political party are not seeking to exclude those of French origin and other ethnic groups. They merely wish, if I may say so, to decide themselves, for they alone constitute universal suffrage.
>
> I am familiar with this theory. Over the seven years that I have been meeting him, M. Tjibaou has not changed. He is a man I respect, whose words go

further than words. But I do not believe that the historical precedence of the Canaques is sufficient to create rights. History against history: the Caledonians of European origin have also, through their toil, transformed that earth, been nourished by its substance, have put down roots. It is inconceivable that one community, confronted by the other, can durably impose its law, without the other and against the other—unless it is through recourse to violence, and there is a limit to violence. Independence, why not? If the population had been homogeneous, that is where New Caledonia would already be, like its neighbors. But independence in the present situation of a breakdown of relations between two populations of comparable size, means civil war, a war without mercy, and hence the crushing of one of the two camps. One can imagine which. The abused rights of the Canaques will only be identified, restored through internal peace, and the guarantor of this peace and of these rights can only be the French Republic. There is no other arbiter. I'm not stating a principle here; I'm recognizing a fact and a fact which ensures salvation for all. . . .

New Caledonia is advancing in the dark, banging into walls, hurting itself. The crisis it is experiencing comprises, in miniature, all the elements of a colonial drama. It is time to put an end to it. It is my hope that, during the coming weeks, the opposing communities will avoid the pitfalls of confrontation. Then I will use the authority confided in me to ensure that the history of France, at the other end of the world, regains its ancient wisdom. (Mitterrand, in Tjibaou 1996, 240–241)

New Caledonia was indeed advancing in the night; metropolitan France as well. On 22 April 1988 an FLNKS commando attacked the police post at Fayaoué, on Ouvéa, resulting in the killing of four gendarmes; then at dawn on 5 May the French military launched their attack on the cave at Goosana, leaving, by the early afternoon, nineteen Kanak militants and two French soldiers dead.

Between April 1987 and April 1988 Jean-Marie addressed one other letter to the French people, in December 1987.[4] It was written in France, in the context of yet another visit to meet President Mitterrand. The perpetrators of the massacre at Hienghène had just been acquitted by a jury that did not include a single Kanak. Bernard Pons was imposing his highly militarized reign over the territory. The United Nations General Assembly had reiterated its support for self-determination, but this time without the votes of the member nations of the European Community, who now favored the Republican logic of citizenship and of one person, one vote. This time the tone of his letter was despairing.

Alas, I have little hope! Little more hope to one day see a community based on friendship among all peoples take form in Kanaky. Today, in effect, there is no longer any justice. . . .

What remains to be done? We must continue what we have begun, but the limits to peaceful action are now apparent. Given the Hienghène verdict, it is no longer possible to stop there. We do not have the right to send our people to the slaughterhouse through mass nonviolent protests that make them easy targets for Fascists thirsty to "have a go with guns."

It is a sad and unfortunate situation, but we can no longer rely on the workings of institutions, nor on the manner in which justice is rendered in our country, to protect us from dying. . . .

I'm feeling very weary, weary of explaining to representatives who are constantly changing; explaining that we are human and that we no longer want others to determine, in place of us, our destiny, that's to say our life and death.

Relations of power no longer favor us when justice expresses itself in the way it has just done. There is nothing new about it; our fathers had the same experience. My tribe's village was burned twice in the course of history. In 1917 my father's mother was killed, the village burned, and I have relatives who died in prison.

I feel very weary faced with the increasing number of victims over the past century. . . .

Our only possible remaining hope is that public opinion finally shifts in France. Condolences and flowers placed on the bodies of victims are fine, but it's not enough. If opinion doesn't change, the government will not modify its policy of oppression on the ground.

I, Jean-Marie Tjibaou, am of no importance. It is the Kanak people that count. I come in their name, to say no, to say it has gone too far. Justice has been rendered in your name, that of the French people. You support such justice. . . . today, the further one goes, the further one is removed, the more Europeans risk being associated with the institutions which destroy all possibility of sharing. And, in this context, you too become a source of despair for our people. When a minister for the Francophonie speaks of us with contempt, how can one avoid posing the question: Should we continue to speak French?

Today there is not much hope left. There are people who have helped and who continue to help us. It's true, but it is not enough. When I say, we must buy guns, if it is legally possible; you know that I am speaking against my nature. However we are struggling for our freedom, and the freedom we demand is for the living, not for the dead. (Tjibaou, reproduced in Milne 1996, 231–232)

It was a dark letter, a last desperate cry for help and, above all, for the understanding that precedes action. It evoked the blind intolerance of political institutions and of those that momentarily take possession of them. For the first time it expressed doubts about the community of language and the larger world to which, by virtue of colonial history, education, and experience, the Kanak belonged. It was as if Jean-Marie sensed he had arrived at the edge of the abyss. A man "who had no wish for death" was now confronted by what he felt to be the unavoidable reality of violent death.

One ray of hope and one thread of solidarity with a small part of France did emerge in the 1980s—with the Larzac. In a geographical sense the Larzac is one of several limestone plateaus, termed in French *causses*, located to the south of the Massif Central and the west of the Cévennes. It is a part of the Rouergue, an ancient province more or less equivalent to the department of Aveyron, and a region that was first revealed to the intellectual and artistic worlds through Georges Rouquier's classic 1946 film *Farrebique*. The filmmaker had shared, over an entire year, the life of a peasant family. In it he described the unbroken cycle of seasons and of generations, and of the dictates of a land that transcends the passing needs of the people who work it. "Farrebique; it is the day-to-day song which mingles with the symphony of the seasons" (www.lesdocs.com/fiches/vid05.htm).

The Larzac is probably best known today for José Bové, one of the charismatic leaders of the *alter-mondialisation* movement, and for the architectural wonder that spans the Tarn gorge in which its regional center, Millau, is located. The highest bridge in the world, it was opened in 2004, and has served to greatly accelerate the flow, along autoroute 75, of tourists traveling south to the warm shores of the Mediterranean and of Spanish fruit and vegetables being delivered to the tables of northern Europe. The autoroute cuts through the very heart of the region, their juxtaposition epitomizing two radically different ways of inhabiting the earth.

Some one thousand square kilometers of high plateau[5] lying immediately to the south of the Tarn, the Larzac is a cold, bleak area in winter, and the economy has for long been based essentially on sheep, more specifically ewes, whose milk is sold to the producers of Roquefort cheese. In the 1950s and 1960s the Larzac sheep farmers were leading semi-subsistence existences with only small flocks of sheep, while as recently as the early 1990s the region "provides, overall, only about 3 percent of the milk used in the fabrication of Roquefort. Yet, the plateau—with its open space, unpolluted environment, and tradition of production by small peasants—remains the symbol of purity and rural wholesomeness that—the industrialists never cease to remind the public—is its *sine qua non*. It is even claimed that the best quality Roquefort is made from the milk of the Larzac sheep fed on grasses native to the *causse*" (Alland with Alland 1994, 6–7). By definition and by tradition the peasant inhabitants struggled to survive, but they were also celebrated by the consumers of the end product of their labors.

Another feature of the Larzac is a military base, established in 1902 over an area of three thousand hectares, and characterized by an agreement that the peasants could graze their sheep within its confines when there were no maneuvers underway. In turn, the military could install their artillery batteries on the commune's land (Alland with Alland 1994, 16), thereby having the possibility of operating over up to one hundred thousand hectares of the *causse*.

By the 1960s the population of the Larzac was in serious decline and also aging rapidly. At the same time use of the military camp was increasing, its facilities being leased out to the armed forces of other European countries. In 1971 Georges Pompidou's minister of defense, Michel Debré, announced his government's intention to expand it to a total of seventeen thousand hectares. This would involve the expropriation of 107 essentially small peasant holdings, a seemingly simple exercise. Reality proved very different, as 103 of the landowners formally opposed the initiative. They and the land they owned became the center of the Larzac militant movement and the focus of a ten-year struggle to thwart the French government. This small core of *purs porcs*—peasant farmers with deep historic roots in the Larzac, for the most part Catholic and conservative—rapidly attracted a broad spectrum of allies: Maoists, hippies, Occitan regionalists, left-wing Catholics, worker-priests, pacifists, *soixante-huitards* (antiestablishmentarians), academics, and union activists. An exceptionally dynamic social movement quickly took form, inspired by the events of 1968 and by a growing ecological and regional consciousness, resulting in it becoming one of the few regions of remote rural France to experience economic revitalization. By virtue of its charismatic internal leaders and prestigious external allies, the movement acquired a remarkable degree of visibility, credibility, and internal cohesion that was unique for so diverse a membership. Of the external allies the most important were probably François Roux, a protestant lawyer from Montpellier but with deep roots in the Cévennes, and Lanza del Vasto, a disciple of Gandhi and an apostle of nonviolence who had established a community at La Borie Noble on the southern margins of the Larzac. Both were committed, in their respective ways, to the promotion of justice through the application of their religious convictions in their daily lives. The one defended in the courts people engaged in civil disobedience—notably conscientious objectors to military service—while the other was founder of L'Arche. This deeply spiritual movement had established a number of small communities in Europe devoted to voluntary simplicity, sharing, reconciliation, and respect, where work, prayer, silence, song, and festivities all had their place. In brief, both men were concerned with the power of truth, opposition to injustice and violence, and respect for the adversary.

Almost from the outset, members of L'Arche joined the opposition to the extension of the military base. Then, in 1972, Lanza del Vasto committed himself to the movement, while expressing a strong cautionary note, if not a condition. "I will make you a gift; the gift of two weeks of my life. During this period I will fast, and you, you will reflect on the action you must take. I suggest to you nonviolent action because this speaks to the conscience of your opponents" (del Vasto, quoted in Roux with Vilacèque 2002, 34).

Lanza del Vasto had been active in most of the major postwar protest movements in France, notably against the war in Algeria and the resort to torture in the course of it, as well as against the possession and testing of nuclear weapons. His strategy was one of active nonviolence and his presence defined the character of the Larzac movement. For some of its members, acting in such a way was the expression of a moral conviction—to be, in a sense, the Gandhians of Europe—while for others it was a tactic in the face of the superior force of the opposition. Endowed with its spiritual and essentially Christian dimension, the Larzac movement attracted the support of the Catholic bishops of Montpellier and Rodez. Retired senior military figures were also attracted to it—Admiral Antoine Sanguinetti and General Jacques Bollardière. François Mitterrand himself was fascinated by the struggle, while Michel Rocard was an active supporter from the outset.

François Roux became involved in the Larzac in the mid-1970s as links developed between conscientious objectors and peasants who returned their military papers. Increasingly involved in human rights issues—first the European Convention on Human Rights and then the Universal Declaration of Human Rights—he started to defend Larzac militants in the courts and to counsel them on initiatives they might take themselves, in the form of *la guérilla judiciaire*. He was the principal legal architect of "combat without violence," and it was a combat that, after ten years of struggle on the Larzac, in the courtroom, and in the streets, proved eminently successful. The struggle was marked by a variety of public and highly symbolic acts: marches, demonstrations, "happenings," and also gestures that exhibited a great deal of humor, as when a flock of ewes invaded the courtroom at Millau or were put to graze beneath the Eiffel Tower.

François Mitterrand, as Parti Socialiste candidate in the 1981 presidential elections, made it clear that, if he was elected, he would abandon the project to expand the military camp. On 10 May 1981 he defeated Jacques Chirac in the second round of the elections. "One of Mitterrand's first official acts, taken against the advice of his minister of defense, was to cancel the extension plan. *He had kept his word*" (Alland with Alland 1994, 66; my italics).

In their struggle against the French authorities the Larzac peasants received support from throughout France and elsewhere in Europe. Comités Larzac were created outside the *causse*, while a Larzac *université* was established there, and academics from Paris came, offering workshops "with" as distinct from "on" the peasants. One of them was the historian and Asian specialist Jean Chesneaux. They practiced committed scholarship, moving between observation and action, and seeking solutions to real-world crises. Links were also formed with peasant and protest movements elsewhere in the world, notably the Polish union Solidarity and the Japanese peasants fighting against the extension of Narita airport. In French prisons Larzac militants met Polynesians opposed to nuclear testing on Moruroa, and in 1979 the lawyer François Roux traveled to Tahiti to defend other Oceanian militants in court. There he experienced for the first time the travesty of justice through outright racial prejudice. He met Tahitian independentists who prayed and sang *himéné*, a lawyer from Nouméa, Gustave Tehio, who defended them, and Kanak militants who had traveled to Tahiti as an expression of solidarity for their fellow Oceanian activists. At this time Roux sensed that victory in the Larzac was close, and he was looking for human rights causes to defend elsewhere in the world.

On the Larzac itself the decision was made, following the 1981 victory and in the light of the experience gained, to offer support and assistance to peasant movements elsewhere, preferably in the third world. Solidarity was the guiding principle. A Fondation Larzac was created and, with the aid of François Roux, the Kanak cause became the focus of its attention, a situation that prevailed until 1989. Roux brought the first Kanak visitor to the Larzac in 1982, and he was first called to Nouméa in 1983 to defend the Kanak of Koindé-Ouipouni, implicated in the killing of two gendarmes in the course of a dispute with a logging company. However, the Hienghène massacre in December 1984 led to the development of close ties between the Kanak and Larzac peoples, this time with Jean-Marie Tjibaou as a crucial actor. Following the massacre, François Roux returned to New Caledonia with Pierre Parodi, Lanza del Vasto's successor at the head of L'Arche, following the latter's death in 1981. On this occasion he first met Jean-Marie Tjibaou.

> I told him about the struggle on the Larzac and about L'Arche. I suggested that the Kanaks attempt to achieve independence nonviolently. He told me to write a letter to him on my return to France and I did so. On my return I got together with Hervé Ott [founder of the Centre de recherche et de formation à la défense civile et populaire non-violente, located at Le Cun] and Pierre Parody [*sic*] in the Cévennes. In our letter we proposed an exchange between the Kanaks and the plateau. The Kanaks wrote to us accepting our proposition and then Hervé went there and did an excellent job teaching nonviolence. After that, a Kanak delegation came to the Larzac where they were very well received. (François Roux, quoted in Alland with Alland 1994, 88)

Jean-Marie was a member of that first delegation, which also included Yeiwéné Yeiwéné and Léopold Jorédié. They came in late April 1985 at a time when the prospect of the Parti Socialiste losing the forthcoming national elections was looming and when President Mitterrand had counseled Jean-Marie to communicate directly with the French people. In these dark times the discovery of the Larzac was a revelation. Face-to-face contact with a group of Larzac militants had been made at a rally in Paris in support of the Kanak cause, Jean Chesneaux being the architect of the meeting and introducing Jean-Marie to them. They invited him to visit the Larzac and immediately a remarkable synergy sprang up between the two communities.

For Jean-Marie the engagement with the Larzac was much more than a simple question of acquiring understanding and support in France; it was as if all the pieces of the Kanak puzzle came together there (figure 18). He encountered a people who had thwarted a state initiative directed to the

FIGURE 18. Jean-Marie on one of his several visits to the Larzac, where he found friends, comfort, and a possible way forward for the Kanak people. *(ADCK-Centre Culturel Tjibaou)*

expropriation of their land, without the loss of a single life. They applied their Christian beliefs in their daily lives. Their movement included a broad range of interest groups and was supported by local representatives of the Catholic Church as well as the mayor of the neighboring town of Millau. Perhaps most significant, it placed culture before the dictates of the economy. It had created collectively owned land banks (Groupements fonciers agricoles [GFA]) to help establish young people on the land and revitalize the rural economy. As in Kanaky, the struggle on the Larzac had been motivated primarily by considerations of dignity and justice, and the desire to maintain the people on the land.

Louis Mapou, now chief executive officer of the Société Minière du Sud Pacifique and a student in France at the time, recalled asking Jean-Marie what he thought of the Larzac delegation he had met at the demonstration in Paris and who had invited him to visit them. He immediately replied, "Did you see their hands?!" (Mapou, pers comm, 20 Jan 1998). The Larzac peasants were the same as the Kanak; Jean-Marie had the sense of discovering "indigenous Europe," in a demographic as well as an ethnic sense. "I can still see him on the occasion of his first visit to the plateau, standing transfixed before this poster which announced, 'We won because we were the weakest'" (Roux with Vilacèque 2002, 63).

People on the Larzac expressed similar sentiments on the occasion of that initial meeting. They are inscribed on a plaque standing on a small piece of land belonging to Le Cun that the people of the Larzac offered in usufruct to their Kanak friends on the occasion of Jean-Marie's last visit in June 1988. He had been in Paris to negotiate the Matignon Accords.

> A man is there who addresses us, slowly,
> the eyes lowered. He draws everything together in
> this spoken word where each individual word appears to be
> chosen especially for us, for this precise
> moment, here. It is a gist of the word that is made to us
> there, a true gift. . . .
> Surprise, emotion, pleasure . . . time stops . . .
> yes, these words are well and truly words which
> prevent time from existing! Between his
> memory and ours, between his history and
> ours something is being woven, between his distant
> island and our stony earth something
> is being formed. And if it were to be a customary
> path?

All the symbolism was there in the Larzac connection: the spoken word, the vocabulary, the attachment to the land, the spirituality—and the humor too. "Jean-Marie officiated at the ceremony. About to cut the ribbon at the entrance to Kanaky-Larzac, he said—with that ironic sense of humor much appreciated by those who knew him—'I take possession of France'" (Alland with Alland 1994, 88). Thus the *rire mélanésien* merged with the *rire Occitan*,[6] serving as another expression of the bond that had been spontaneously established between an indigenous and a peasant people, the one Oceanian and the other European. That bond was vested in the distinctive but at once familiar rhythms that are authentic expressions of the close interweaving of society and seasons, of a people with their inherited earth.

When Jean-Marie arrived that first time on the Larzac it was evident he wanted to learn as much about their experience as they wished to know about his. According to Marizette Tarlier, in whose house he always stayed, he was fascinated by their attachment to the land and their practice of non-violence, that they were Europeans who understood in a political sense the nature of the Kanak struggle, and that they had been able to establish young people on the land. They were Catholics like him, and he was also impressed that the clergy supported them in their struggle, as did the mayor of Millau. Indeed, in order to give an official character to each of Jean-Marie's visits to the Larzac, the mayor always formally welcomed him at the Town Hall. What fascinated him most of all was that they had won, in their battle against the French state and in their project to revitalize Larzac society and economy. He was curious about everything—sheep, cheese, small farmers, the land banks (GFA), the fact that Marizette and her husband, Guy,[7] had lived for many years as planters in the Central African Republic, had experienced that country's passage to independence, and had stayed on without difficulty.

> We had in common the struggle for freedom that is grounded in the earth; we are, like them, peasants and we well understand their struggle, tied to the occupation of the land, first of all as a means of survival, of livelihood. And also the fact that it is the battle of a minority against a cultural majority. We are first and foremost peasants, who work the earth. We experience the same feelings when the military take possession of our very lands, when we are repressed by them. I believe that the people of the Larzac experience in the same way as us the struggle here.
>
> The support of the Larzac is very important to us, sentimentally and politically. It is a good example for us, because the struggle drew them together even more strongly. They won because they roused the conscience of the majority. (Tjibaou 1996, 214)

These sentiments were expressed to a reporter from the *Journal des Objecteurs* (a publication of the French conscientious objectors movement). They reveal how much Jean-Marie was impressed by the similarities between the two situations and "that it was necessary to defend the land in order to transmit ideas." He was also deeply impressed that the people of the Larzac had won precisely because they had not resorted to violence. At the same time his Larzac hosts, Marizette and Guy Tarlier, were also very conscious of the need to temper his enthusiasm by insisting on the differences between the two places. The Larzac was not a colony, and their movement was only faced with the riot police (CRS), whereas the Kanak were confronted by the army.

However, the extent to which the Larzac influenced Jean-Marie in his beliefs and actions in the last years of his life remains unclear. Did it turn him into a pacifist as is often intimated? In a sense, the question irritated him profoundly, journalists often posing it at the height of the *événements* in New Caledonia. His response to them was unambiguous. "Nonviolence, for us, is not a doctrine, only an occasional strategy, dictated by the circumstances and which pays off for us. For how long, I have no idea. The political right, right from the beginning, plans repression. They provoke us into reacting, which in turn allows them to hit our movement hard and silence it. We are more intelligent than they are, and our actions are designed to increase the awareness of our people, but also to bring national and international public opinion to recognize the justice of our struggle and to obtain their support" (1996, 228).

Jean-Marie was always a pragmatist and never a purist. He was not simply defending a just cause before the long arm of the state; he was increasingly confronted by other groups, on the ground, who were concerned to thwart the aspirations of his people by acting as much outside as within the law. He had to adapt his strategy to a constantly evolving situation in New Caledonia. As he said to François Roux, "Nonviolence, yes; but with the gun at our feet" (Roux with Vilacèque 2002, 64). Nevertheless, he was increasingly weary of violence and of the repeated loss of lives, and he sought ways to put an end to both. So, at one point, under his direction, the FLNKS proposed a peaceful mass march for the length of the Grande Terre, from Poum to Nouméa, to signal the Kanak people's opposition to the referendum Bernard Pons planned for September 1987. It would have been along the lines of those undertaken by Gandhi and Martin Luther King Jr. However, given the strong military presence in the form of *nomadisation*, the idea was rapidly abandoned in favor of fifteen local marches. Even some of these smaller marches were violently suppressed.

Jean-Marie most certainly got valuable ideas from the Larzac. He also acquired substantial legal assistance to fight in the courts of Nouméa, and a number of young Kanak received training in the philosophy and practice of nonviolence at Le Cun. However, perhaps more than anything else, the Larzac served as an emotional refuge for him and for his close collaborators in the difficult years from 1985 to 1988. Whenever they went to Paris they suffered, by virtue of it being a cold, anonymous city, but also because they found themselves, particularly during the period of cohabitation between Mitterrand and Chirac, in an overtly hostile negotiating environment. The Larzac was a place where they could rest and recharge their batteries. Jean-Marie would call the Tarliers from Paris to ask "Can I come to the bush?"! It helped restore his confidence in the French people. His last public words to the people of the Larzac, expressed on 19 June 1988 on the occasion of a tree-planting ceremony on the plot of land given to the Kanak people (figure 19), ended with the affirmation:

> Today we are particularly happy to be here and to share your meals because *it is the sign that we are humans.* . . .
> KANAKY LARZAC
> A pathway that is now inscribed in tradition

These words, too, are inscribed on the plaque that stands on the site, because "Jean-Marie said, at each visit, 'On the Larzac, I feel like I am in the tribe. . . . Here one feels good, the earth breathes'" (Chesneaux 1989, 24; my italics).

FIGURE 19. Kanaky Larzac: The plot of land symbolically offered to the Kanak people in the aftermath of the Ouvéa crisis. The tree in the foreground was planted by Jean-Marie in June 1988. Marie-Claude came a year later to lay the first stone of the *casselle,* the dry-stone shelter that for long served as a dwelling, sheepfold, or to store equipment on the *causse. (Eric Waddell)*

9   *From Ouvéa to Matignon, and Back to Ouvéa*

> Jean-Marie lowers his eyes. His voice, strained with emotion,
> becomes weaker. Is he thinking of his own brothers, killed in the
> ambush at Hienghène? "We had to choose: to continue killing
> one another or to build the future. . . ." Once again, the former
> priest made his choice: "Between a poor agreement and killing
> one another, we preferred not to kill one another."
> Alain Rollat, *Tjibaou le Kanak*, 264

As DAWN BROKE on the morning of 5 May 1988, the elite of the French
armed forces launched an assault on the cave at Goosana. Their objective
was to release the twenty-three hostages taken following the bungled attack
on the police post at Fayaoué some thirteen days earlier. Fourteen of them
were gendarmes captured on 22 April, eight were French military, and one a
magistrate, all of whom had been taken hostage—or had allowed themselves
to be taken hostage—in the course of negotiations with the hostage-takers.
One hundred and thirty soldiers were directly engaged in the action, backed
by helicopters. Ouvéa had been closed to the press since the beginning of
the crisis, the village of Goosana was occupied, villagers had been beaten if
not tortured, and property had been damaged. Although no formal state of
emergency had been declared, such was the reality on the ground. Bernard
Pons, the minister of DOM-TOM, was present on the island to witness what
one New Zealand observer described as "the scene of the bloodiest operation by a European army in the Pacific since World War Two" (Small 1997,
63). Following a second attack around midday, the outcome was nineteen
Kanak and two French soldiers killed, with among the former, a twenty-
two-year-old "tea boy" from Goosana, one of several who delivered food
and drink on a daily basis to all the occupants of the cave. According to
witnesses, another Kanak, Vince Lavelloi was summarily "executed," while a
third, Alphonse Dianou, was "allowed to die," both after the hostage-takers

had surrendered to the military. All but one of the Kanak who died in the military operation were in their twenties and thirties. In all it is estimated that up to three thousand shots were fired, tear gas and hand grenades were thrown, and a flamethrower was used to "neutralize" a machine gun that had been taken, along with other weapons, from the armory at Fayaoué.

Thirty-three Kanak were taken prisoner by the military during the operation, and twenty-nine of them were almost immediately flown to France and placed in five different prisons in and around Paris. Medical examinations on arrival there revealed that eight of them had been beaten, spent long periods in chains, and had cigarette burns on their skin. They had arrived in France in the same state as they had been taken prisoner, often in shorts and torn T-shirts, and without any personal possessions. Djubelly Wéa was among them. The principal victims of the drama—those who were held responsible for the detention of the hostages, those whose village was occupied by the military, and those who were systematically humiliated and who figured among the dead—were from Goosana. Once again they were the martyrs.

The overall tone, the strategy adopted to resolve the hostage-taking crisis in Ouvéa, and the brutality that surrounded it had been set by the prime minister at the time, Jacques Chirac, and by Bernard Pons. Falling between the first and second rounds of the presidential elections in France, the Ouvéa crisis served to fuel a bitter electoral confrontation between François Mitterrand and the Parti Socialiste on the one hand, and Jacques Chirac and the Rassemblement pour la République on the other. Adding fuel to the fire, the latter were actively courting the votes that had gone to Jean-Marie Le Pen and his extreme right-wing Front National in the first round.[1] As prime minister, Jacques Chirac was in charge of the government of France and, specifically, the armed forces. He, not President Mitterrand, had the responsibility of addressing the crisis. In opting for armed confrontation rather than negotiation he was almost certainly motivated by partisan political considerations as distinct from the overriding interest of the state. There is no doubt that a nonviolent outcome would have been possible. Members of the military favored it. Right from the second day of the crisis, direct contact had been established between the leaders of the Union Calédonienne—Jean-Marie Tjibaou, Yeiwéné Yeiwéné, and Léopold Jorédié—and the hostage-takers. Jean-Marie was also in contact with Edgard Pisani, who was a special adviser to François Mitterrand at the time. In the course of the exchanges between the UC leaders and the hostage-takers, three conditions were rapidly formulated for liberation of the hostages: the withdrawal of the military from Ouvéa, the canceling of the 24 April elections in New Caledonia, and the nomination by the president and the prime minister of a mediator. In subsequent exchanges between Jean-Marie Tjibaou and Edgard Pisani, the conditions were reduced to the immediate transport of the hostage-takers to Paris, imprisonment, and a fair trial, in return for liberation of the captured gendarmes. The hostage-takers themselves were convinced until the very end that they would be visited by French television journalists and have the opportunity to voice their grievances to the public. As the days passed it became increasingly evident that this was the only possible way of escaping the clutches of a hostile military and political leadership. However, no such occasion was provided, for Ouvéa was effectively isolated from the rest of the world. In the circumstances a nonviolent outcome was inconceivable.

The vocabulary used by Jacques Chirac, Bernard Pons, and Jean-Marie Le Pen from the very beginning of the crisis was an inflammatory one: "insurrection," "armed struggle," "terrorism," "barbarity," "guerrilla warfare." . . . Further, as far as the French military was concerned, their "honor" was at stake, with some of them at least being motivated by considerations of "vengeance." Bernard Pons arrived in New Caledonia on the night of 23–24 April with full authority accorded by Chirac to determine the actions to be taken. His logic was unfailing: the FLNKS and the Kanak independence movement as a whole had to be crushed. In his mind there was never any question of conducting negotiations with the hostage-takers or the FLNKS. It was the logic Pons had imposed on New Caledonia since his appointment as minister of DOM-TOM a little more than two years earlier, and its direct consequence had been a spiral of increasing prejudice, sectarian violence, and injustice. Confronted by an intransigent political regime, the Kanak were rapidly losing any remaining faith in the institutions of democracy and the integrity of the French state.

In a very real sense the outcome of the hostage taking at Fayaoué and the violent assault on the cave at Goosana had been sealed in Nouméa on 29 October 1987, with the acquittal of the perpetrators of the 1984 ambush at Hienghène. On learning of the judgment Jean-Marie had, with frightening premonition, announced, "It's logical. That means one can shoot down Kanaks like dogs. . . . There will be no justice for the Kanaks as long as there is no independence. That means that justice can only be achieved through the barrel of a gun. The Kanak people must, as of now, prepare themselves" (quoted in Plenel and Rollat 1988, 16). The same event and the same realization had prompted Alphonse Dianou to leave the seminary in Suva, return to New Caledonia, engage first in the promotion of nonviolent action among young people within the Union Calédonienne, and then, at the end, take charge of the hostage-takers in the cave. This final decision no doubt also explains why elements in the French military purposely left him to die outside the cave after he had given himself up.

An adolescent shows the letter Alphonse Dianou left for an aunt prior to his departure for Ouvéa, some two months ago. Fifteen or so lines written in capital letters with a few small letters scattered here and there in the middle of the words. . . . The former seminarian; the advocate of nonviolence who was arrested after the brutally suppressed manifestation of September 1987 on the Place des Cocotiers, in Nouméa; he who had never been seen with a weapon in his hand, "not even a stone," speaks only of "fighting until death": "Even if we need to fight to eternity, from eternity to eternity, we will fight, we will fight to the end." And he concluded with a "Take heart!" and an elaborately laced signature. On his treasured photocopy, the boy had penciled, without attention to spelling, "Pray for us."[2] (Plenel and Rollat 1988, 188–189)

With the hostage taking at Fayaoué and the attack on the cave at Goosana, New Caledonia had moved a second time to the brink of civil war. Directly caught in the sights of the presidential elections, the drama of the Kanak people had also finally attracted the attention of the French public at large and of metropolitan human rights groups. SOS-Racisme and the Ligue des droits de l'Homme both demanded that an independent enquiry be held into the manner in which the crisis was handled. New Caledonia had ceased to be an obscure, distant French territory.

Jean-Marie himself was weary, weary of being systematically confronted by injustice, weary of the mounting hatred of the Kanak people displayed by vocal and influential elements of the local European and immigrant communities, and weary of having to repeatedly explain and justify expectations and actions to innumerable politicians, government officials, and journalists from France, seemingly without ever being understood. Given Chirac's refusal to negotiate with "terrorists," he and his close collaborators within the Union Calédonienne had vested their hopes in the hostage-takers being able to hold out until 8 May, when it was expected that François Mitterrand would be reelected. But even that option had failed. Further, the vast majority of those who had died on Ouvéa were Kanak, three of them in circumstances that suggested "extra-judicial" killings. The situation in the hours following the release of the hostages could not have appeared more desperate for his people. Nevertheless, the rapid succession of events that followed led to New Caledonia and France, Kanak and Caldoche stepping back from the void.

On 8 May François Mitterrand was reelected president of the Republic, with 54 percent of the votes compared to 46 percent for Jacques Chirac. The result put an end to two years of cohabitation between a left-wing president and a right-wing prime minister. The outcome was also a crushing defeat for the Right, its worst result since 1958, when the Fifth Republic was established. Two days later the president appointed Michel Rocard as prime minister, immediately delegating to him the urgent task of seeking a solution through dialogue to the New Caledonian crisis. Both events were prudently welcomed by Jean-Marie, in part no doubt because, in New Caledonia, the vast majority of Kanak had abstained from voting, while the rest of the electorate had voted massively in favor of Chirac.

From a Kanak perspective, Michel Rocard was a well-received nomination. He was a social democrat committed to the constant interweaving of ideas and action, and to the resolution of conflicts through negotiation rather than violence. Negotiation necessarily meant compromise, and compromise could provide the foundations for a shared future. In a sense, his was a very Melanesian approach to conflict resolution, insofar as it was based on the premise that all parties have legitimate interests and grievances. Rocard was also a Protestant, which meant not simply sharing the religion—and the religious intuitions—of the majority of Kanak,[3] but also possessing, in the context of metropolitan France, a distinctive education and culture, together with the heritage of having been a member of an oppressed minority. As a Socialist and a Protestant he was a declared anticolonialist and, significantly, an opponent of a highly centralized state. In other words, his approach to New Caledonia was dictated as much by personal cultural preoccupations as by broad economic and organizational considerations. In the 1960s he had been one of the architects of the *deuxième gauche* in France, a different Left that was committed to decentralization and to local organization. In addition, he had been active in the events of May 1968 and had subsequently become involved in the Larzac crisis. On the election of François Mitterrand as president in 1981 he was appointed minister of regional planning (Aménagement du territoire) and given the responsibility of visiting that bleak and obstinate plateau to elaborate on the new government's decision to abandon plans to extend the military base. For him, the occasion was memorable.

> Today's reader will have great difficulty imagining the unique, fabulous and amusing spectacle which took place at the time and which we will no doubt never see again. There were a large number of activists on the plateau. . . . It was like in May 68; not a single cloud in the sky. The Republican police motorcyclists, in full regalia, slowly opened the way, in the midst of militants who were singing and waving masses of banners and placards, to allow the passage of the official procession. Which official procession, jolting along a bad dirt road, consisted of four tractors almost hidden under the flags, followed by a solitary official car, a black Renault, mine, then again half-a-dozen tractors. The formal ceremony was cut short by the cheering. We took our revenge with the libations. (Rocard 2003a, 27)

In an intellectual and figurative sense, the paths of Jean-Marie Tjibaou and Michel Rocard had crossed on the Larzac (figure 20). Perhaps their respective visions of a just and welcoming society, of a way around violence, had found common ground there as well?

Rocard assumed personal responsibility for New Caledonia, and within a week of his appointment as prime minister he formed a group whose purpose was to reestablish dialogue between opposing parties in the territory. It was composed of six personalities drawn from different political and reli-

FIGURE 20. Michel Rocard, the man who gave his word and in whom Jean-Marie expressed confidence. *(ADCK-Centre Culturel Tjibaou/ Gamma)*

gious spheres, whose specific mission was to establish the bases on which an agreement could be reached between the Kanak and European communities as to their common future. Monsignor Paul Gilberteau was rector of the Institut Catholique de Paris, Jacques Stewart was a pastor and president of the Fédération protestante de France, while Roger Leray was a Freemason and former grand master of the Grand Orient de France. The other three members were senior civil servants: Christian Blanc, the head of mission and Edgard Pisani's secretary-general for New Caledonia in 1984–1985, Jean-Claude Périer, former head of police and military justice, and Pierre Steinmetz, who had been a chargé de mission in the cabinet of prime minister Raymond Barre. All could be characterized as men motivated by moral considerations and committed to action based on a capacity to listen rather than on ideology based on prior knowledge and abstract understanding. They also mirrored the principal actors and interest groups in New Caledonia.

Arriving in Nouméa on 20 May, this ecumenical mission was given until 29 June—the date of Rocard's inaugural address at the Council of Ministers—to satisfy two purposes. "[T]he principal objective of this mission is to restore peace among the citizens, peace that has been seriously threatened. But its aim is also to lay, for the future, the foundations of a 'common accord between the communities'" (Freyss 1995, 63).

As in the immediate aftermath of the massacre at Hienghène, Jean-Marie opted for peaceful dialogue rather than violent riposte. Three weeks after the assault on the cave at Ouvéa, he agreed to meet the dialogue mission. On this occasion, according to Alain Rollat, a peace plan was submitted to him that would include a constitutionally guaranteed referendum on independence for New Caledonia.

> Christian Blanc . . . was finding it extremely difficult to figure out his host's [Jean-Marie Tjibaou] position. He decided therefore, in the course of a lengthy private conversation, to add an idea of his own making to the propositions he had to submit to the two opposing camps. So he got the impression of being caught out when Jean-Marie said to him in the course of the evening, at Tiendanite: "Then if it's like that, we're agreed!"
>
> The prime minister's emissary had just proposed the idea of guaranteeing the future of the territory by negotiating a peace plan, the content of which would be constitutionally guaranteed by the organization of a national referendum, and Jean-Marie had just accepted it on the basis of a simple, instinctive reflex. (Rollat 1989b, 259)

Whether Jean-Marie's reflex was motivated by confidence or despair, or by a mix of both, will never be known. With respect to confidence, the return of the Parti Socialiste to power in France and the reelection of François Mitterrand as president meant that he probably sincerely hoped that the legitimate aspirations of the Kanak people would finally be recognized. In terms of despair, he no doubt understood that, once again, his people had paid the price in blood of challenging the implacable logic of democracy and the authority of the state, that there was a limit to the number of deaths they could sustain, that perhaps their only hope lay in compromise. However Freyss also noted that he "admitted in July 1988 that FLNKS mobilization in favor of the active boycott had been very uneven, badly organized and was globally weak. The limited success of the 'March' organized during the summer of 1987 to peacefully protest the Pons referendum (this March was a direct allusion to the 1930 Salt March, a campaign of civil disobedience organized by Mahatma Gandhi), together with failure of the Pacific Games boycott, had revealed the gulf that existed between the weakness of Kanak political organization and the population's deep attachment to the struggle for its dignity" (1995, 62).

The experience of Ouvéa had revealed that the Kanak people were locked in a downward spiral where they were pushed to act outside the law, in a more and more violent and desperate manner. In turn the state was reacting in an increasingly heavy-handed and confrontational way, as demonstrated by the decision to use the elite of the French armed forces rather than the police to resolve the latest crisis. Since 1986 more and more of these forces had been stationed in New Caledonia, required to act in what was for them an unfamiliar situation; military honor had been soiled on several occasions. The French political leadership and senior civil servants had demonstrated over the last two years that it was impossible to resolve the situation through a narrow application of the Constitution. And in Ouvéa, the Kanak people had once again demonstrated that they did not have the means to successfully engage in physical resistance. They possessed neither the organizational nor the military capacity to effectively protest or even to resist. New Caledonia had reached a turning point where the only options were reconciliation or bloody and prolonged sectarian violence. The possibility of outright civil war was nourished by the memory of Algeria and the image of Northern Ireland, as well as the growing presence of armed militia groups in the territory.

Within a span of three short weeks the dialogue mission met with more than twelve hundred people and heard, time and again, that enough blood and tears had been spilled. "They listen to the Caledonians evoking their day-to-day problems, recounting their past and affirming their attachment to this land. They make more and more symbolic gestures, kneel before the graves of the victims of the attack at Ouvéa, respect custom and meet gendarmes" (Pitoiset 1999, 181). The mission took great care to adopt a cultural approach to the different communities, recognizing their specificities, respecting their differences, listening to their aspirations and, without a doubt gaining a considerable degree of respect and confidence in the process. Nowhere was off limits for them, not even Goosana or the mass grave at Hwaadrila. Respects were paid and customary gestures made. Their visit to Ouvéa on 25 May was followed, the next day, by a meeting with Jean-Marie at Hienghène and a visit to his tribe at Tiendanite, which involved a brief but vital stop at the memorial to the December 1984 ambush. According to Plenel and Rollat, at his initial meeting with the dialogue mission, Jean-Marie expressed yet again his analysis of the situation and his aspirations, with the hope that, following the return of a socialist president and government to power in France, they would no longer fall on deaf ears. "He reminded them that 'the Kanaks demand their native land there where their home is' and it is essential therefore 'to find, seated around the table, a binding answer to the claim.' According to him, institutional solutions must be found 'in the short-term, the medium-term and a longer term that remains to be determined.' It is necessary moreover, he said, 'to try to find out how to address this question among Kanaks but also with the non-Kanaks insofar as people are worried about independence'" (Plenel and Rollat 1988, 195).

Jean-Marie's position was consistent with his long-standing convictions—of *espérance* (hope, faith), the search for dialogue, achieving political independence—and at the same time laying the foundations for a viable and welcoming independent nation. What appeared to be changing in the aftermath of the bloodbath on Ouvéa and the return to power of the Parti Socialiste in France was the position of Jacques Lafleur, the president of the RPCR. The actions of the ecumenical mission to New Caledonia, and the confidence created by sending it, were no doubt a crucial factor in this shift, for his several loyalties found ample expression in its composition. Two of the civil servants, Périer and Steinmetz, were closely associated with the right wing of the French political spectrum, while, as a Protestant and a Freemason, Lafleur found ready interlocutors in Stewart and Leray. Following his own meeting with the dialogue mission, Jacques Lafleur stated on Radio Rythme bleu, the aggressively loyalist radio station in Nouméa:

> The people of this territory have lost the habit of talking, of working together. This state of affairs can't last for a whole lifetime. For those who seek a racist independence, in the name of the first occupier (of the land), they must inevitably assume their share of the sacrifices to be made. If we insist on that point of view, it means that we too have to give something and, to be specific, we must consent freely to making certain sacrifices. Responsibilities must be shared, each of the opponents must feel at ease in his area of responsibilities; these responsibilities must be broad; the state must provide these realms and these people with every chance of succeeding. In such case there is every reason to have hope for New Caledonia. (Quoted in Plenel and Rollat 1988, 197–198)

For the first time the state proposed, if not indeed demanded, dialogue, and both Kanak and Caldoche leaders rose to the occasion. It was, of course, what Jean-Marie had been seeking right from the start—within the Catholic Church, in his seminars on Melanesian culture, in Mélanésia 2000, in choosing to act politically within the Union Calédonienne, in refusing to respond by taking vengeance in the face of physical and judicial violence, and in seeking inspiration and guidance in the Larzac. However, for Jacques Lafleur it was the first time—the first gesture of recognition, the first sign of a desire to listen and to question, and the first expression of hope for a shared and mutually respectful future for New Caledonia. He too indicated he was ready to extend his hand in a gesture of friendship and a search for compromise. Was it a question of nobility and wisdom, or perhaps, like Jean-Marie, a simple expression of the fact that he too was weary and that he had finally recognized that there was no other way forward? Both were no doubt traumatized by the events on Ouvéa, frail, and motivated by their transcending responsibility to the territory as a whole.

Not surprisingly, events moved extremely rapidly from this point. The bases of an agreement were outlined while the dialogue mission was still in New Caledonia, essentially through discussions among three individuals: Christian Blanc representing the French state, Jean-Marie for the FLNKS, and Jacques Lafleur for the RPCR. On 15 June the Kanak and Caldoche leaders met for the first time since the July 1983 roundtable at Nainville-des-Roches. This time it was at a private meeting in Paris with Prime Minister Rocard, and it resulted in a commitment to engage in formal negotiations between FLNKS and RPCR delegations beginning within a week. They were held at the Hôtel Matignon, the prime minister's official residence in the seventh arrondissement. Starting at 7:30 PM on Saturday 25 June, they took the form of a blitz, the tone and precise circumstances of which were set by Michel Rocard. "Food for several days has been prepared, and there are numerous mattresses in various rooms and lounges. . . . My opening words came as a shock: 'Lady, Gentlemen. We are here to choose peace or war for the territory. We have all the time that is needed; it's Saturday evening; my first meeting is on Tuesday at 3 PM. There is sufficient food, and all that is needed for dozing or sleeping. But there won't be another meeting. No one will leave here or telephone until an agreement or a disagreement is recorded. I alone will, naturally, keep the President of the Republic informed" (Rocard 2003b, 397–398). By 3:30 AM the following morning an agreement had been reached and a declaration was signed by all three parties, wherein the RPCR and the FLNKS

> have recognized the urgent need to contribute to the establishment of civil peace in order to create the conditions whereby the various populations will be able to choose freely and confidently their future, exercise control over their destiny.
>
> This is why they have agreed to the [French] State assuming once again responsibility for the administration of the Territory, for the next twelve months.
>
> The delegations have, furthermore, promised to submit to and to solicit the agreement of their respective leaderships with regard to the prime minister's propositions as to the future evolution of New Caledonia. (quoted in Plenel and Rollat 1988, 252)

While the seven members of the RPCR delegation (which included Jean-Marie's brother-in-law and member of his 1982–84 Governing Council, Henri Wetta) signed the declaration, only five of the independentists did: Jean-Marie, Yeiwéné Yeiwéné, Caroline Machoro (Eloï's sister), and Edmond Nékiriaï for the FLNKS, together with Nidoish Naisseline for the LKS, the last perhaps against his better judgment, "understanding too late that the core of the agreement had been established, with Christian Blanc, prior to this meeting, and that he had been attributed, unsuspectingly, a mere onlooker's role" (Rollat 1989b, 263). For his part, Léopold Jorédié, "who didn't want 'to be trapped by the French'" (Rollat 1989b, 262–263), refused to append his signature to the document.

At 10 AM a press conference was held and the agreement made public. A powerful evocation of reconciliation between the leaders of two peoples who had been to the verge of civil war was provided by a photograph of Jean-Marie Tjibaou and Jacques Lafleur warmly shaking each other's hand (figure 21). The image traveled around the world and was immediately en-

FIGURE 21. The handshake with Jacques Lafleur, at the Hôtel Matignon on the morning of 26 June 1988, that in hindsight sealed for the foreseeable future the political destiny of New Caledonia and the personal fate of Jean-Marie. *(ADCK-Centre Culturel Tjibaou/ Gamma)*

graved in the minds of Kanak and Caldoche alike in New Caledonia—for better or for worse, since it would seal the political destiny of the territory and the personal fate of Jean-Marie. In respecting the deadline and reaching an agreement, Michel Rocard met the challenge he had set for himself and imposed on both the dialogue mission and the FLNKS and RPCR delegations. On 29 June he made his inaugural address to the Council of Ministers, and the projected agreement was a key part of it.

Negotiations as to the precise content of the agreement continued for several weeks, concluding with the signing on 20 August of the Oudinot Accord. These subsequent negotiations were conducted and signed by seven representatives of the FLNKS: Jean-Marie and Edmond Nékiriaï, both present on the earlier occasion, together with Rolland Braweao, Kotra Urugeï, Paul Néaoutyine, Louis Mapou, Charles Pidjot, and Raphaël Pidjot. Several of the new signatories would assume crucial roles in the years to follow. The document itself was written by François Roux, the Protestant and pacifist lawyer from Montpellier who had defended first the Larzac cause and, subsequently, many Kanak militants and victims,[4] and who had been instrumental in bringing the nonviolent struggle on the *causse* to Jean-Marie's attention.

These two agreements, of 26 June and 20 August, taken together have come to be known as the Matignon Accords. They had to be ratified by a national referendum, and they involved immediate institutional reforms and investment strategies favoring those parts of New Caledonia where the Kanak constituted the vast majority of the population, together with the delayed holding of a referendum on the future political status of the territory. The agreement covered cultural, economic, and political issues of direct concern to both Kanak and European communities—in its commitment to a geographical and ethnic redistribution of power and wealth, in directly addressing the independence issue, in bringing peace to a deeply wounded place, and in demonstrating a willingness on the part of the two communities to work together. Specifically the accords recommended:

1. The division of New Caledonia into three provinces, Nord, Sud, and Loyauté, each with elected governments and a broad range of responsibilities in such areas as education, health, agriculture, forestry, urban planning, public infrastructures, and so on, as well as the authority to generate revenue through taxes;
2. A territorial congress comprising the elected members of the three provincial assemblies;
3. A regional development strategy directed toward the spatial rebalancing of the territory's economy in favor of the two predominantly Kanak provinces, Nord and Loyauté;
4. A referendum on independence to be held in 1998, that is in ten years' time, with the electoral roll "frozen" to those registered in 1988, together with those of their children who had become adults in the intervening period;
5. The direct administration of the territory by France for a twelve-month period, to permit the new structures to be put in place and the policies to become effective, but also to dislodge the RPCR from a situation of control of all the democratic institutions in New Caledonia, this aberrant situation having resulted from the latest electoral boycott by the FLNKS.

Michel Rocard also made a number of verbal commitments to the FLNKS at the June negotiations, notably to provide amnesty for all those Kanak held responsible for the hostage taking on Ouvéa, and to impose strict controls on immigration. Amnesty was subsequently extended to all those responsible, prior to 20 August 1988, for what might be described as politically motivated assassinations. It included killings perpetrated by French gendarmes and military or loyalist militia as well as by Kanak independentists. Thus it put an end to any further investigations into the deaths of, for example, Pierre Declercq, Eloï Machoro, and Alphonse Dianou, as well as of the gendarmes at Fayaoué.

From Jean-Marie's perspective the agreement had the merit of favoring accelerated development in the two Kanak and independentist provinces. In particular, the proposed federal structure would provide considerable experience in government for his people. It would also result in a broad range of development initiatives and massive investment in infrastructures outside Nouméa and the southern part of the Grande Terre. In short, the agreement came very close to recognizing the existence of his people while providing grounds for interethnic reconciliation.

In some respects the accords evoked a simple return to the institutional arrangements that had existed prior to the March 1986 election of Jacques Chirac and the appointment of Bernard Pons as minister of DOM-TOM. But in the promise of a referendum and control of immigration it could realistically be conceived as a stepping-stone to viable independence for Kanaky a decade later. In this respect it was faithful to Jean-Marie's conviction, "It is too easy to leave by the front door of independence and to come back to beg at the side door of mendacity" (quoted by Rocard 1989, 15). Furthermore, given that Jacques Lafleur and the RPCR signatories were party to the search for a consensual future, the political climate within New Caledonia showed signs of changing for the first time since the Kanak independence movement had taken form in the late 1960s. Hadn't Jacques Lafleur himself pronounced the words, "We know of no hope for our children other than here"?[5] Nevertheless, Jean-Marie was well aware that it was a very uneasy compromise and that the struggle was far from over. The aim was to win the referendum in 1998 and, in the interim, put an end to sectarian violence and lay the foundations for a viable, sustaining peace. However, these were hardly sufficient grounds for suggesting that the handshake with Jacques Lafleur and the signing of the Matignon Accords inspired confidence.

For Louis Mapou, Jean-Marie was a fine strategist who both understood his own people well and knew how to react in difficult situations. He was a man who would listen quietly to debate and to criticism, who would let the others do the talking, then draw his own conclusions and make a decision. Like many great leaders, he was a solitary person, even a loner, whose cultural and political strength was derived from his capacity, in the words of François Burck, "to say something which he had nourished in silence." His ability to withdraw, to reflect in silence—thereby entering into communication with the ancestors—was, of course, a distinctly Melanesian quality: "Wisdom is to know how to be silent" (François Burck, pers comm, 22 Jan 1998). Yet precisely for these reasons Matignon was a terrible experience for Jean-Marie. He had left New Caledonia for Paris with firm instructions from the FLNKS not to sign anything, but simply to evaluate the situation and report back. His obligation was first to consult and only then to act, on the basis of a collective decision. However, he signed on the night of 25–26 June. Certainly it was only a general agreement, with the details to be worked out in the following weeks, yet in signing he banked on something abstract—hope, and the possibility of creating a new society in a shared land. He signed at the expense of an express commitment and calendar that would lead the Kanak people to independence. It was an act of courage and a risk of immeasurable proportions.

According to Caroline Machoro, Jean-Marie addressed a letter to the prime minister at the outset of the negotiations (pers comm, 28 April 2008).

> These negotiations are not only concerned with the finalizing of the internal status of a territory of the French Republic; they are also a process whereby the Kanak people rediscover their dignity in the context of a sovereignty that is restored to them. These negotiations involve in the first instance the French state, which has for the past 134 years controlled the destiny of New Caledonia, and the representatives of the Kanak people. That is to say the state cannot hide behind a role of arbiter. It is not judge but actor. Given the humiliations and suffering we have just experienced, it is not possible for us to embark the Kanak people immediately on a path that does not offer the clear perspective of the acquisition of sovereignty. We are a people who have always been fooled. (quoted in Rollat 1989b, 265)

Jean-Marie was undoubtedly "seduced" by Michel Rocard, to an extent that surprised even Rocard himself. "On the Kanak side, where it is clear that I benefited from a surprising show of confidence, I thought for a long time that it was the fact of my being a Protestant that was appreciated. Above all however, and Jean-Marie Tjibaou alluded to it later, it was my well-established history, since the Algerian war, of being an anticolonial activist which was helpful in crossing, in full respect for these people, a barrier that they had hardly ever opened in the past to other French governments" (Rocard 2003b, 402). However, the problem was that the new prime minister was a regionalist but not a nationalist, and he harbored a very different vision of the future of New Caledonia. "[T]he recognition of the dignity of a minority people is in no way incompatible with belonging to the French Republic. It is a bit my dream. It is also the hope for which I am working" (Rocard, quoted in Lenormand 1991, 155).

Michel Rocard had a different agenda that was not immediately evident to Jean-Marie. Rather he felt, for the first time perhaps, that he could trust the word of his French interlocutor, for he sensed that he was speaking to a political leader who understood him and empathized with him. Whether the other members of his negotiating team shared these sentiments is another matter, and even for Jean-Marie the illusion was rapidly transformed into dismay. In this sense, according to Louis Mapou, Matignon proved to be a terrible experience because, once back in New Caledonia, in recounting it to close collaborators, Jean-Marie could only say "I was trapped. I thought it was good" (Mapou, pers comm, 20 Jan 1998). François Burck remarked that he was completely distraught and unable to sleep at night (pers comm, 22 Jan 1998). He came asking, "What do we do?" François answered, "We carry on," and Jean-Marie went away. The response was not far removed from Yeiwéné Yeiwéné's "I'm frightened" (Rollat 1989b, 265), formulated immediately following the signature of the accords and, more prophetically, his comment the next day, "It's the black hole. If Jean-Marie falls into it, I fall with him" (quoted in Freyss 1995, 63).

The last section of the published collection of Jean-Marie's speeches, writings, and interviews is entitled "Ouvrir la voie" (Opening the Way) (Tjibaou 1996, 265). It presents the sentiments expressed and the initiatives taken during the last year of his life. As always it is founded on the notion of hope—that France will decolonize New Caledonia, that a just society will be created for all the inhabitants of the new nation, and that the wounds of the past will be healed. In what turned out to be the final months of his life, he referred to himself and his immediate family, in the context of his much larger Kanak "family." "My family is somewhat hostage to my public life, because I come and go. My mother's uncles, the uncles in my village; I would say that my family is in a sense the aim of my life, but it is my family and all the other families that I try to serve. That means doing everything, and if possible succeeding, so that people are happy with me and, above all, are happier than me" (Tjibaou 1996, 284). His thoughts also extended to the spiritual and material drama of the *petits Caldoches,* which, in some respects, was not far removed, from that of the Kanak people. "The violence of these lost people is terrible; it's terrible because they have lived in ghettos. They don't know anything else, and they find themselves in a state of being rejected, condemned" (Tjibaou 1996, 290).

His vision embraced and engaged that of Jacques Lafleur. "The promise Jacques Lafleur is making is to hand down to his children, a future in their country but also a country where the Kanak are the majority. So, it's a future with us. That's not stated in any text but it is the real significance of the documents that have been submitted to us" (Tjibaou 1996, 268). At the same time he evoked the drama of the newly independent nations of Africa. "We had a lot of admiration for Sékou Touré and [Thomas] Sankara. But at the time of the Matignon Accords, I thought once more about these African countries and their experience of decolonization: political power can only be possessed if you are organized, economically and financially. Sankara was something of a lone voice in the desert. The African countries have been suffocated by the West, and their leaders no longer have the courage to walk beside their people. . . . What is insidious is the fact that it is the Blacks themselves—whether they be Africans or Oceanians—who are the agents of impoverishment of their peoples" (Tjibaou 1996, 304).

Very occasionally he publicly expressed real bitterness about the Matignon Accords, notably in a revealing interview with the *Sydney Morning Herald* journalist Sarah Walls that bears the caption "French swindled us: FLNKS leader," published on 7 January 1989. He voiced his anger about the criteria to be used for drawing up electoral lists for provincial elections planned for 1989 and 1995, because restrictions would only be imposed in the 1998 referendum, despite the agreement reached in June. He also revealed his doubts about the French government's intention to hold a referendum in ten years' time: "The Left has never decolonized." Finally, in the same interview, he expressed uncharacteristically cynical ideas about Jacques Lafleur—that his participation in the accords can be summarized as "He's loading nickel"—and about the loyalists in general—that they participate simply "because they want the money from the accords—the money, the calm, the business. That's all that interests them" (Tjibaou 2005, 285). The use of the word *swindled* in the caption was not a *Sydney Morning Herald* editorial fabrication; it was the term he used himself in the interview. By this stage, he was fully conscious that political success was conditional on freezing the electoral roll and holding a referendum in ten years' time. Even more important than these legislative instruments, it depended on a political and moral commitment "wherein everyone agrees to the Melanesians constituting an absolute majority" at the time of the referendum (Tjibaou 1996, 268). It was an extraordinarily fragile edifice. By April 1989 his explanation was much more down-to-earth: "If I signed, it is quite simply because we didn't have any more sugar, any more rice . . . the soldiers, the insecurity; they were perhaps signs of Providence? But for us it was quite concrete. It was that or moving on to the stage of guerrilla warfare. In order to make that choice you need to have the means" (1996, 303).

Not surprisingly, all along he had to struggle against the doubts and recriminations of key elements in the Kanak community. Publicly at least, he appeared to rationalize and to accept them with remarkable equanimity. "It is the lot of every leader to be criticized; it's a sign of good health. If they don't listen any more, if they have shut themselves off, not only denying rumours emanating from the crowd, but also from the mounting fears, cries, tears and also joys of the people they claim to represent, the leaders no longer have any inkling of the problems; and they are screwed" (Tjibaou 1996, 279). Yet, in the many moments of extreme solitude that were now his lot, when he was confronted by repeated manifestations of incomprehension and hostility on the part of his own people, Jean-Marie would sometimes angrily respond, "To those who affirm that I signed (at the expense of the dead), I say, 'You can go to hell'"[6]—alluding in no uncertain terms to the two brothers he had lost in the massacre at Hienghène in December 1984.

In a political agreement that drew both leaders toward the center of the political spectrum, Jean-Marie Tjibaou had much more difficulty than Jacques Lafleur in justifying his actions. Lafleur had lost the French elections but gained a cessation of hostilities in New Caledonia. More important, he had obtained a ten-year postponement of any decision concerning its political destiny. In contrast, Jean-Marie had won the elections, put an end to what was becoming increasingly a bloodbath for the Kanak people, and found a respectful interlocutor in the person of the new prime minister. But he had also agreed to delay any possibility of independence for a further ten years. With hindsight—and from a somewhat cynical perspective—Jean-Marie had obtained ten years to prepare a viable Kanak independence, while Lafleur had gained ten years to make independence unnecessary, and the French state had engineered a remarkably astute agreement.

Occasional public outbursts and private disclosures of pessimism apart, Jean-Marie insisted from the outset that the Matignon Accords were a "wager." He defended them in such terms when he returned from Paris to report to the FLNKS Convention, held first at Thio on 17 July and then adjourned for a week and transferred to Hwaadrila on Ouvéa, because of the deep divisions created by his gesture. Approval, painfully but ultimately acquired, allowed him to return to Paris (Oudinot) in mid-August with a new delegation, negotiate modifications to the initial agreement, agree on a series of "accompanying measures" essentially economic in nature, and sign the final document. The recommendations had then to be submitted to a national referendum for approval by the entire French—metropolitan and overseas—electorate, to be held on 6 November 1988. That critical date would "freeze" New Caledonia's electoral list for the vote on independence to be held a decade later.

Jean-Marie had to use all of his oratorical skills and talent as a *rassembleur* (unifier) to convince, at the same time making clear he would willingly abandon the leadership of the independence movement if his position were disavowed. In that case, "I will go back home, to Hienghène, and plant yams" (Rollat 1989b, 270). He was staking his political career, and perhaps his life, on the lonely commitment he had made at the Hôtel Matignon in the early hours of 26 June. Two minority party members of the FLNKS, the FULK and PALIKA, openly contested the proposed agreement. At a third convention, held at Houaïlou in September, the FULK continued to distance itself from the majority position, while even the majority, in ratifying the accords and inviting the Kanak people to vote yes in the upcoming referendum, stressed that the accords offered no guarantee of their fundamental demand for independence. In contrast, Jean-Marie was much more successful in convincing his own UC party of the merits of an approach that involved preparing for independence through the establishment of solid economic foundations for the Kanak people.

For Ouvéa, the people of Goosana, and Djubelly Wéa in particular, this political outcome was treated as yet another humiliation. The tribe as a whole had suffered in mind and in body during the brief French military occupation, while Djubelly himself had been unjustly accused of orchestrating the hostage taking, tortured, and then imprisoned in France. To add insult to injury, as far as Djubelly was concerned, Jean-Marie declined his request to participate in the FLNKS negotiating team at the Hôtel Matignon, even though he had been released from prison and was still in Paris. Neither he nor the people of Goosana were consulted at any stage in the subsequent negotiations, even though their sons, and those of fellow Ouvéans, had died at the hands of the French military.[7] To cap it all, any possibility of independence was delayed yet again. In brief, they felt abandoned if not deeply betrayed by the rest of the independence movement and especially by the Kanak of the Grande Terre. Their militants had died for nothing.

Regardless of the latest tragedy, Djubelly made it clear that the liberation struggle must continue. If, on the one hand, he had gone from failure to failure in recent years, becoming increasingly embittered and intransigent in the process, he also harbored one last dream: that Ouvéa would declare unilateral independence in 1989, with the expectation that Maré and Lifou would quickly follow. The year 1989 was of considerable symbolic significance in that it would mark the two-hundredth anniversary of the Declaration of the Rights of Man and the Citizen, a document that lay at the foundations of the French Revolution and served as a direct source of inspiration for many national and international declarations that followed.

Djubelly's deep sense of humiliation pointed to another fracture line between Goosana, collectively frustrated for deep historical reasons, and the larger independence movement. Djubelly was personally marked by his Fiji experience. There, in the course of his studies he had learned of the theology of liberation, and through the Nuclear Free and Independent Pacific movement he experienced radical political discourse and talk of unilateral action. The ideas were formulated by fellow Oceanians from the newly independent nations of the Pacific, and all expressed in what he saw as the unifying language of the region, English. Not surprisingly he quickly became active in PALIKA, the most ideologically rigid and uncompromising of Kanak political parties—it promoted "scientific socialism"—engaging in politics at the local and regional levels. In a sense PALIKA was a natural political choice for him because as a young man he had been a member of the Foulards Rouges, a movement also marked by an imported radicalism.

Intransigence meant that by 1988 Djubelly had withdrawn from the larger political and religious institutional spheres, with the exception of the local FLNKS *comité de lutte,* and even this committee had the particularity of being limited to Goosana rather than embracing the whole commune, as was the practice elsewhere in the territory. This focus on a small, tight-knit community had the advantage of drawing together individuals and, in Djubelly's case, brothers who had joined different political parties—notably FULK, UC, and PALIKA. The tribe and the village had progressively become both a fortress and a model, with its dynamic École populaire kanak

(ÉPK),[8] its cooperative bakery and copra drier, and its barricades across the road leading to the village. As of June 1988 this distinctiveness was reinforced by taking the ÉPK schoolchildren to the cave, as a sign of respect for the martyrs and so that the lessons of the immediate past would not be forgotten.

The Wéa brothers had a reputation for being "very enterprising, progressive. They were always the most advanced in everything. Djubelly was the very first pastor to study in Fiji. He was a journalist at the same time, for the newspaper *La France Australe*. He always had ideas that were a little revolutionary, if not harebrained. I believe that the first Melanesian business to have been created on Ouvéa was theirs. At the time they had buses, cars. They always set themselves apart by being in the forefront" (Loueckhote 1999, 61). The brothers were not motivated by personal economic gain so much as the aim that their tribe should become a model for the Kanak people. Social and economic justice and an overriding concern to eliminate the inequalities that too often mark "development" and "progress" were their objectives. For Djubelly in particular, the boundary between religion and politics was diffuse if not nonexistent. Urgency and a logic of confrontation meant that independence would almost inevitably be a unilateral act in his eyes. It was necessary to prepare for it, to count exclusively on one's own resources, to be self-sufficient, and to accept the reality that the new nation would be poor.

This recent experience makes Ouvéa a most distinctive place in the eyes of many observers. Beneath the seemingly calm exterior—of a bucolic Pacific Island atoll—lay a marked degree of intransigency and a potential for violence related to a sense of being ahead of the rest of Kanaky in the independence movement—more innovative, more lucid, and more impatient. Goosana in particular prided itself on its integrity and was always concerned to defend its honor. This implacable logic led the tribe's *comité de lutte* to declare its opposition to the Matignon Accords, to call for the boycott of the November 1988 referendum, and to maintain the barricades at the entry to the tribal land.

If Jean-Marie spent the months following the signature of the Matignon Accords urging his people to vote yes on 6 November, the results only confirmed the fragile nature of the peace that had been agreed to in Paris four and a half months earlier. Although the accords were endorsed by 80 percent of voters, only 38 percent of the electorate actually went to the polls. It was France's worst turnout in a national referendum since the Second World War. More seriously, while electors voted massively in favor of the accords in metropolitan France, the portrait was very different in New Caledonia. There, while 63 percent of the electorate went to the polls, some 43 percent of voters rejected the proposal. In Nouméa and the Province Sud this figure rose to over 60 percent. Though close, the victory in New Caledonia was attributable largely to the Kanak independentist vote that Jean-Marie had solicited. Conspicuously, on Ouvéa 54 percent of those on the electoral rolls chose not to vote, with the boycott significantly higher at Goosana.

In the aftermath of the Ouvéa crisis and the signing of the Matignon Accords, the tribe confirmed that it had retreated into silent grieving, nourishing its sense of being profoundly misunderstood and perhaps bitter, for it was clear to them: "Consider the case of 1988; if all the regions had supported the action taken by the people of Ouvéa, I believe that, since 1988, we would be independent. We have moved back thirty years, just when we were on the finishing line. Do you call that solidarity?" (M Wéa 1999, 51). This lucid analysis on the part of Djubelly's brother also pointed to the extreme marginality of the tribe's position. They were a mere two hundred people at Goosana, Djubelly Wéa at their head, who "understood" what had really happened and were condemned to suffering what for them was both a local human and a territory-wide political tragedy. The population of Ouvéa as a whole amounted to a mere 2,800 individuals. Although the victory of the center of the political spectrum was assured, its cost was the isolation of the margins. Again, the risk for Jacques Lafleur was far less than for Jean-Marie Tjibaou. Whereas Lafleur's margins were overtly violent and racist, they were now confronted only by the remote possibility of an independent Kanaky. What for them was a lull was, by contrast, a source of bitterness for the others.

In the last few months of his life, between the referendum of 6 November 1988 and the "big black hole" of 4 May 1989, Jean-Marie spoke constantly of the need to lay the economic foundations for independence and to ensure that the Kanak people win the referendum on the political destiny of the country to be held a decade later. He stressed that France would make no gifts, and how it was necessary to continue the combat during the intervening period. This combat was economic as much as political, the ultimate goal being the effective exercise of power.

> No one will make you gifts. You will only have the fruits of your struggle. We are fighting to take the place which is rightfully ours. In order to gain power we must first invest in the economy. We have always viewed it to be a source of alienation. Now we have to take our places on the boards of directors in order to be present and to do battle. We must establish businesses, economic activities: coffee, fisheries, and so on, but above all we need to work independently and responsibly. Kanak and socialist independence first of all means that each person must assume more responsibility, so that living conditions in the country are improved, for it to be more beautiful, for us to be proud of it, so that Kanaky flourishes. (Tjibaou 1988, 1–2)

These ideas were expressed on the occasion of the nineteenth congress of the UC, held at Gélima (Canala) in mid-November 1988, and he added that the model for this economy had to be a Kanak and not an imported one.

"We remember our dead, we have our manner of thinking, of dancing. We have ways of dancing, ways of thought, styles of poetry, a sense of propriety, values. In other words, we have a way of being in this world. All that needs to be asserted" (Tjibaou 1988, 2). Cultural specificity also had to be affirmed in a manner that embraced those who had voted no in the referendum, "because they know the roots of this land" (Tjibaou 1988, 2). The goal was economic power, but never at the cost of cultural alienation or the loss of respect or of self-respect.

Nothing had changed with regard to Jean-Marie's vision and strategy. The discourse was the same, with the possible difference that the weariness of two years of violent confrontation with Chirac and Pons had rendered it a little less political and a little more poetic. The same determination was in his speeches, mingled with a sense of greater calm, but his words also veiled the tension that marked his people, for expectations were high, and the deep sense of impatience and anger was for some too hard to bear. Both Jean-Marie and Djubelly, together with their kin at Hienghène and Goosana, had the interests of the Kanak people and of Kanak culture at heart, but the one had agreed to aspire to economic power and a viable national independence as a long-term objective while the other strove for local self-sufficiency in the context of third-world independence as an immediate goal. Both were also confronted by the return to power of a Parti Socialiste that sustained the dream of decolonization—and the impossibility of realizing that dream.

The fragility of the independence movement was demonstrated in municipal elections held in March 1989, with the UC presenting separate lists from the FLNKS and, in several cases, even joining forces with the RPCR to win a municipality. Nevertheless, momentum was maintained because it had been agreed to assess progress under the accords in 1992. As Jean-Marie said in his opening speech to the *comité directeur* (management committee) of the UC at Poindimié on 29 April 1989, "The countdown has begun" (1989d, 10).

A little less than two weeks before the Poindimié meeting, the journalist Lêdji Bellow had interviewed him. In her article, entitled "Tjibaou: Sa dernière entrevue," she described the setting of what was to be the "last conversation." "We leave the table. Marie-Claude had offered us some large fish, which she had caught that very morning in the river that enters the ocean in front of the house. Jean-Marie, who insisted on honoring our presence, had produced a bottle of Bourgogne a French friend had offered him a year ago, to accompany his wife's fried fish and the manioc cooked in coconut milk. And we talk about many things" (Bellow 1989b, 29). He spoke of the interactions between Christian and indigenous faiths, of Western and traditional medicine, of the signs of Providence, of the drama of the independent nations of Africa, and of the courage and lucidity of Sékou Touré and Thomas Sankara, of the need to train in new skills, and to prepare his people to be free . . . "to invest in grey matter so that the people, with the help of the colonizer, free themselves intellectually, sociologically, psychologically. Forming such people, that's a bit our ambition. . . . One can allow oneself such an ambition in a small country where no one is starving, where no one is dying of cold. People must be well trained, be smart and able to create. So that they can say they are missionaries and they must be messengers for future generations, standard bearers in the protection of the planet." He repeated what he had insisted on so many times, "I am for a tradition that asserts its place in the modern world." At this last publicly recorded feast[9] he announced, with characteristic warmth and simplicity:

> Me, I'm ephemeral, but I must do everything in my power, everything I can in order that the country I hand down to my sons is the most beautiful of countries, a country where there is wealth, wealth in thinking, in wisdom, in flowers, in food. So that there is plenty, if possible. Our objective is to be self-sufficient. Wherever one may be, one has the same responsibility with regard to present and to future generations. (Tjibaou 1996, 305)

A little over two weeks later he was at Hwaadrila, on Ouvéa, to mark the end of the period of mourning for the nineteen young Kanak who had been killed at Goosana. Standing on the grounds of the *chefferie* just across the road from the mass grave, he made a customary gesture on the part of the political bureau of the FLNKS and the other visiting delegations, offering cloth, Kanak money, and yams. He spoke of unity, of pain, of loss, and of freedom, repeating the words an elder had voiced shortly before him, "the living blood flows and it continues to live. And we rush forward because this blood of the dead is living, it calls out to us, it is our blood, it is the blood of those who demand freedom for our people" (Tjibaou 1996, 308).

A few minutes later Djubelly stepped from the crowd, shot and killed Jean-Marie and Yeiwéné at point-blank range. In one cataclysmic act the martyr became the assassin, and the Provisional Government of Kanaky lost, in the person of its president, its *âme dirigeante* (guiding spirit), and in that of its vice president, his most loyal of allies. One belonged to the Grande Terre, and the other to the Loyalties. Djubelly Wéa was in turn shot and killed by one of Jean-Marie's bodyguards, all three thereby joining the nineteen militants lying in their shallow grave set against the backdrop of the lagoon. In all probability, it was a gesture designed to put a brutal end to the ambiguity created by the signing of the Matignon Accords, by deepening the wound within the Kanak community between a majority who favored dialogue, compromise, and patience, and a minority who sought immediate unilateral independence.

10 The Measure of the Man

Then a silent revolt rose up in us, black hole before the knell of our
men who were falling one by one with, in front, these mocking smiles
and this one-sided justice. Inexorably, inevitably, they sped through
time like those shooting stars which disappear too quickly into
infinity, leaving behind them a trail of blinding light. So we had to
delve deep into ourselves, to seek and to draw on the source of life,
in order to rise again and continue to advance.
Marie-Claude Tjibaou 2002, 11

THE DEATHS OF Jean-Marie and of his indefectible lieutenant, Yeiwéné,
resulted in a spontaneous outpouring of grief of unexpected dimensions.
According to newspaper reports, more than twenty thousand people turned
out on 7 May to pay their respects to the deceased outside the cathedral in
the center of Nouméa, where their funeral was held, and along the road
leading to the town's airport. In other words, well over 10 percent of the
territory's population gathered around them prior to their final journey
to their respective tribal homes, Jean-Marie to Hienghène, on the Grande
Terre, and Yeiwéné to Maré, in the Loyalty Islands. Of this number, an estimated eight thousand accompanied the cortege from the morgue to the
cathedral and then on to the airport at Magenta, the silence broken only by
outbreaks of deep, unrestrained sobbing surging from the crowds assembled
along the route. The hearse was preceded by a young man bearing the flag
of Kanaky, and behind the vehicle a seemingly endless line of people advanced hand-in-hand along one side of the road. While the mourners were
massively Kanak, interspersed among them were Caldoche and metropolitan French, Wallisians, and others drawn from New Caledonia's broad array
of ethnic communities. As the aircraft rose into the air and the two companions in combat and in life were finally separated, Franck Wahuzue, adviser and friend of Yeiwéné and an ex-RPCR militant ventured, "Jean-Marie
returns to the earth. Yeiwéné to the earth." For his part, Olivier Couhe,
the French journalist who recorded the observation, described the sense of

disorientation that marked those left behind. "Jean-Marie and his faithful lieutenant dead, it's the void. '*With them it is everything which vanishes*' lament the activists met by chance; '*the symbol, the leaders, hope, all that is gone. What will become of us?*'" (Couhe 1989, 17; emphasis in original).

Couhe's coverage of the funeral for the French weekly news magazine *Politis, Le Citoyen* formed part of a collection of articles written by close observers of the Kanak and New Caledonian scene. In his brief introduction, the editorialist Bernard Langlois recalled that Djubelly Wéa visited their offices in Paris following his release from prison in June 1988. He had come to pay customary respects and to thank *Politis* for its support of the Kanak cause. The simple gesture led Langlois to conclude his text with the observation, "His terrible, long prepared, extraordinarily staged decision [to commit the murders] appalls us, crushes us. We mourn for Jean-Marie Tjibaou and Yeweine Yeweine [*sic*] and we salute their memory. But that does not mean their murderer is a swine or a madman. One is always wrong to forget that History is tragic" (1989, 11).

The funeral was attended by official delegations from New Caledonia and throughout the region: the Papua New Guinea minister for foreign affairs, Michael Somare; the sister of the prime minister of Vanuatu, Hilda Lini, and the foreign minister, Donald Kalpokas; the president of French Polynesia's territorial government, Alexandre Léontieff; the Australian minister for foreign affairs, Gareth Evans; and the New Zealand deputy prime minister, Geoffrey Palmer, to name only a few. Jacques Lafleur and Dick Ukeiwe, his faithful Kanak lieutenant, were present, together with the entire RPCR *état-major* (leadership). Michel Rocard came from France, at the head of a large delegation of politicians and senior civil servants. In a sense, perhaps Rocard's attendance at this public ceremony in the capital was of greatest symbolic and political significance. He spoke at the airport, after customary respects had been paid by the various Pacific Island delegations, his voice charged with emotion.

> I remember Jean-Marie Tjibaou on the night of 25 June 1988, when we had just laid the foundations of this dream, in signing the Matignon Accords. The air was mild and, in crossing the grounds of the Hôtel Matignon in the dark, you said to Yeiwéné Yeiwéné, who was walking in front of you, "Watch out for the big black hole." I heard it, and Yeiwéné replied "Whatever happens, we are there together."
>
> Yes, peace is a journey that is more unpredictable, more uncertain and, in its own way, riskier than war or violence which, they, are so obvious in their progression and in their results.

He went on to speak of courage, of vision, and of history, as well as of the principles vested in the Matignon Accords, which were designed to put an end to violence.

> The first of these principles is that Caledonia is too small for all its children not to have their rightful place, in the way that each of the posts of the high chief's house plays its role in ensuring the solidity of the whole. And if there is a central house post, it can only be that of the democratic state. The second principle is that there is no destiny of any worth in misery. Jean-Marie once said "I don't want an independence that will put us on the list of the ten poorest UN countries." His great international visibility . . . enabled him to gauge the submission which generally accompanies the poverty of nations. And he added: "It is too easy to leave by the main door of independence and to return to seek favors at the rear door of begging." Sovereignty, dignity, they are in the first instance those borne in one's head: that is our third principle. (Rocard 1989, 15)

His speech revealed a fine comprehension of Melanesian values, particularly with respect to the spoken word and the ancestors. This quality can be attributed, variously, to the political skills and wisdom of Michel Rocard, to his choice of close advisers, and to his Protestant origins and faith. It also helps explain why the Parti Socialiste had always generated such high expectations on the part of Jean-Marie and the FLNKS leadership. In his homily, Rocard quoted President Mitterrand, both his memorable "Les mots vont plus loin que les mots" (The words go further than words)—which was inscribed in his response to Jean-Marie's "Letter to the President," penned shortly before the crisis on Ouvéa—and his response to the news of the double assassination. "As the President says, and I quote him, we will all be accountable for this heritage. And it is henceforth our responsibility to be vigilant with respect to it, in the way that one takes great care of the yams that ensure the harvest for the coming years and for the coming generations" (Rocard 1989, 15).

Michel Rocard made it clear that he understood the vital importance of keeping his word, *tenir parole*.

Jean-Pierre Aïfa, mayor of Bourail, of Algerian (Kabyle) origin, and Jean-Marie's accomplice in the era of a gentler, avowedly multiracial Union Calédonienne, spoke just before the prime minister, introducing a new dimension that would mark reflections and syntheses in the weeks and months to follow: the parallels between Jean-Marie and other great men who had preceded him. In posing the rhetorical question as to whether Jean-Marie was a "terrorist," he advanced the name of George Washington, who had been described in such terms, as had the members of the French Resistance during the Second World War (quoted in Andreani and Bobin 1989, 7).

In the following days and weeks, a multitude of articles in newspapers and weekly and monthly magazines in France and in the Pacific were devoted to Jean-Marie, while individual testimonies came from across the French political spectrum, the Larzac, L'Arche, the Grand-Orient de France, senior civil servants, journalists, indeed from many of the people he had encountered in the course of his short public life. None was indifferent to the moral strength, the political intelligence, and the stature of the leader, and all recognized that Jean-Marie was a man of dialogue and peace who consciously put his own life at risk and who paid the highest price, that of a violent death.[1]

A number of the writers recalled that both Mahatma Gandhi and Martin Luther King Jr had been assassinated, and for similar reasons, for they too were men of dialogue who had sought to break their particular spirals of violence and to put an end to savagery. François Mitterrand reinforced the parallel in a speech on 8 May commemorating the liberation of Orléans by Jeanne d'Arc in 1429: "Those who resemble him are, at all times, more vulnerable than others. Those who have chosen to remain open to dialogue, to prepare avenues for peace with honor, they—today's news reminds us of it—are often the first to fall. Later—but too late—one realizes how much they are missed" (quoted in *Le Monde,* 10 May 1989, 9).

The intellectual Jean Chesneaux insisted on Jean-Marie's capacity to *transcend:* "By virtue of his dual capacity to fully assume his Melanesian identity and to profoundly assimilate our Western culture, Jean-Marie had arrived at a *universality* which is superior to ours. That was the key to his intellectual strength, his political sense, his humor, his charisma, his warm simplicity" (quoted in *Spécial Kanaky* 1989, 3; emphasis in original). In the same special issue, produced by the French Association Information et Soutien aux Droits du Peuple Kanak (AISDPK), under the title "It is Jaurès who has been assassinated once again,"[2] Jacques Thibault evoked the "overwhelming sense of the dismal repetition of injustice, 'this sort of maliciousness of history' which puts down, well before their time, the great combatants of humanity. As if by design it is at the moment when they are most needed by the peoples they serve that the Luther King, the Jaurès, the Tjibaou disappear. The Kanak people are condemned to silence, as were yesterday the Black people of the United States, as in 1914 were the French working people. . . . In these times, when hopes and abominations traverse the planet like tornadoes, free people have no need for supreme chiefs or for saints, but in the near future they risk being cruelly short of wise combatants" (Thibault 1989, 4).

Other names would emerge in the months and years to follow, of individuals who shared similar values, aspirations, and strategies to those of Jean-Marie: the Algerian Ferhat Abbas and the Burkinabean Thomas Sankara, together with Nelson Mandela and Isaac Rabin. All were leaders of integrity who espoused nonviolence and pluralism. In advancing such names, the many commentators, friends, and allies were striving to get the measure of the man, to define the contours of his greatness. History, universality, integrity, faith are noble terms that are not easy to translate into the reality of particular experiences and places, particularly when Jean-Marie himself rarely made reference to other political leaders and never openly evoked any models. According to François Burck, he probably admired a few leaders

FIGURE 22. Jean-Marie's customary burial ceremony at Tiendanite on 8 May 1989.
(ADCK-Centre Culturel Tjibaou)

who were not slaves to oppressive, imported ideologies, but one thing is certain, "Jean-Marie would have cried victory at the fall of the Berlin Wall" (Burck, pers comm, 22 Jan 1998).

In seeking to position Jean-Marie in the universe of visionaries and values, it is revealing to consider the customary burial, held at Tiendanite on 8 May (figure 22). It was an intimate ceremony, in the presence of several thousand people, essentially Kanak who had come spontaneously from throughout the territory to bid him farewell. In addition, Oscar Temaru was there—the independence leader and, briefly, president of French Polynesia—together with political allies from the past, such as Jean-Pierre Aïfa. Those with whom he had shared the present were there in force—François Burck, Gérald Cortot, Léopold Jorédié, Paul Néaoutyine, Armand Pala—as were the representatives of a younger generation who would occupy key roles in the years to come, notably Raphaël Pidjot and Louis Mapou. Five Catholic priests were also present, with Father Rock Apikaoua officiating. A multitude of speeches and customary gestures were made, to which the tribal spokesman responded, mentioning the crucial importance of offerings of cloth and money—both Kanak and modern—as expressions of solidarity. Without custom there is no dignity, no identity—one is no longer Kanak. He spoke of their profound sense of loss and disarray, "Today the

Kanak people no longer have a head. When one is without a head, one is in the dark. One doesn't know where to turn."[3]

Such views were, of course, shared by the FLNKS speakers, but they gave an avowedly political dimension to them. The words of the priests were very different. They stressed that although Jean-Marie had left the Church, he had continued to serve, and such was the true sense of sacerdotalism. He had remained faithful to his religious convictions to the end. In his homily, Father Apikaoua insisted on the religious as distinct from the political nature of Jean-Marie: he spoke of hope as distinct from loss and failure. For his brother priests Jean-Marie was profoundly Christian. "It was a part of his life which he didn't talk about . . . because it was a part of his being. He ceased serving as a priest but he remained profoundly a priest, outside the institution of the Church. He was the father of his people until the end. He was, in a certain sense, a pontiff who built bridges between men, cultures, beliefs. He had a profound respect for people. He possessed the ability to speak in such a way as not to be indecent. Even when he was shocked, he was capable of expressing his anger, his disagreement with such elegance. He was a man who always held his head above water" (Apikaoua, pers comm, 20 July 1994).

Whether Jean-Marie would have been comfortable with such statements, or with the parallels with other great figures of the twentieth century, is another matter. By nature, by conviction, and by strategy, he was opposed to all forms of appropriation. If he had repeatedly insisted that "it is we who determine our socialism," so, as the years passed, he expressed increasing indifference to the preoccupations of the Catholic Church and with its incapacity to espouse the Kanak people's quest for dignity. He was perhaps "a priest for eternity" in the eyes of those officiating, but he was first of all a Kanak, who had entered the living world at Tiendanite in the presence of the ancestors, and who had been designated by custom to lead his people forward. Had he been born into the Protestant faith he might, conceivably, have remained a pastor to the end. However, even that hypothesis is questionable, for, while he necessarily turned in many directions "in his search to understand," he was dominated by no ideology, no profession, no institution, the Church included. He was a pragmatist firmly grounded in a local reality but with a vision that embraced all peoples and all places. This unswerving conviction had guided him in his actions and explained why he was simultaneously a man of the people and a man of peace.

Father Apikaoua related a Chinese parable moments before the coffin was lowered into the earth. "Great men resemble large trees, and when large trees fall in the forest, they make a lot of noise. Two large trees have fallen in the Caledonian forest. They have made a great deal of noise. This noise can be heard at the four corners of the earth. But when the sound of the falling of these great trees ceases, we must listen, we must listen intensely, because there is something that makes no noise. When the forest grows, it makes no noise. Will you truly be a part of this forest, which grows and will give life to our country?" (Apikaoua, pers comm, 20 July 1994).

Despite the many moving testimonies delivered in the intimacy of the tribe, Jean-Marie was not held in universal esteem by Kanak. The unity he achieved was always a fragile one and the criticism was not limited to Goosana or the nineteen martyrs who had died at the cave. The searing remark penned by Léopold Jorédié following the signature of the Matignon Accords—"The slave agreed to shake hands with his master in order to reconcile the French" (Jorédié 1988)—was simply the tip of the iceberg. The radical fringe of the independence movement, represented by the FULK and PALIKA, and of the union movement, represented by the Union Syndicale des Travailleurs Kanaks et des Exploités (USTKE), together with many young Kanak, were all culturally more distant from France and often, at the other extreme, from the reservations. For them Jean-Marie was a "bourgeois Melanesian," a man of unacceptable compromise and even of questionable integrity who sought to transform the French colonial order from within rather than to confront it from outside and eliminate it. Such people were increasingly ill at ease with what was rapidly taking the form of a cult of Jean-Marie's memory they considered was masterminded from France.

Younger Kanak wanted heroes. For them it was not Jean-Marie Tjibaou and Yeiwéné Yeiwéné who fitted this image, but Eloï Machoro and Djubelly Wéa, for they had died "in combat." Both were *purs et durs* (strict hardliners), who favored physical confrontation, if not outright war, in their quest for immediate and nonnegotiable independence. Their aim was the reconquest of an ancestral land. More seriously, in the eyes of some of these young, impatient idealists, both heroes had been "sacrificed" by the FLNKS leadership—by Jean-Marie and Yeiwéné.[4]

Existing rivalry among Kanak leaders had little to do with ideology or strategy. Jean-Marie's charisma resulted in an ascendancy over his peers that effectively eclipsed other talented and ambitious individuals, making for considerable jealousy in some cases. Measured criticism, when formulated, was surprising in both its variety and its contradictions. Gabriel Païta, as a member of the Union Calédonienne and the FLNKS until 1984, was a close associate in the early years. However, opposed to violence, he distanced himself from the independence movement, creating the obscure Parti Fédéral d'Opao. In his view, Jean-Marie was politically suspect and had limited knowledge of Kanak culture.

> It is usual today to speak highly of Yeiwéné, of Tjibaou, or of Machoro. That's post mortem glory! But weren't they seeking above all to seize power? Everyone, from now on, praises Tjibaou, but his career followed a tortuous path in our history. . . . Jean-Marie, who had above all been trained to be an auxiliary teaching brother, had been obliged to compensate for his shortcomings (in terms of studies at the seminary) through sociology and through all he learned

in preparing Mélanésia 2000. (Païta, quoted in Cazaumayou and de Deckker 1999, 155)

No doubt Tjibaou wanted, then, to appropriate this Kanak culture of which he had so little knowledge, which he knew so poorly. He wished to immerse himself in it. (Païta, quoted in Cazaumayou and de Deckker 1999, 117)

René Guiart, the son of French anthropologist Jean Guiart and of a Kanak mother from the Loyalties, was a young independentist militant in the 1980s, more attracted by the radical confrontational approach of Eloï Machoro than by Jean-Marie Tjibaou's seemingly never-ending quest to discuss and to negotiate. His observations are equally equivocal but, in a sense, diametrically opposed to those of Païta.

Jean-Marie is an adept of traditional discourse, accumulating symbolic assertions and being capable of unashamed recourse to less heroic realities. This discourse can be inadequate in a historic phase where the opponents are no longer the old-style partners but the fraction of racists and unscrupulous Europeans allied with the heads of these frigid monsters that are modern states. Jean-Marie's training as a priest meant he had developed a capacity to reflect more than to act. He thrived on the word, watching out for the utterances of his partners of the moment in order to gain maximum benefit, but without always really distinguishing word from action. He was often indifferent to material contingencies. (R Guiart 2001, 304)

He readily attributed tasks to European collaborators—Metropolitans or Caledonians—without envisaging the need to take special precautions. His vocation was to negotiate—he would do it until the last minute, including at hell's gates—but he did it in the Oceanian way. . . . Jean-Marie Tjibaou, behind the colorful and symbolic language used, and the system of references which were apparently a little outdated and which he hid behind when he was cornered and seeking room to maneuver, is the man who demonstrates the greatest capacity to devise or to accept compromises, even perfectly clumsy ones. In so doing, he provoked constant suspicion on the part of the younger generation which he never gave himself the means to control and which tended to surpass him by their initiatives. (R Guiart 1991, 139)

In his critique of Jean-Marie's philosophy and style, René Guiart highlighted an important weakness that he shared with other Melanesians who sought to negotiate with those in power in France, namely, their limited understanding of a remote and alien political universe.

They were unfamiliar with its history, and in particular with that of the French workers' movement and the Left. Their references were specific to the colonial history of New Caledonia. They acted somewhat blindly in Paris, learning quickly, and always having the same difficulty of being able to situate in a realistic perspective the words and deeds of our politicians. They still believe too easily in the promises and they tend to place every event in the context of a utopian vision of the future, in conformity with the traditional Kanak discourse which consists of dramatized symbols and epic descriptions. . . . They don't understand French legal language and are frightened to death by written agreements, on the one hand because written documents have always been used to deceive the Kanak, and on the other because they tend to wish to preserve at all costs and in all circumstances their freedom to decide. (R Guiart 1991, 139)

This observation is an important one. Almost certainly an element of naivety pervaded Jean-Marie's thoughts and actions, a naivety that might also be termed innocence—or generosity. He was imbued, perhaps more consciously than many of his French counterparts, with a sense of history and of justice and inspired by revolutionary ideals. In a specifically French intellectual and political milieu, he believed that both the colonized and the colonizer must be treated with respect and their honor remain untarnished. This dual preoccupation led him, in negotiating the Matignon Accords, to suggest 14 July 1989 to Prime Minister Rocard as the date on which the new status for the territory would come into effect. Contributing in this way to celebrations to mark the bicentenary of the French Revolution and the associated Declaration of the Rights of Man and the Citizen would show Republican ideals to be entirely compatible with the aspirations of the Kanak people, each nourishing the other. In this respect, the reference was as important to the "hero" as it was to his "assassin," Djubelly Wéa, who was similarly influenced by French revolutionary ideals.

In the last year of his life, Jean-Marie repeated ceaselessly that the Matignon Accords were simply a stepping-stone on the road to independence, that the struggle was far from over. The agreement had brought peace, provided guarantees, and ensured that solid economic foundations would be established, in order to ensure a viable independence at a predetermined date for a country to be called Kanaky. Yet with his death it was as if the hands of the clock ceased to turn, for it left the Kanak people orphaned, deprived of a readily identifiable leader with his charisma, tact, and vision, who possessed the ability to take them collectively forward. "J-M Tjibaou had gambled on making use of the Accords to develop the Kanak of today and to construct the independence of tomorrow: a perilous route where it is was necessary to advance with care; a complex procedure requiring a profound sense of dialectics. J-M Tjibaou, in combining great pragmatism and a deep reflection on Mankind, was more than anyone else this dialectician that the Kanak world needed in order to maintain their difficult course. There are other leaders; ones will be found to take over, but it will take time, a lot of time" (Freyss 1995, 65).

Almost two decades have passed since the signing of the accords, and it is possible to obtain some measure of their impact, and of the wisdom of

Jean-Marie's judgment and strategy. In 1999, Anne Pitoiset offered a provisional assessment. "Ten years after Matignon, peace has made history. The state is relinquishing part of its sovereignty and the political leaders—RPCR and FLNKS—are being granted considerable autonomy, accompanied by the permanent transfer of important responsibilities. The Nouméa Accord is similar to that of Belfast. It handles with care the susceptibilities of one another. The Caledonians possess from now on the principal tools required for their development. It remains for them to choose the route that will lead them there. Once again, it is a confrontation of two logics" (Pitoiset 1999, 194–195). In the case of the majority of Caldoches that logic is, inevitably, one of a commitment to unrestrained economic growth largely based on neoliberal principles, while for the majority of Kanak it is the continuing desire to blend traditional and market economies with a view to ensuring that benefits flow to the population as a whole rather than to a select, racially defined few. "The S in FLNKS stands for the independence of our land, translated into an economic system that is opposed to the exploitation of our inheritance exclusively for the benefit of a small number of people. For us, this S is also intimately linked to Kanaky. There is not a single reference to doctrines developed by others. We will write our socialism ourselves" (Tjibaou, quoted in Winslow 1995, 9). Both positions are tempered by, on the one hand, the emergence of a new Caldoche political elite and, on the other, the birth of a Kanak petty bourgeoisie. The Caldoche actively seek to integrate New Caledonia within the Pacific region with respect to commercial ties and institutional arrangements while still remaining closely associated with France. For the Kanak, economic and environmental issues increasingly take precedence over direct political concerns, although independence is still a declared objective.[5]

The achievements of the past fifteen to twenty years are considerable. Two of New Caledonia's provinces are unequivocally in Kanak hands, and they possess the financial means to promote major economic initiatives. The ambitious plan to geographically rebalance the economy, by providing basic infrastructures, investing in small and large-scale development projects, and training a new generation of managers, all in favor of the two "Kanak" provinces, remains on course. Thus far the results are, not surprisingly, focused on the Province Nord and largely limited to the establishment of an urban development pole at Koné-Pouembout, the construction of a new 65-kilometer-long cross-island road, the Koné-Tiwaka, and, perhaps most important, the creation of the Société de Financement et d'Investissement de la Province Nord (SOFINOR). A direct outcome of the Matignon Accords, SOFINOR was established in September 1990 with the specific objective of promoting economic development through investment in key sectors of the economy, thereby actively contributing to the geo-economic rebalancing of the Grande Terre. One of its first initiatives was to acquire the Société Minière du Sud Pacifique (SMSP) from Jacques Lafleur. Ownership was then apportioned to the Province Nord and the Province des Îles on a 95:5 basis. Two ore-bearing massifs were purchased the following year, while in 1998 the rich Koniambo massif was obtained in exchange for the smaller Poum massif. In both cases the French state played a key financial and mediating role. The avowed objective of the SMSP is to ensure that a significant part of the territory's nickel extraction and processing is in Kanak hands, with the benefits flowing to the population as a whole. Within five years of its purchase, the SMSP had become the island's major exporter of nickel ore, and it has been poised for several years now to build a nickel smelter in association, as a majority partner (51:49), with a major international mining group, Xstrata. If the project comes to fruition it will result in a major economic boom in the Province Nord and in Koniambo becoming one of the world's leading producers of refined nickel.[6]

It is now principally in the crucial minerals sector that the Kanak seek to collectively enter the corridors of power, undermine the control that the Province Sud and the Caldoche community exercise over the national economy, and engage directly in the modern international economic system. Jean-Marie recognized very early in his political career that the economic emancipation of New Caledonia and of his people necessitated that they become major actors in nickel production and that the ore be processed within the country rather than massively exported. SMSP was one of the major fruits of his endeavors and its first director, Raphaël Pidjot, a nephew of Roch Pidjot, was in a very real sense Jean-Marie's heir, building the future within the framework of the global market economy. Tragically Raphaël, along with three other SMSP personnel, died in a helicopter crash in November 2000. In early 2006, Louis Mapou, one of the signatories of the Matignon Accords and for a number of years director of the agency responsible for rural development and land reform in the territory (ADRAF), was appointed managing director of the company.

If the SMSP constitutes Jean-Marie's most important economic legacy, in terms of both symbol and act, the Tjibaou Cultural Center, on the outskirts of Nouméa, is probably his most significant cultural legacy. Like the SMSP and its engagement in the global mining industry, the Tjibaou Cultural Center has been the subject of controversy—on account of its luxurious and monumental character, by virtue of its location in "Nouméa la Blanche," because its construction was financed by the French state, and because, according to some, it is poorly frequented by Kanak. Yet unquestionably it constitutes the fulfillment of another of Jean-Marie's dreams. He had expressed the desire to establish a Kanak cultural center in Nouméa at the Hôtel Matignon negotiations, and Michel Rocard had agreed in principle to it, although only verbally at the time. Jean-Marie's death precipitated events.

Why did Jean-Marie insist that the center be in Nouméa? The reasons are at once multiple and simple. Located on the Tina Peninsula, some eight

kilometers from the center of Nouméa, it occupies the site on which the Mélanésia 2000 festival was held. As explained in chapter 5, this was a defining
event in the emergence of a modern Kanak collective consciousness. It was
also a public manifestation of the desire to engage in intercultural communication within New Caledonia—an explicit invitation to the population of
European descent to build a shared future. To have a cultural center in Nouméa was a way of investing the "White" city, occupying one's rightful place
in the present, and contributing actively to the construction of the future.
Located in the capital, the center could also assume the role of a cultural
crossroads embracing the Pacific and worlds beyond. It was another, essential, feature of the rebalancing initiative, with the emphasis in the north of
the Grande Terre placed on the economy and in the south on culture. The
remarkable logic and elegance of the project made it entirely consistent with
Jean-Marie's actions since entering the public arena in 1975. In the words
of Marie-Claude Tjibaou, the center's president, "it symbolizes the recognition and the existence of the people of the Kanak land" (1998, 9).

In a very real sense establishing the center in Nouméa meant returning
to a part of the country from which the original Kanak landowners had
been evicted in 1856 in order to establish the colonial settlement of Port-
de-France (changed to Nouméa in 1866) and where residence by Kanak was
forbidden by law until 1946. It symbolizes the ultimate stage in the reappro-
priation of the Grande Terre by the indigenous inhabitants of the land. It
also recognizes that Nouméa is, increasingly, a magnet for migration, to the
extent that, according to the present director, the city has already become
"the biggest Kanak tribe in New Caledonia" (Emmanuel Kasarhérou, pers
comm, 29 July 2000). This trend is unlikely to be reversed, regardless of the
outcome of the geo-economic rebalancing program.

Pressure from Paris led the City of Nouméa to transfer the ownership
of 8 hectares of land to the Agence de Développement de la Culture Kanak
(ADCK) in order for it to construct the cultural center. The agency itself was
a direct outcome of the Matignon Accords. Established in 1989, its mission
with regard to the Kanak people is to promote scientific research, create
new forms of cultural expression, observe and accompany the evolution of
cultural norms and practices, and establish international cultural exchange
programs. Within a year, its activities had become largely focused on the
creation of the Tjibaou Cultural Center, an initiative undertaken jointly with
the French government as one of its *grands projets présidentiels* (presidential
grand projects). It is a French tradition that each president provides a legacy
of great architectural works. François Mitterrand already had several to his
name, including the Grand Louvre (with its glass pyramid entrance), the
Arche de la Défense, and the Bibliothèque nationale de France. He unhesi-
tatingly added what was initially described as the "Centre culturel kanak"
to the list, in the process replacing "kanak" by "Tjibaou." This semantic
shift "offered above all the advantage of euphemizing the enterprise and

freeing the Center of an unduly 'ethnic' image" (Bensa 2000, 35), which sat poorly with Republican values. As Alban Bensa pointed out, Mitterrand was as astute as ever in his commitment to the venture. "He who was sometimes called 'the prince of ambiguity' no doubt had in mind the dual objective: to contribute to increasing the influence of France in the Pacific while, at the same time, restoring the flouted identity of a population that had been brutally colonized by the same France" (Bensa 2000, 34). Bensa went on to say that the president probably also had in mind what he considered to be the principal political challenge of the twenty-first century, for France and for the global community, namely of addressing the complex web of relations that exist between nationality and citizenship.

The appointment of Marie-Claude Tjibaou as president of the ADCK from the outset in 1989 was another artful compromise in managing Kanak-French relations. Coming from a staunch loyalist background and having developed in her life with Jean-Marie considerable skills in both communication and bringing disparate forces to act together, she was, from both perspectives, particularly well suited to pursue his goals.

As with all *grands projets présidentiels,* selection was made through an international competition where 10 architects out of a total of 170 who had expressed interest were invited to submit proposals. The Italian Renzo Piano's submission was selected in mid-1991. Two years later funding was approved by the French government; construction commenced in early 1995 and was completed in May 1998. The Tjibaou Cultural Center became a reality ten years after the signing of the Matignon Accords and in the year that had been chosen for the referendum to determine whether New Caledonia would accede to independence or not.

By any standard, the building that Renzo Piano created is a great architectural achievement as well as a remarkable manifestation of modern Kanak identity as conceived by Jean-Marie. The goal Piano had set himself was to express, through architecture, Kanak identity and aspirations—a world where past, present, and future are closely interwoven, as are the built and natural environments. He was also concerned to create the impression of an unfinished work, a *chantier perpetuel.* In this way the structure can be interpreted as a direct reference to that most pregnant and most widely quoted of Jean-Marie's affirmations, "Notre identité est devant nous" (Our identity is before us). At the same time Renzo Piano sought to place the structure in context, as an expression of a larger reality. In a radio interview conducted on the day of its opening, he stressed, "It was not a question of constructing a building but a place" (Piano, quoted in Bensa 2000, 197). He went on to explain that the gesture and the repetition of the gesture are eternal for the Kanak, not the building itself (figure 23). The site must be a place where customary acts are performed in the spirit of a constantly evolving culture.

What the architect created, with the help of French anthropologist

FIGURE 23. "An unfinished work": The Tjibaou Cultural Center, on the Tiga Peninsula with the outer suburbs of Nouméa in the background. *(ADCK-Centre Culturel Tjibaou)*

Alban Bensa along with Marie-Claude Tjibaou, Octave Togna, and several other Kanak counselors, was a central unenclosed walkway set astride the crest of the Tiga Peninsula. It evokes a village layout with the central *allée* (avenue) leading up to the chief's residence. On the lagoon side are a series of low, flat-roofed structures—amphitheater, administrative offices, and so on—while on the side that faces out to the ocean and to the prevailing winds are ten soaring wooden structures resembling unfinished *cases*. Varying from twenty to twenty-eight meters in height, their curved forms and open character emerge from the surrounding vegetation likes sails reaching to the sky. They serve variously as galleries, lecture hall, media center, café, and classroom. To enter the cultural center, visitors follow a long pathway, a *chemin kanak,* that winds along the inward flank of the peninsula and suggests, through reference to the land—both mineral and vegetable, food and medicinal plants—the founding myths of a people. The pathway proceeds in five stages, from origin to renaissance, as explained in the brochure prepared for the opening ceremony in May 1998. "This pathway evokes a ritual key which opens to the new—the Center Tjibaou—without abandoning the old, which are the foundations of our society and our culture" (ADCK 1998).

    If the inspiration is traditional and the materials used in the building are simple—with abundant use of wood as distinct from concrete—it is also technically sophisticated in that what are effectively *demi-cases* facing onto the lagoon and open sea are formed out of vertical staves with valves behind them that open and close. These sail-like structures "filter the sun, capture the light, and tame the wind, letting a refreshing breeze pass within" in response to changing atmospheric conditions (Décamp 1998, 58). By employing ultramodern technology, Renzo Piano succeeded in creating a building that is alive, moves, accommodates, and responds to nature.

The center is neither a museum nor a mausoleum. Modern media and the creative arts are its raison d'être, set in the Kanak earth and in the presence of the ancestors. The mix is faithful to another of Jean-Marie's convictions, that *both memory and forgetting* are required to build the future, a future that is open. On this point Renzo stressed that the only possible justification for building the Tjibaou Cultural Center in so small a country as New Caledonia was "to do it for the whole world" (quoted in Bensa 2000, 199).

However, global reach has perhaps been achieved at the cost of local rootedness. Jean-Marie wanted the Nouméa cultural center to reach back into the entire Kanak earth as well, where it would nourish and be nourished by a network of smaller centers throughout Kanaky. In reality only two have taken form, one at Hienghène and the other at Maré. Both have difficult existences, and their relationship with the Tjibaou Cultural Center is, in a way, tenuous. On the other hand, school groups from throughout New Caledonia come to the center, typically staying several days on the site. The frequent presence of young children—principally but not exclusively Kanak—excitedly learning about their own civilization, watching videos, playing with computers, browsing in the library, and being guided around the site—underlines how the center is grounded in the country and how Jean-Marie's other objective is being addressed.

The Tjibaou Cultural Center is not the only way in which the oeuvre of Jean-Marie is inscribed in a global future. He continues to inspire the Larzac, in southern France, notably two of its most remarkable personalities. José Bové, one of the leaders of the altermondialist movement, frequently expresses his debt to him and to the Kanak people as a whole in their affirmation of local communities, local identities. He considers their search for dignity and respect and their desire to be collectively inscribed in the future of the earth to be an expression of "the universal quest of [all] peoples" (Bové 2002, 68). The lawyer François Roux, who, after the struggle on the Larzac, became an ardent defender at the international level of human rights and justice through nonviolent action, likewise continues to be inspired by Jean-Marie, seeing in the text of the 1998 Nouméa Accord a clear recognition by France of the extent of Kanak suffering, a commitment to right the wrongs of the past, and an action that has effectively created peace between peoples.[7]

Even so, if the 1998 Nouméa Accord was, for François Roux, a reason to celebrate, it is uncertain whether Jean-Marie would have shared his unbridled enthusiasm. The official opening of the center, on 4 May 1998, marked in a most dignified manner the tenth anniversary of his assassination. But the principal political commitment of the Matignon Accords was not respected. There was no independence to celebrate in 1998, only a cultural center.

Jean-Marie had succeeded in convincing a skeptical FLNKS to support the Matignon Accords precisely because it proposed a program with a predetermined calendar that would lead to a vote on the issue of self-determination, to be held in 1998. Further, by establishing a restricted electoral list, the agreement offered the prospect of the Kanak constituting a majority on that occasion. They would be in a position to determine, by democratic means, the political future of their ancestral land. Both the agreement and the strategy were based on the French government making an unprecedented decision with regard to voting rights. Only in the case of the referendum in Djibouti had France showed a willingness to "bend" its Constitution, and there the voting was restricted to those who had been resident in the territory for a minimum of three years. In New Caledonia, the required period of residence was set at ten years, and it differed radically from Djibouti with respect to the presence of a massive settler population, principally of French origin.

In his speech at Jean-Marie and Yeiwéné's funeral, Prime Minister Rocard had announced, "The Matignon and Oudinot Accords, at the foot of which Jean-Marie Tjibaou and Yeiwéné Yeiwéné had, in signing, committed the word of their people; the law which is the outcome of the Referendum of 6 November 1988, whereby the French people as a whole have expressed their commitment; I hereby swear that they will be scrupulously applied, in their spirit and in their word" (1989, 15). Yet, come 1998, no referendum was held.

This time the reasons for the volte-face lay in large part with the Kanak themselves. No political leader with the charisma of Jean-Marie had emerged to unite and give a clear direction to the independentist forces, leaving the FLNKS fraught with internal tensions. Most important, however, the demographic profile of New Caledonia had not evolved sufficiently to provide the Kanak community with any possibility of winning a referendum. The 1996 census revealed them to constitute only 44 percent of the total population, with the Europeans comprising 34 percent. In this situation the other immigrant communities, notably the Polynesians from Tahiti and Wallis and Futuna, exercised a critical balance of power and were massively in favor of a continuing French presence as a source of security for themselves. In addition a significant Kanak minority—perhaps 20 percent—remained avowedly loyalist. So, negotiating from a position of weakness, and in the interests of maintaining peace and a semblance of unity among peoples and political parties, as well as of pursuing the development of the two Kanak-dominated provinces, the Kanak leadership opted for a new agreement in place of the intended referendum.

The political arena in France had also changed significantly since 1988. The last two years of François Mitterrand's reign, from 1993 to 1995, were marked by a second period of cohabitation with the political right, this time with Edouard Balladur as prime minister. Though Balladur was much less confrontational than Jacques Chirac, the president's authority was significantly undermined, his deteriorating health simply augmenting the "fragility" of his reign. Then, in 1995, Chirac won the presidential elections. Within two months of taking power, he ordered the resumption of nuclear testing in the Pacific, marking the return of a geopolitically aggressive France eager to affirm its global aspirations. Fortunately for New Caledonia, his wings were clipped by the victory of the *gauche plurielle* (the socialist and communist parties, the greens and the left-wing radicals) in the 1997 legislative elections, resulting in a third period of cohabitation that prevailed until 2002. This time the tension was between a right-wing president and a left-wing prime minister, Lionel Jospin.

With both Kanak and loyalists constrained in their aspirations and their actions, a France that once again teetered between the left and right poles of its political spectrum, and a president who was increasingly distant from the management of the affairs of the nation, the situation in the lead-up to the 1998 deadline was not auspicious. In response to the hesitations of the principle actors, Jospin opted for a consensual approach to negotiations. His strategy was successful, and on 5 May 1998—the tenth anniversary of the military assault on the cave at Goosana—the Nouméa Accord was signed. The fruit of over two years of meetings between French government representatives, the FLNKS, led by Roch Wamytan, and the RPCR, led once again by Jacques Lafleur, it is in many respects a remarkable document, despite all parties having reneged on the promise of a referendum on independence. The preamble to the agreement clearly recognizes the existence of a Kanak people and a Kanak civilization. It speaks of their ties to the land and their distinctive social fabric. It recognizes them as a founding people who have suffered deeply from colonialism and the arrival of immigrant populations. Further, it affirms:

> The time has come to acknowledge the shadows of the colonial period, even though it was not devoid of light. The shock of colonization constituted an enduring trauma for the original inhabitants. Clans were deprived of their name at the same time as their land. . . . This dispossession led to an identity crisis. . . . the Kanak artistic heritage was denied or plundered. . . . The Kanak were driven to the geographical, economic, and political margins of their own land . . . and this could only incite rebellion, which in turn provoked violent repression. . . . Colonization undermined the dignity of the Kanak people. (Legifrance 1998)

The tone, the spirit, and even the words of Mélanésia 2000 and, in particular, of the stage play *Kanaké,* written largely by Jean-Marie, are there—the intentions too: "Decolonization is the way of reestablishing a durable social bond between the communities that live in New Caledonia today" (Legifrance 1998). Some twenty-three years after it was voiced for the first time, *Kanaké*'s "plea for the future" was heeded. The tide of violence had receded in New Caledonia, with the colonizer finally recognizing the presence and admitting to the suffering of the colonized.

The accord, signed on the day following the official opening of the Tjibaou Cultural Center, recognizes the existence of custom and of customary status and envisages the creation of a *Sénat coutumier.* It confirms the progressive transfer of key political responsibilities from France to New Caledonia, together with the creation of a New Caledonian citizenship. It introduces the concept of "shared sovereignty," of privileging the employment of long-term residents of the territory, and of "freezing" the electoral roll essentially to people resident in New Caledonia since 1988.

Reassuring though the initial commitment was with regard to the restrictive electoral roll, it was almost immediately contested by the Constitutional Council in France and brought to the attention of the European Court of Human Rights.[8] Even more ominous, the agreement to postpone the referendum on the political future of the territory for a further fifteen to twenty years gave many independentists the clear impression that the accord served simply to seal the territory's destiny and that there would never be an independent Kanaky. Certainly the last line of the preamble evokes the possibility of "full sovereignty" for New Caledonia. However, the loyalist signatories and, no doubt, the French government hoped that by then it would have become redundant, in large part thanks to the creation of a significant Kanak middle class committed to the market economy and bound to the institutions of what has become, by virtue of the accord, a *pays d'outre-mer* as distinct from a *territoire.* Whether the term itself constitutes a mere semantic sleight of hand or confirms the acquisition of a form of internal self-government, not unlike that of the Cook Islands in relation to New Zealand, is yet to be determined.

One of the devisers of the preamble to the Nouméa Accord was François Roux, the lawyer who had introduced Jean-Marie to the Larzac, who was a member of the legal collective that had acted on behalf of the victims of the 1984 Hienghène massacre, and who had played a key role in writing the Matignon Accords. As a devout Protestant, a deeply committed pacifist, and an opponent of all forms of injustice, he affirmed that the introductory statement constitutes "one of the finest crowning achievements of everything I believe in" (Roux 2002, 72).

The pertinence of his judgment is in a large part supported by the large turnout in the referendum held in New Caledonia in November 1998 to approve the accord. Over 74 percent of those registered exercised their right to vote and, of that number, 71.8 percent voted in favor. Further, even in the Province Sud and the capital, Nouméa, the proposed accord obtained majority support. This electoral response constituted a very significant advance over the referendum that had been held ten years earlier. It demonstrated that the two dominant communities in New Caledonia had evolved from confrontation to consensus, thereby fulfilling one vital aspect of Jean-Marie's dream. A second aspect of his dream concerned the progressive acquisition of economic power during the decade leading up to 1998. During the mid-nineties, the focus had shifted to the acquisition of sufficient mining rights to make a projected nickel refinery in the Province Nord economically viable, an initiative that proved successful. However, the third, key aspect of his dream of political emancipation remained suspended in an indefinite future.

In his 2003 account of the Matignon negotiations, Michel Rocard alluded to the Nouméa Accord: "The problem of independence will be raised anew in fifteen years. But at this point a large part of the explosive character of the situation will have been removed. . . . The problems remaining in New Caledonia are serious, but they are principally those of underdevelopment" (2003b, 402).

The words speak for themselves. From a Parti Socialiste perspective, France was successfully engineering a shift from political emancipation to economic development for the Kanak people, thereby alleviating the risk of further interethnic conflict in New Caledonia. However, the reelection of Jacques Chirac as president in April 2002 suggests that the reality is far more complex and, for the Kanak, even more problematic. The Socialist candidate in the presidential elections (and outgoing prime minister), Lionel Jospin, was defeated in the first round, having been outdistanced by Jean-Marie Le Pen of the Front National. The generalized concern to defeat an extreme right-wing candidate resulted in 82.2 percent of the votes going to Chirac in the second round. This resounding victory, together with the end of cohabitation with a Socialist prime minister, allowed Chirac a free hand to impose his particular style of leadership. While his attention was initially focused on Iraq and pleas for a "multipolar world" as an alternative to increasingly aggressive US unilateralism, he soon turned to New Caledonia. During a three-day visit in late July 2003 he pleaded in favor of dialogue and reconciliation as well as economic rebalancing. However, he was also confronted by angry Kanak demonstrators, and he expressed no remorse for the violent military assault on the cave at Goosana. To add insult to injury, although he visited the Loyalties, he did not travel on to Ouvéa from Lifou "because of timetable constraints" (Fulda 2003, 6). Finally, he indicated, in the course of his visit, that he would address the question of New Caledonia's electoral list before the end of his presidency.

Concerns regarding the criteria for inclusion in the electoral list were compounded by growing controversy about the incorporation of a question on ethnic identity in the upcoming census. In response to grievances formulated by a high-profile athlete born in metropolitan France but raised in New Caledonia, Jacques Chirac was clear. "The idea to have someone tick their ethnic origin is downright scandalous and totally contrary to the principles of the [French] Republic. The Republic does not recognize people according to their origin, it only recognizes French citizens. I can only condemn in the most severe manner the initiative that may have been taken to have people tick this box in a census; this is totally illegal and immoral" (Decloitre 2004).

Initially planned for July 2003, the census finally took place in September 2004, without the ethnic question. Even in its absence an estimated 10 percent of the population refused to respond, among them a large number of metropolitan French who considered they were being condemned to the status of second-class citizens in New Caledonia, particularly with regard to access to employment. Justification for avoiding any reference to ethno-racial criteria is, of course, provided by the French Constitution where all citizens are recognized as equal and indistinguishable before the law. However, this omission now results in an aberrant situation where the state refuses to gather statistics pertaining to an essential parameter of New Caledonian identity, one that is of crucial political significance. The most recent census statistics on ethnic (or community) identity in New Caledonia were collected in 1996. The direct implications for the establishment of the electoral list, as well as for the territory's political destiny, are critical. Although the French Congrès du Parlement approved, in February 2007, the freezing of the electoral list for the 2009 and 2014 elections in New Caledonia to those registered in 1998, there is continuing doubt as to whether that decision will be respected when the time comes. Inscribed in the Constitution at the end of Chirac's presidential reign, and hence not easily changed, its passing was vigorously opposed by loyalist leaders. Chirac's successor, Nicolas Sarkozy, has yet to show his colors with respect to France's overseas possessions. However in June 2007 the new secretary of state for Outre-Mer, Christian Estrosi, made a characteristically sibylline statement when questioned by a *Les Nouvelles Calédoniennes* journalist as to the new government's intentions. "Our government does not then wish to encourage an outcome that would separate New Caledonia from the Republic. At the same time the Nouméa Accord is recognized by our Constitution and we will therefore apply it loyally and in the spirit of consensus which must preside over its application" (Estrosi 2007).

Despite the continuing ambiguity about political institutions and electoral matters, significant progress has been made on other fronts. With regard to education, moves have been initiated to introduce a primary school curriculum that reflects local realities and provides for teaching in at least some of New Caledonia's indigenous languages. Further, in January 2007 the Territorial Congress unanimously approved the creation of an Académie des Langues Kanak. Such initiatives not only restore dignity to the Kanak people, but they also permit the transmission and sharing of local knowledge. Progress toward official reconciliation is exemplified by the installation of a 12-meter-high Kanak totem, or Mwâ Kaa, at Baie de la Moselle in Nouméa. Engraved on a stone at the foot of the totem is a phrase inspired by the preamble to the Nouméa Accord, "the future must be the time for a shared identity in a common destiny." The totem was officially unveiled on 24 September 2005, for long the day on which "taking possession" of New Caledonia by France was celebrated, and now called Citizenship Day.

Yet all these initiatives occlude the failure to satisfy Jean-Marie Tjibaou's fundamental demand. In strictly political terms it can even be argued that the Kanak have gained little more than what they lost in the 1960s. Worse, the order of priorities established by the FLNKS has been reversed, as Jean-Marie himself admitted in the days immediately following the signature of the Matignon Accords. "[T]he current project throws into question the issue that has always been of central concern to us, that is, first sovereignty, then cooperation agreements for the control of training and development" (Tjibaou, quoted in Bobin 1988, 8). Indeed, this chronological inversion of the FLNKS priorities and strategy, imposed by the accords, had led one member of the Union Calédonienne executive to respond to Jean-Marie's initial presentation of the agreement, in early July 1988, with the angry (and, with hindsight, perceptive) cry, "The training of administrative officers over a ten-year period will lead to the emergence of a Kanak bourgeoisie. It is a strategy of integration with a view to silencing nationalist demands!" (Anon, quoted in Bobin 1988, 8).

This fear and this political reality prompted Roch Wamytan, signatory of the Nouméa Accord, to go to New York on his own initiative in October 2005 to address the Fourth Commission of the United Nations. Former president of what he termed a now "imploding" FLNKS, he announced, "I am calling for the vigilance of your organization with regard to the emancipation process launched in my country. . . . The future of the Kanak people, a colonized people, is under your responsibility. Help our people to terminate colonialism, this historical parenthesis, with dignity" (Wamytan 2005).

Whether his plea will be heard depends, of course, on the situation in New Caledonia itself as well as the sentiments and aspirations of his own, Kanak, constituency. The FLNKS has been without an elected leader for several years now, while Jacques Lafleur has been sidelined politically, breaking with the RPCR in December 2005 to form, a few months later, a new but minor political party, the Rassemblement pour la Calédonie.[9] From 2004 to 2007 the RPCR itself (officially known as the Rassemblement-UMP since 2002) ceased to occupy center stage in New Caledonia, having been replaced by Avenir Ensemble, composed essentially of RPCR dissidents, opposed to independence but in favor of increased autonomy and open to dialogue and collaboration with Kanak independentists. From 2004 to 2007 Marie-Noëlle Thémereau, representing Avenir Ensemble, served as president of congress, with Déwé Gorodey, representing the FLNKS, as vice president. However, the 2007 legislative elections were marked by a rapprochement between Avenir Ensemble and the RPCR, resulting in a return to the corridors of power of hard-line loyalist interests. Harold Martin, the president of Avenir Ensemble, has succeeded Marie-Noëlle Thémereau as president of congress, Déwé Gorodey continues to serve as vice president, and power-sharing remains the leitmotif, but in a context where the RPCR once again exercises significant influence.

Unquestionably, dialogue and reconciliation have become dominant features of the New Caledonian landscape following the signing of the 1988 and 1998 accords. The Kanak have entered the city, and major economic development projects have been initiated, political power is shared, geographical rebalancing is underway, the school curriculum gives consideration to local realities. Yet all this has been achieved at great cost, not only of numerous violent and senseless deaths, the scars and the memory of which remain, but also of an increasingly devastated natural environment. The creation in 2001 of a Kanak environmental movement in the Province Sud, Rhéébù Nùù, and its repeated legal challenging of the Goro nickel project, together with the establishment of a Resource Management Council by the Customary Senate, indicate that Kanak militancy is taking a new form and, in the process, directly addressing another of Jean-Marie's wishes—to bequeath "the most beautiful of countries" to future generations. With INCO, now the Canadian subsidiary of a Brazilian multinational,[10] in the process of constructing in the Province Sud what it asserts to be "perhaps the largest single mining project ever constructed in the world" and Xstrata poised to develop its own massive project in the Province Nord in partnership with SMSP, time is running out. The risk of even more massive environmental damage in the name of rapid economic development designed to integrate the Kanak people into, and share the benefits of, the contemporary global economy is now considerable.

This new, overriding preoccupation, where economic interests take primacy over political ones and where cultural concerns are once again condemned to the margins, inevitably brings attention back to a troubling dilemma underlying the Ouvéa crisis, from the hostage taking at Fayaoué to the military assault at Goosana, ending with the assassinations at Hwaadrila. Anne Tristan, who lived in Goosana from December 1988 to March 1989, offered a poignant assessment of what was, perhaps, really at stake in the tragic confrontation between Djubelly Wéa, on the one hand, and Jean-Marie Tjibaou and Yeiwéné Yeiwéné on the other.

> Since May 1988 some had accepted the compromise of the Matignon Accords in order to ward off death, physical death, that which had struck at the cave at Goosana. For Kanaky to exist, it was necessary to wait until all generations want

to break with France. Others had rejected the compromise in order to ward off death, cultural death. For Kanaky to exist it was no longer a question of awaiting this already promised and already deferred self-determination. . . .

Voices were clashing in the name of unity, divisions were not following the contours of pressure groups but were cutting across them. Jean-Marie Tjibaou and a part of the Union Calédonienne was tending for the most part toward the first way in order achieve independence. Djubeli and Gossana [*sic*] had chosen instead the second. *But each within himself experienced the contradiction in its entirety*. . . .

Only the dead remain, and they alone bear witness of this Time of the Whites that has installed itself between them. And all those who came close to them mourn, not one or the other but the three. In haste or slowly, it is always the Time of France which divides. (Tristan 1990, 283, 286; my italics)

It is a poignant judgment, formulated by a radical journalist and political activist, who was herself something of a *passeur,* able to cross divides and read the world from "the other side." From her perspective it was Michel Rocard rather than Djubelly Wéa (or even, from an Ouvéan perspective, Jean-Marie Tjibaou) who was the "assassin" because, by virtue of the Matignon Accords and the active promotion of economic development as distinct from political emancipation, metropolitan France had successfully divided the Kanak people, for years to come, even perhaps indefinitely.[11] At the same time she clearly recognized the distinctive realities and contradictions that both Jean-Marie and Djubelly struggled with. Even so, to imply that Jean-Marie was prepared to compromise on "moral death" in order to bring an end to "physical death" is to gravely misjudge the person. It is patently clear from his words and his actions that he was in no sense prepared to accept the spiritual or moral death of his people or of their land simply for the sake of economic power and the partitioning of the country. Dignity, to be restored through the acquisition of political independence, is precisely what he spent his life struggling for—from the seminary to the cathedral in Nouméa, on to his studies in France, and once back on the only earth that he and his people knew. He was fully conscious that the only possible path to follow, fraught as it was with risks, was the one that led his people away from violent confrontation with the other, more recent, inhabitants of the Kanak earth. To return, to seek to live in a past that was the exclusive domain of the Kanak people was no longer conceivable. In seeking to maintain themselves, to survive, they were condemned to sharing the present and to embracing the future, hopefully also to making a contribution to it, as local participants in a global community. In this respect, he was deeply convinced that "the distinctive feature of culture is for it to be shared" (Tjibaou 1996, 295) and that his people's particular knowledge and experience were one small part of the heritage of all mankind.

Jean-Marie was a man with deep philosophical convictions who believed that the wealth his people had to offer to those who exercise power in today's world was in no way confined to nickel. The Kanak "way of being" offers a sense to both life and death in a world dominated by a West that is disenchanted and has lost its soul, but which remains blinded by its absolute power and the belief in its universality. Jean-Marie knew full well that his people must eat to their satisfaction and that they must possess the tools necessary to control the future and be heard by others.

In June 2006 Jacques Chirac inaugurated his own *grande œuvre,* the Musée du Quai Branly in Paris, dedicated to the arts of the indigenous peoples of Africa, Asia, Oceania, and the Americas. In his speech, he emphasized its role in restoring dignity, respect, and recognition to peoples that have, through time, been brutalized and exterminated because of the insatiable greed of conquering civilizations. By virtue of the objects displayed there, the museum "proclaims that no one people, no one nation, no one civilization draws on or epitomizes mankind's brilliance. Each culture enriches it with its part of beauty and of truth, and it is only in their constantly changing manifestations that the universal which draws us together can be seen. . . . More than ever, therein lies the destiny of the world" (Chirac 2006, 5, 7). Jacques Chirac was in large part responsible for the violent confrontations during the period 1986–1988 in New Caledonia, culminating in the massacre at the cave at Goosana and, ultimately, the violent deaths of Jean-Marie Tjibaou and Yeiwéné Yeiwéné, as well as of their assassin Djubelly Wéa. Do these words, expressed in the closing months of his reign, reveal his own cruel contradictions, or rather that Jean-Marie's *parole* is now heard on distant European shores?

Jean-Marie has passed to "the other side of the mirror" and joined the ancestors, but his word certainly lives on and that, no doubt, is what he desired. He knew full well that the *parole* is at the origin of and determines the *geste*—the act. It is binding, with one having no sense or meaning without the other. France's unfulfilled words and shallow memory have been a constant source of frustration and bitterness for the Kanak people, while Djubelly's desperate act removed two leaders and, provisionally at least, broke the spirit of an entire movement.

*   *   *

A Togolese friend, who is now a political refugee in the United States, surprised me some time ago by affirming that he knew about Jean-Marie. Intrigued, I sought an explanation, and he responded, "Most young African nationalists of my generation follow and experience on a day-to-day basis the contemporary history of our Black brothers throughout the world. Sometimes we are deeply marked by it. My hope is that one day the peoples of the earth may live in sincere fraternity, in honest and reciprocal respect, and in peace."[12]

Notes

Introduction: The Challenge of Writing about Jean-Marie Tjibaou

Unless otherwise noted, all chapter-opening epigraphs are from Jean-Marie Tjibaou.

1. The contextual explanations for this very different judgment are presented in chapter 1.

2. Both articles arose from the same visit with Jean-Marie Tjibaou and family, at Hienghène and Tiendanite, 15–17 April 1989, some two weeks before his assassination at Ouvéa.

3. In the ultimate irony, the French commandos responsible for its sinking operated from a yacht named *Ouvéa!*

Chapter 1: "The Big Black Hole"

Principal Sources: Howe 1977; Lange 2006; *Mwà Vée* 1999; Plenel and Rollat 1988; Rollat 1989b; Shineberg 1967.

1. These terms are used by the people of Tanna (Vanuatu), *man-ples* referring to those who are rooted in the land, in memory, and in magic, as distinct from "drifting men," who are increasingly numerous and "have neither roots nor true homes, they are 'modern people' committed to the physical and spiritual wandering of the people beyond the seas" (Bonnemaison 1997, 13).

2. The French terms *indépendantiste* (person favoring independence, member of the independence movement) and *loyaliste* (person loyal to France) are here translated respectively as independentist and loyalist.

3. Jean-Marie never wrote his speeches. At the most he would note a few key words on a sheet of paper.

4. In André Tangopi, Djubelly Wéa had an accomplice who was believed to have fired one of the shots and was arrested after the killings and imprisoned until February 1990. While his name figured in initial press reports, it disappeared rapidly from the public eye, and no mention was made of him in the 2004 reconciliation between the people of Ouvéa, Hienghène, and Maré.

5. His decision was possibly motivated by the brutal killing of Eloï Machoro, the FLNKS "war commander," by French military sharpshooters in January 1985.

6. According to Aizik Wéa, three young men from the Goosana tribe were sent as catechists to Papua toward the end of the nineteenth century, and Djubelly tried to find out what became of them.

7. Goshen (Gosen in Hebrew) was given as grazing land to the descendants of Jacob. It was there that the Lord protected the children of Israel from the last of the seven plagues that struck in the rest of Egypt, and it was there that they prospered. (See *Exodus,* 8 and 9.)

8. No one at the University of the South Pacific seemed to have been aware of Djubelly's dream to establish a campus on Ouvéa.

9. Djubelly made this assertion in the film *Les chemins de la réconciliation* (Trubert 1989).

10. This effacing of a certain "Englishness" in the Loyalties was probably only achieved in the 1920s or 1930s.

Chapter 2: The Roots of Identity

Principal Sources: Besset 1989; Garnier 1871; Godin 2003; Mokaddem 2004; Rollat 1989b; Saussol 1979; Shineberg 1967; Tjibaou 1989c, 1996.

1. See the special issue of *Mwà Véé* (46/47, 2004) for a detailed account of the reconciliation ceremonies at Hienghène, Maré, and Ouvéa and of the events leading up to them. An earlier issue of the same magazine addresses the delicate reconciliation process on Ouvéa itself (*Mwà Véé* 25, 1999).

2. All of these are customary exchange items serving to seal relationships. *Balassor* is a woven vegetable fiber cloth, rather like tapa.

3. Gustave Kanappé, letter to governor dated 30 October 1881, quoted in Duroy 1988, 59–60.

4. A fracture between Bwaarhat and the inland tribes had occurred in 1917, when the high chief Bwaarhat failed to give aid during the rebellion against the French.

5. Jean-Marie was subsequently given to the Church to become a priest, while his second brother, Louis, was given to the Goa, and his third, Vianney, to the Bwaarhat chiefdom, thereby placing his generation at the center of a powerful network of alliances at Hienghène (Jean Pipite and Emmanuel Tjibaou, pers comm, 17 July 2006).

6. Not surprisingly, very few photographs exist of Jean-Marie as a student or a priest, and to my knowledge, none has to date been published. Hence the intrinsic value of figures 4 and 5, despite their poor condition. I am much indebted to Emmanuel Tjibaou for having located them.

7. In fact it was more than ten years since he had left.

8. The language of the people of Hienghène is Pijé, Fwaî being Jean-Marie's mother's language. Nevertheless, the point stands.

Chapter 3: *C'était la logique du système*

Principal Sources: Ataba 1984; Lenormand, Gauthier, Guiart, and Martin 1969; Leymang 1969; Mathieu 1995; Raluy 1990; Rollat 1989b; Sénès 1985; Tjibaou 1989c.

1. *C'était la logique du système.*

2. Declaration on the Granting of Independence to Colonial Countries and Peoples, UN General Assembly resolution 1514 (XV) of 14 December 1960.

3. For a portrait of the man and of his writings, drawn shortly after his death and principally from the perspective of the Catholic Church in Oceania, see Lenormand, Gauthier, Guiart, and Martin 1969, 189–199.

4. History and Psychology of the Melanesians. According to Bernard Gasser and Hamid Mokaddem, editors of a recent edition of the thesis, "This dissertation should have been published by *Présence africaine* in 1966 with a title something like '*Calédonie d'hier, Calédonie d'aujourd'hui, Calédonie de demain*' [Caledonia Yesterday, Caledonia Today, Caledonia Tomorrow]. The author had already had it prefaced by the deputy Roch Pidjot" (Anova 2005, back cover). In the new edition, the editors revert to Father Apollinaire's preferred surname, Anova, as opposed to Ataba, which was inscribed in the civil register and used in the earlier edition of his thesis.

Chapter 4: The Desire to Understand

Principal Sources: Bastide 1975; Clifford 1982; Comité Maurice Leenhardt 1978; Godin 1989; Lenormand 1990–1991; Ravelet nd; Rollat 1989b; Tjibaou 1989c, 1996.

1. On gaining independence in 1980, the country adopted its present name, Vanuatu.

2. The Foulards Rouges (red scarves) was a political group favoring independence founded in 1969 by students returning from France. Groupe 1878 was a protest movement formed in 1974 by radical young Kanak.

3. The ÉPHÉ was renamed the École des Hautes Études en Sciences Sociales (ÉHÉSS) in 1975.

4. Leenhardt's humanity, indeed his humility, is well expressed in an anecdote related by James Clifford in his biography of the man: "In a classroom at the Sorbonne, a skeptical student confronts the missionary-anthropologist: 'But, *M. Le Pasteur,* how many people did you *really* convert during all that time out there?' Leenhardt strokes his finely combed, abundant grey beard, then replies with a shrug: 'Maybe one.' His blue-grey eyes often contained a hint of amusement; he liked to provoke. There can be little doubt that the 'one' in question was himself" (Clifford 1982, 1; italics in original).

5. Frequenting the Collège Coopératif was, in itself, an important experience for Jean-Marie. An "open university," it was dedicated to adult education in the broad field of social and economic development. Motivated by principles of justice and respect for cultural differences, hence of solidarity in the broadest sense, it was concerned to link research and action, to find creative responses to new challenges and issues. Henri Desroche, its founder, Roger Bastide, and many more of the educators who converged on the college were committed Christians, both Catholics and Protestants. They practiced "a sociology of hope" and were, in a very real sense, "Christians without a Church." Desroche was a former Dominican priest. The college environment evoked Melanesian values and practices of cooperation and solidarity that affirmed some of Jean-Marie's core expectations in going to study in France. Interestingly, a close collaborator of his in the organization of Mélanésia 2000, Philippe Missotte, subsequently became director of the college. Images from New Caledonia and quotations from Jean-Marie now figure in some of its promotional literature, as do references to Paolo Freire and Julius Nyerere.

6. Alban Bensa, although fifteen years younger, attended the same seminars

at the ÉPHÉ as Jean-Marie, but had little contact with him and had no idea at the time that he would himself end up having a deep professional involvement in New Caledonia.

7. François Burck was one of the priests present on that occasion. As *père supérieur* at the seminary, in 1972 he advised his superiors that he wanted to teach contemporary philosophy. In consequence he was relieved of his responsibilities and sent to Canala and Thio as a priest. He too subsequently left the Church and turned to political action.

Chapter 5: From Applied to Committed Anthropology

Principal Sources: Chappell 2003; Freyss 1995; J Guiart 1996; *Journal de la Société des Océanistes* 1995; Lagadec, Perret, and Pitoiset 2002; Mathieu 1995; Missotte 1995.

1. Notably in Russia, Canada, Australia, and Indonesia.

2. French colonials born in Algeria.

3. All population figures are from Christnacht 1987.

4. This did, indeed, happen, with Papua New Guinea gaining independence in 1975, followed by Solomon Islands in 1978, and Vanuatu in 1980.

5. For a detailed description of the Foulards Rouges and what is described as "The Kanak Awakening," see Chappell 2003.

6. "Reconnaissance" in the French original, broken into syllables: "re-connaissance," or re-born-with.

7. Missotte described the failure of the Caledonia 2000 project in some detail in his thesis (1985, 526–532).

Chapter 6: Contrasting but Complementary Civilizations

Principal Sources: Tjibaou 1976, 1981.

1. The Black Americans, The Near and the Distant, and Applied Anthropology.

2. Information on the circumstances surrounding Jean-Marie's address and the subsequent publication of the transcript were provided by Moniale Chrysostome (formerly known as Marie-Joëlle Dardelin) (pers comm, 21 Nov 1996).

3. This anecdote is recounted in an article entitled "Tjibaou, le sage de Hienghène" that appeared in the newspaper *Libération* shortly after Jean-Marie's death and signed "M.K. et J-M.H." (5 May 1989, 6–8). It is reproduced in Mokaddem 2005, 379.

Chapter 7: New Caledonia or Kanaky

Principal Sources: Duroy 1988; R Guiart 1991; Lenormand 1991; Rollat 1989b.

1. Interestingly, Jean-Marie was not present at the meeting.

2. Parti Socialiste Français, Declaration of 9 Nov 1979, quoted in Pitoiset 1999, 173.

Chapter 8: The One Remaining Hope

Principal Sources: Alland with Alland 1994; Roux with Vilacèque 2002.

1. Bastia is the main port and commercial center of Corsica. Although it has been part of metropolitan France since 1768, a number of sometimes-violent independence movements are active on the island.

2. See Milne 1996 for a detailed discussion of Jean-Marie Tjibaou's political discourse with regard to France.

3. Published in *Témoignage Chrétien* on 13 April 1987 under the title "Lettre ouverte aux Français par Jean-Marie Tjibaou," it is reproduced in Milne 1996, 230–231.

4. The letter was published in *Témoignage Chrétien* on 14 December 1987 under the title "Tjibaou: Appel aux Français." It is reproduced in Milne 1996, 231–232.

5. The Larzac is situated at an altitude of between 560 and 920 meters.

6. Melanesian laughter merged with the laughter of this (Larzac) region of southern France.

7. Guy Tarlier was one of the principal architects of the Larzac revolt. He died in 1992.

Chapter 9: From Ouvéa to Matignon, and Back to Ouvéa

Principal Sources: Freyss 1995; *Mwà Véé* 1999; Plenel and Rollat 1988; Rocard 2003b.

1. In the first round of the presidential elections, held on 24 April, François Mitterrand had obtained 34.1 percent of the vote and Jacques Chirac 20 percent. They were followed by Raymond Barre with 16.5 percent and Jean-Marie Le Pen with 14.4 percent. Since only the first two entered the second round, there was a very real possibility that Chirac could, in attracting the votes cast for the other right-wing candidates, defeat Mitterrand.

2. "Prié pour nous" in French.

3. Jacques Lafleur, the head of the RPCR and "spiritual leader" of the European community, was a Protestant as well.

4. Notably at the trial of the perpetrators of the December 1984 massacre at Hienghène. Alexander Alland wrote, regarding the Matignon Accords, François Roux, and the Larzac: "It will be news to the French public to discover that this agreement was written (with, to be sure, the close consultation of Jacques Lafleur and Jean-Marie Tjibaou) by François Roux! It is no exaggeration to say that the Larzac played a major role in bringing peace to New Caledonia" (Alland with Alland 1994, 90).

5. Noël Gohoup, retired gendarme from Maïna (Hienghène) and UC militant recalled these words of Jacques Lafleur, stressing how they revealed a commitment on the part of the two leaders "to work together in the same spirit" (Gohoup, pers comm, 30 Jan 1998).

6. Mapou, pers comm, 20 Jan 1998.

7. Although only two of those who died at the cave were from Goosana, the tribe considered all nineteen Ouvéans killed by the French military to be their dead.

8. At its height the school had an enrolment of close to five hundred children.

9. Related in a second article written by Lêdji Bellow (1989a).

Chapter 10: The Measure of the Man

Principal Sources: Bensa 2000; Cugola 2003; R Guiart 1991, 2001; *Politis, Le Citoyen* 1989; Roux with Vilacèque 2002; Tristan 1990.

1. The one significant discordant voice among them, not surprisingly, was that of Jean-Marie Le Pen. He declared, "An adept of terrorism, Jean-Marie Tjibaou met a terrorist's death" (quoted in "Les réactions après le double assassinat d'Ouvéa," *Le Monde,* 6 May 1989, 8–9).

2. Jaurès was both a politician and a philosopher who played a key role in unifying the socialist movement in France at the turn of the twentieth century. An avowed internationalist, he was assassinated by a nationalist in 1914 for his opposition to the war and to French colonialism.

3. The words are transcribed from the RFO-Nouméa television coverage of the funeral at Tiendanite.

4. Jean Guiart elaborated on this point in a *postface* to an article written by his son René, on Eloï Machoro (R Guiart 1991, 138–139).

5. The possible long-term implications of the imposition of a logic of development and of the attendant birth of a Kanak petty bourgeoisie are explored in a brief but important paper by Umberto Cugola (2003).

6. The initial agreement was made with a Canadian multinational, Falconbridge. However in August 2006 that company was taken over by a Swiss multinational mining group, Xstrata, the latter becoming, in the process, the world's fourth largest refined nickel producer. What this takeover means for the partnership with SMSP in the development of nickel mining and of the Koniambo processing plant in the Province Nord remains unclear, although in February 2007 the company announced its intention to engage in "early construction activity" on the site.

7. See Roux 2002, 71. François Roux acted as one of Zacarias Moussaoui's legal defense team. Moussaoui was condemned to life imprisonment by a US court in May 2006 for the role he was accused of playing in the attacks of September 2001 on the World Trade Center and the Pentagon.

8. The court rendered an equivocal decision in 2005, affirming that voting restrictions were justified, given the tormented political and institutional history of New Caledonia, but that a ten-year residency restriction would appear a priori to be excessive.

9. RPC is, not surprisingly, the original name of the RPCR, which Jacques Lafleur founded in 1977.

10. In January 2007 INCO, a Canadian multinational, became a wholly owned subsidiary of Companhia Vale do Rio Doce, a Brazilian company, and is now called CVRD Inco Ltd.

11. Interestingly Thomas Ferenczi, in his review of Rocard's 2000 collection of essays and speeches, characterized him as being a "virtuous Machiavelli" (Ferenczi 2000, 10).

12. Folikoue André Teko, pers comm, 22 June 2005.

References

ADCK, Agence de Développement de la Culture Kanak
    1998   *Loje catùmê mê naa ni.* Program for opening ceremony of the Tjibaou Cultural Center, 4 May. Nouméa: ADCK.

Aldrich, Robert
    1990   *The French Presence in the South Pacific, 1842–1940.* Honolulu: University of Hawai'i Press.
    1993   *France and the South Pacific since 1940.* Honolulu: University of Hawai'i Press.

Alland, Alexander, Jr, with Sonia Alland
    1994   *Crisis and Commitment: The Life History of a French Social Movement.* Yverdon, Switzerland: Gordon and Breach.

Andreani, Jean-Louis, and Frédéric Bobin
    1989   L'hommage des Canaques et des notables. *Le Monde,* 9 May.

Anova, Apollinaire
    2005   *Calédonie d'hier, Calédonie d'aujourd'hui, Calédonie de demain.* Presentation and notes by Bernard Gasser and Hamid Mokaddem. Nouméa: Expressions–Mairie de Mondou.

Apollinaire, Père [Anova]
    1969   Deux exemples de réflexions mélanésiennes: 1. L'insurrection des Néo-calédoniens de 1878 et la personnalité du grand chef Ataï; 2. Pour une économie humaine. *Journal de la Société des Océanistes* 25:201–237.

Aporonou, Simon
    1986   Université des EPK [Études populaires kanak]. *Bwenando* 46:14, and *Bwenando* 47:13.

Ataba, Apollinaire Anova
    1984   *D'Ataï à l'indépendance.* Preface by François Burck. Nouméa: EDIPOP.

Bastide, Roger
    1967   *Les Amériques noires.* Paris: Payot.
    1970   *Le prochain et le lointain.* Paris: Éditions Cujas.
    1975   *Le sacré sauvage, et autres essais.* Paris: Payot.
    1998   *Anthropologie appliquée.* Paris: Éditions Stock. Reprint; first published in 1971.

Bellow, Lêdji
    1989a   Trois jours avec Tjibaou. *Jeune Afrique* 1480:38–39. Paris. Weekly news magazine.
    1989b   Tjibaou: Sa dernière entrevue. *Jeune Afrique* 1481:28–29.

Bensa, Alban
    1990   *Nouvelle-Calédonie: Un paradis dans la tourmente.* Paris: Découvertes Gallimard.
    1998   *Nouvelle-Calédonie: Vers l'émancipation.* Paris: Découvertes Gallimard.
    2000   *Ethnologie et Architecture: Nouméa, Nouvelle-Calédonie, le Centre Culturel Tjibaou, une réalisation de Renzo Piano.* Paris: Adam Biro.

Bensa, Alban, and Éric Wittersheim
    1996   Introductory texts and comments. In J-M Tjibaou 1996, 17–25.

Besset, Jean-Paul
    1989   Tjibaou 'le' Kanak. *Politis, Le Citoyen* 61:21. Paris. Weekly news magazine, now called *Politis.*

Bobin, Frédéric
    1988   Après l'Accord de Matignon sur la Nouvelle-Calédonie du 26 juin 1988: La démarche conciliatrice de M. Tjibaou se heurte au scepticisme des militants indépendantistes. *Le Monde,* 6 July.

Bonnemaison, Joël
    1997   *Les fondements géographiques d'une identité. L'archipel du Vanuatu. Essai de géographie culturelle, livre II. Les gens des lieux. Histoire et géosymboles d'une société enracinée: Tanna.* Second, revised edition. Paris: Éditions de l'ORSTOM.

Bové, José, with Gilles Luneau
    2002   *Paysan du monde.* Paris: Fayard.

Burck, François
    1984   Preface. In Ataba 1984.
    1989   Introduction. In J-M Tjibaou 1989c, 8.

Cazaumayou, Jérôme, and Thomas de Deckker
    1999   *Gabriel Païta, témoignage kanak: D'Opao au pays de la Nouvelle-Calédonie.* Paris: L'Harmattan.

Chapman, Murray, and Jean-François Dupon, editors
    1989a   *Renaissance in the Pacific.* Special issue of *Ethnies* 4 (8-9-10). Published simultaneously with 1989b.
    1989b   *Renaissance du Pacifique.* Special issue of *Ethnies* 4 (8-9-10).

Chappell, David
    2003   The Kanak Awakening of 1969–1976: Radicalizing Anti-Colonialism in New Caledonia. *Journal de la Société des Océanistes* 117:187–202.

Chesneaux, Jean
    1989   Tjibaou le paysan. *Politis, Le Citoyen* 61:24–25.

Chesneaux, Jean, and Nic Maclellan
    1992   *La France dans le Pacifique: De Bougainville à Moruroa.* Paris: La Découverte. English version published in 1998 as *After Moruroa: France in the South Pacific,* by Nic Maclellan and Jean Chesneaux (Melbourne: Ocean Press).

Chirac, Jacques
    2006   Speech delivered at the inauguration of the Musée du Quai Branly, Paris, 20 June. Press release. Paris: Présidence de la République.

Christnacht, Alain
    1987   *La Nouvelle-Calédonie.* Notes et études documentaires 4839. Paris: La Documentation française.

Clifford, James
    1982   *Person and Myth: Maurice Leenhardt in the Melanesian World.* Berkeley: University of California Press.
Comité Maurice Leenhardt, editor
    1978   *Commémoration du centenaire Maurice Leenhardt, 1878–1954: pasteur et ethnologue.* Nouméa: Comité Maurice Leenhardt.
Connell, John
    1987   *New Caledonia or Kanaky? The Political History of a French Colony.* Pacific Research Monograph 16. Canberra: National Centre for Development Studies, Australian National University.
Couhe, Olivier
    1989   Avec eux, c'est tout qui disparaît. *Politis, Le Citoyen* 61:17–18.
Cugola, Umberto
    2003   Perspectives pour une décolonisation en Nouvelle-Calédonie. *Journal de la Société des Océanistes* 117:273–280.
Dardelin, Marie-Joëlle
    1984   *L'avenir et le destin: regards sur l'école occidentale dans la société kanak.* Travaux et documents de l'ORSTOM 173. Paris: ORSTOM.
Décamp, Florence
    1998   Nouvelle-Calédonie: le Centre, près de la lagune . . . *Air France Magazine* 11:48–59.
Decloitre, Patrick
    2004   Controversial Census Begins in New Caledonia. *Oceania Flash,* 1 September.
De Gaulle, Charles
    1944   Speech delivered at Brazzaville conference, 30 January. http://gaullisme.free.fr/DGBrazzaville.htm [accessed 28 July 2005]
Desroche, Henri
    1975   Les récurrences du sacré. Preface. In *Le sacré sauvage, et autres essais,* by Roger Bastide, 7–10. Paris: Payot.
Dobbelaere, Georges, and Jean-Marie Tjibaou
    1975   "Les symboles de l'histoire: kanake," a play in three acts. In *Mélanésia 2000, Festival des arts mélanésiens, Nouvelle-Calédonie, Nouméa du 3 au 7 septembre 1975,* 15–32. Program booklet.
Duroy, Lionel
    1988   *Hienghène, le désespoir calédonien.* Paris: Bernard Barrault.
Estrosi, Christian
    2007   Christian Estrosi: "L'accord de Nouméa dans un esprit consensuel." Interview by David Martin, *Les Nouvelles Calédoniennes,* 23 June. http://www.info.lnc.nc/caledonie/20070623.LNC9282.html [accessed 24 June 2007]
Ferenczi, Thomas
    2000   Un Machiavel vertueux. *Le Monde,* 23 June.
Fortune, Kate
    2000   The Pacific Way. In *The Pacific Islands: An Encyclopedia,* edited by Brij V Lal and Kate Fortune, 486–487. Honolulu: University of Hawai'i Press.

Freyss, Jean
  1995   *Économie assistée et changement social en Nouvelle-Calédonie.* Paris: Presses universitaires de France.
Fulda, Anne
  2003   Ouvéa: "Si c'était à refaire. . . ." *Le Figaro,* 26–27 July.
Garnier, Jules
  1871   *Voyage autour du monde. La Nouvelle-Calédonie (côte orientale).* Second edition. Paris: Henri Plon.
Gauthier, Jacques
  1996   *Les Écoles Populaires Kanak.* Paris: L'Harmattan.
Godin, Patrice
  1989   Tjibaou le vivant. *Politis, Le Citoyen* 61:22–23.
  2003   Ba men duup. PhD dissertation draft manuscript. Nouméa.
Guiart, Jean
  1996   Avant et après le festival *Mélanésia 2000:* le contexte. *Journal de la Société des Océanistes* 102 (1): 91–112.
Guiart, René
  1991   La vie et la mort d'un héros kanak: Eloï Machoro. *Journal de la Société des Océanistes* 92–93 (1–2): 129–139.
  2001   *Le feu sous la marmite.* Nouméa: Le Rocher-à-la-Voile.
Guidieri, R, editor
  1985   *Livre blanc sur la Nouvelle-Calédonie.* Paris: L'Antenne.
Howe, K R
  1977   *The Loyalty Islands: A History of Culture Contacts 1840–1900.* Canberra: Australian National University Press; Honolulu: University Press of Hawaii.
Jorédié, Léopold
  1988   "L'esclave a accepté de serrer la main de son maître" nous déclare M Jorédié, numéro trois du FLNKS. *Le Monde,* 2 July.
Journal de la Société des Océanistes
  1969   *Les missions dans le Pacifique.* Special issue, *Journal de la Société des Océanistes* 25.
  1995   *Mélanésia 2000—Dossiers—Documents et témoignages.* Special issue, *Journal de la Société des Océanistes* 100–101.
Lagadec, Gaël, Cécile Perret, and Anne Pitoiset
  2002   Nickel et développement en Nouvelle-Calédonie. In *Perspectives de développement pour la Nouvelle-Calédonie,* edited by Cécile Perret, 21–42. Grenoble: Presses Universitaires de Grenoble.
Lange, Raeburn
  2006   *Island Ministers: Indigenous Leadership in Nineteenth Century Pacific Islands Christianity.* Canberra: Pandanus Books.
Langlois, Bernard
  1989   Les Justes. *Politis, Le Citoyen* 61:11.
L'Avenir Calédonien
  1990   Roch Pidjot: Un témoin de la lutte de libération du peuple Kanak vient de nous quitter. *L'Avenir Calédonien,* special issue, 24 December.

Leenhardt, Maurice
    1930   *Notes d'ethnologie néo-calédonienne.* Notes et mémoires vol 8. Paris: Institut
               d'Ethnologie.
    1947   *Do Kamo.* Paris: Gallimard.

Legifrance
    1998   *Accord de Nouméa.* http://www.legifrance.gouv.fr/WAspad/UnTexteDeJ
               orf?numjo=PRMX9801273X [accessed 4 July 2007]

Le Monde (Paris)
    1989   M Mitterrand associe Jeanne d'Arc et toutes les victimes de l'intolérance.
               Le Monde, 10 May.

Lenormand, Maurice
    1990–91 In Memoriam, Roch Pidjot. *Études Mélanésiennes* 28:9–21.
    1991   Décolonisation ratée—Indépendance avortée. *Journal de la Société des
               Océanistes* 92–93 (1 and 2): 141–155.

Lenormand, Maurice, Père Nicolas Gauthier, Jean Guiart, and Msgr Martin
    1969   Le Père Apollinaire, prêtre calédonien. *Journal de la Société des Océanistes*
               25:189–199.

Levallois, Michel
    1995   Mélanésia 2000—Un festival très politique. *Journal de la Société des Océ-
               anistes* 100–101: 125–127.

Leymang, Gérard
    1969   Message chrétien et mentalité néo-hébridaise. *Journal de la Société des
               Océanistes* 25:239–255.

Loueckhote, Simon
    1999   Simon Loueckhote, homme d'Ouvéa. Interview. *Dossier: Usooköu: Ou-
               véa, le temps de la réconciliation.* Special issue of *Mwà Véé* 25:59–65.

Malaurie, Jean
    1999   Hummocks, sentinelles de notre planète. *Le Monde diplomatique,* Octo-
               ber, 28.

Marr, David
    1991   *Patrick White: A Life.* Sydney: Random House Australia.

Mathieu, Jean-Luc
    1995   *La Nouvelle-Calédonie. Que sais-je?* Second edition. Paris: Presses Univer-
               sitaires de France.

Milne, Lorna
    1996   Jean-Marie Tjibaou: Turning the Outside In. In *The Language of Leader-
               ship in Contemporary France,* edited by Helen Drake and John Gaffney,
               195–232. Aldershot: Dartmouth Publishing.

Missotte, Philippe
    1985   Endogène et exogène en développement mélanésien de Nouvelle-
               Calédonie. PhD dissertation, École des Hautes Études en Sciences So-
               ciales, Paris.
    1995   Le Festival Mélanésia 2000—septembre 1975: Activation et réactiva-
               tion socio-culturelle canaque en Nouvelle-Calédonie. *Journal de la So-
               ciété des Océanistes* 100–101: 59–100.

Mokaddem, Hamid
    2000   A Itè Nââdo. Le sacré dans l'oeuvre écrite d'Apollinaire Anova et Jean-

Marie Tjibaou. In *Religion et sacré en Océanie: Actes du 12e colloque CORAIL,* edited by Frédéric Angleviel, 67–82. Paris: L'Harmattan.

2004   *L'œil du Père Rouel.* Nouméa: Éditions Expressions.

2005   *Ce Souffle venu des Ancêtres . . . L'œuvre politique de Jean-Marie Tjibaou (1936–1989).* Nouméa: Expressions–Province Nord.

Mwà Véé

1995   *Il y a 20 ans . . . Mélanésia 2000.* Special issue of *Mwà Véé* 10. Nouméa. Quarterly.

1999   *Dossier: Usooköu: Ouvéa, le temps de la réconciliation.* Special issue of *Mwà Véé* 25.

2004   *Pardon et réconciliation à Hienghène, Maré, Ouvéa.* Special issue of *Mwà Véé* 46/47.

Narakobi, Bernard

1980   *The Melanesian Way.* Boroko: Institute of Papua New Guinea Studies; Suva: Institute of Pacific Studies, University of the South Pacific. (Revised and reprinted 1983.)

Pidjot, Rock [*sic*]

1976   La Nouvelle-Calédonie au bord du naufrage. *Le Monde,* 11 June. Reproduced in Rollat 1989b, 147–150.

Pitoiset, Anne

1999   *Nouvelle-Calédonie: Horizons Pacifiques.* Paris: Éditions Autrement.

Plenel, Edwy, and Alain Rollat

1988   *Mourir à Ouvéa: Le tournant calédonien.* Paris: Éditions La Découverte.

Politis, Le Citoyen

1989   Collection of articles by Bernard Langlois, Jean-Paul Besset, and others, commenting on the assassination of Jean-Marie Tjibaou and Yeiwéné Yeiwéné. *Politis, Le Citoyen* 61:10–29.

Pwârâpwéwé, Bwënga Raymond

1995   Après Mélanésia 2000, on a commencé à respecter les kanak. *Journal de la Société des Océanistes* 100–101: 147–149.

Raluy, Antonio

1990   *La Nouvelle-Calédonie.* Paris: Karthala.

Ravelet, Claude

nd   Bio-Bibliographie de R Bastide. http://www.unicaen.fr/mrsh/lasar/ bastidiana/BIO-BIBLIO.html [accessed 6 August 2005]

Rocard, Michel

1989   Michel Rocard à Magenta. *Les Nouvelles Calédoniennes,* 8 April.

2003a   Un spectacle unique et fabuleux. In *1973–2003: Du Larzac à l'altermondialisation.* Special issue of *Politis* 761–763: 26–27.

2003b   Souvenirs d'une négociation. In *François Mitterrand et les territoires français du Pacifique (1981–1988),* edited by Jean-Marc Regnault, 387–402. Paris: Les Indes Savantes.

Rollat, Alain

1989a   Djubelly Wéa continuait 'sa' guerre . . . *Le Monde,* 6 May.

1989b   *Tjibaou le Kanak.* Lyon: La Manufacture.

Roux, François, with Jacky Vilacèque

2002   *En état de légitime révolte.* Montpellier: Indigène éditions.

Saussol, Alain
   1979   *L'Héritage: Essai sur le problème foncier mélanésien en Nouvelle-Calédonie*. Publication de la Société des Océanistes 40. Paris: Musée de l'Homme.
   1986   Du front pionnier à la réforme: colonisation et problèmes fonciers en Nouvelle-Calédonie (1853–1985). *Cahiers d'Outre-Mer* 39 (155): 275–311.

Sénès, Jacqueline
   1985   *La vie quotidienne en Nouvelle-Calédonie de 1850 à nos jours*. Paris: Hachette.

Shineberg, Dorothy
   1967   *They Came for Sandalwood: A Study of the Sandalwood Trade in the South-west Pacific 1830–1865*. Melbourne: Melbourne University Press.

Small, David
   1997   Prospects for New Caledonia: The Challenge of Ouvea. In *Emerging from Empire? Decolonisation in the Pacific: Proceedings of a Workshop at the Australian National University, December 1996*, edited by Donald Denoon, 60–68. Canberra: Division of Pacific and Asian History, Research School of Pacific and Asian Studies, Australian National University.

Spécial Kanaky 3
   1989   Kanaky: Douleur, Indépendance, Paix. Supplement in *Témoignage Chrétien, Campagnes Solidaires, Non-Violence Actualité* et al, Association Information et Soutien aux Droits du Peuple Kanak, 11 May. Paris. Supplement to various newspapers.

Spencer, Michael, Alan Ward, and John Connell, editors
   1988   *New Caledonia: Essays in Nationalism and Dependency*. St Lucia: University of Queensland Press.

Thibault, Jacques
   1989   C'est encore Jaurès qu'on a assassiné. In *Spécial Kanaky* 3:4.

Tjibaou, Jean-Marie
   1975a   Présentation. In *Mélanésia 2000*, 5–6. Program brochure for Festival of Melanesian Arts, Nouméa, New Caledonia, 3–7 September.
   1975b   Le mythe dans la société canaque. In *Mélanésia 2000*, 33–36. Program brochure for Festival of Melanesian Arts, Nouméa, New Caledonia, 3–7 September.
   1975c   L'avocat du diable à cœur ouvert avec: Jean-Marie Tjibaou. Interview, *Journal Calédonien*, 10 September.
   1976   Recherche d'identité mélanésienne et société traditionnelle. *Journal de la Société des Océanistes* 53 (32): 281–292.
   1978a   Hommage à Maurice Leenhardt. In *Commémoration du centenaire Maurice Leenhardt, 1878–1954: pasteur et ethnologue*, edited by Comité Maurice Leenhardt, 93–98. Nouméa: Comité Maurice Leenhardt.
   1978b   Pourquoi ce livre? In Tjibaou, Missotte, Folco, and Rives 1978, 5.
   1981   Être Mélanésien aujourd'hui. *Esprit* 57:81–93.
   1982   J-M Tjibaou: Le développement et danger. *L'Événement*. Irregular supplement to *L'Avenir Calédonien* 2, 15
   1985a   Entretien avec Jean-Marie Tjibaou. *Les Temps Modernes* 464:1587–1601.
   1985b   Discours d'ouverture de Jean-Marie Tjibaou. Sixteenth Congress of Union Calédonienne, Arama, 9–11 November. Taevas, 2.

1986   Jean-Marie Tjibaou, kanak. Interview by Marguerite Duras. *L'Autre Journal* 13:12–17. Paris. Weekly.

1987   Déclaration du Président Jean-Marie Tjibaou sur l'assassinat de Léopold Dawano. *Bwenando* 96/97: 12.

1988   C'est au peuple de décider. Nineteenth Congress of Union Calédonienne, Gélima-Canala, 11–12 November. Sofasi Mwaâârögu, 1–2. Nouméa. UC broadsheet.

1989a   Les dernières paroles publiques de Jean-Marie Tjibaou. *Kanaky* 18:40. Paris. Association Information et Soutien aux Droits du Peuple Kanak (AISDPK) broadsheet.

1989b   Il y a un an déjà . . . Handwritten notes in Le Président Jean-Marie Tjibaou pressentait-il le pire? *L'Avenir Calédonien,* no 997, 3. Nouméa. UC broadsheet.

1989c   Le message de Jean-Marie Tjibaou. Interview by Jacques Violette. Special issue of *Bwenando,* no 121–124.

1989d   Discours d'ouverture de Jean-Marie Tjibaou au comité directeur de l'UC, 29 April at Poindimié. *Kanaky* 18:10.

1989e   The Renaissance of Melanesian Culture in New Caledonia: An Interview with Jean-Marie Tjibaou (March 1984). In Chapman and Dupon 1989a, 74–78.

1989f   La renaissance culturelle mélanésienne en Nouvelle-Calédonie. Entretien avec Jean-Marie Tjibaou (mars 1984). In Chapman and Dupon 1989b, 76–80.

1996   *La présence kanak,* edited by Alban Bensa and Éric Wittersheim. Paris: Éditions Odile Jacob.

2005   *Kanaky.* Writings translated from the original French by Helen Fraser and John Trotter. English edition of Tjibaou 1996. Canberra: Pandanus Books.

Tjibaou, Jean-Marie, Henry Azapunia, Jacques Iekaw, Basil Citre, and Philippe Missotte

1975   *Vers Mélanésia 2000.* Booklet prepared for Festival d'art Canaque de Nouvelle-Calédonie, Mélanésia 2000—Nouméa, 3–7 September 1975. Nouméa: Graphical.

Tjibaou, Jean-Marie, Philippe Missotte, Michel Folco, and Claude Rives

1976   *Kanaké: mélanésien de nouvelle calédonie.* Papeete: Éditions du Pacifique.

1978   *Kanake: The Melanesian Way.* Papeete: Éditions du Pacifique.

Tjibaou, Marie-Claude

1995   Tous vibraient de la même force, de la même conviction. *Journal de la Société des Océanistes* 100–101: 117–123.

1998   Le symbole de la reconnaissance. In *Ngan jila/centre culturel Tjibaou,* edited by Octave Togna, 9. Nouméa: ADCK.

2002   Préface. In Roux with Vilacèque 2002, 11–12.

Tristan, Anne

1990   *L'Autre Monde: Un passage en Kanaky.* Paris: Gallimard.

Trubert, Jean-Michel

1989   *Les chemins de la réconciliation.* VHS, color, 40 minutes. Paris: DEFAP/ Présence Protestante.

Violette, Jacques
    1989   Préambule. In J-M Tjibaou 1989c, 4–6.
Waddell, Eric
    1992   Review of *Renaissance in the Pacific,* edited by Murray Chapman and
                Jean-François Dupon. *The Contemporary Pacific* 4 (1): 216–218.
Wamytan, Roch
    2005   New Caledonia: Still a Colony Despite Accord. Speech delivered at
                Fourth Commission of the United Nations, 10 October. http://www
                .archives.pireport.org/archive/2005/October/10-27-com.htm   [ac-
                cessed 5 Nov 2005]
Wéa, Djubelly
    1977   An Education for the Kanak Liberation. Bachelor of Divinity thesis,
                Pacific Theological College, Suva.
Wéa, Maki
    1999   Statement in Rencontre à Goosana. *Dossier: Usooköu: Ouvéa, le temps de
                la réconciliation,* 39. Special issue of *Mwà Véé* 25:38–58.
Winslow, Donna
    1995   Indépendance, savoir aborigène et environnement en Nouvelle-
                Calédonie. *Journal of Political Ecology* 2:1–19.

Index

Page numbers in **boldface** refer to illustrations.

About the Author

Eric Waddell is a Canadian (Québec) citizen who first set foot in the Pacific in 1963, to work in the New Guinea Research Unit. A geographer by training (Oxford, McGill, and the Australian National University), the focus of his Pacific Island research has progressively evolved from agricultural systems and the environment to issues of cultural identity in a world without frontiers. He has taught at McGill and Laval universities in Québec, and at the University of Sydney and the University of the South Pacific in Oceania. He has also held visiting positions at the Australian National University and at the universities of Hawai'i, New Caledonia, and Canterbury. He is currently an adjunct professor in the Geography Department at Laval and an honorary professor in the School of Geosciences at Sydney.

OTHER VOLUMES IN THE PACIFIC ISLANDS MONOGRAPH SERIES